I0818438

Menachem Kipnis

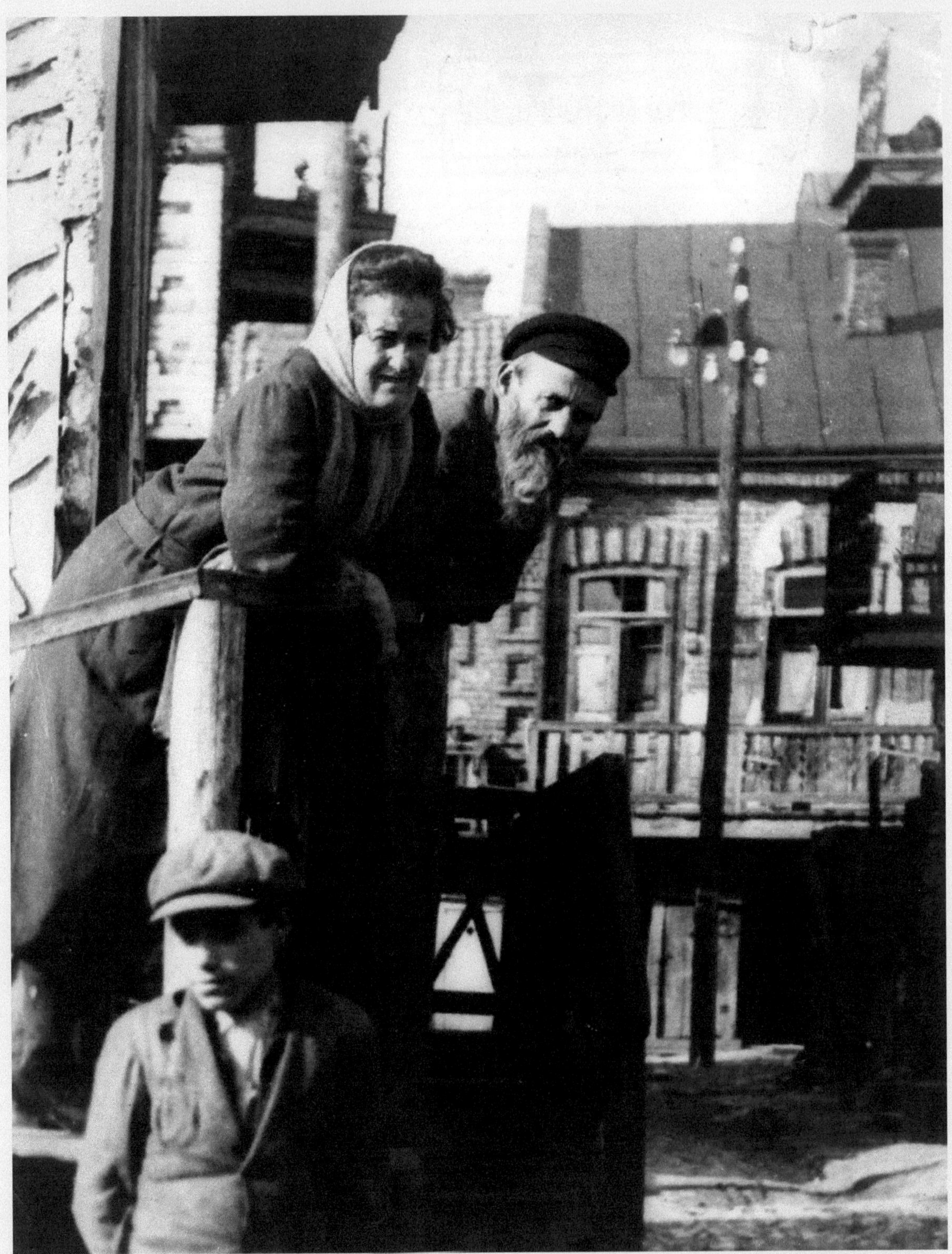

Menachem Kipnis

Yiddish Folklore and Photographs from Interwar Poland

EDITED BY SHEILA E. JELEN

Translated by Raphael Finkel

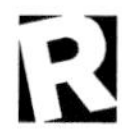

RUTGERS UNIVERSITY PRESS

New Brunswick, Camden, and Newark, New Jersey

London

Rutgers University Press is a department of Rutgers, The State University of New Jersey, one of the leading public research universities in the nation. By publishing worldwide, it furthers the University's mission of dedication to excellence in teaching, scholarship, research, and clinical care.

ISBN 978-1-9788-4610-4 (cloth)
ISBN 978-1-9788-4611-1 (epub)

Cataloging-in-publication data is available from the Library of Congress.
LCCN 2025036499

A British Cataloging-in-Publication record for this book is available from the British Library.

∞ The paper used in this publication meets the requirements of the American National Standard for Information Sciences—Permanence of Paper for Printed Library Materials, ANSI Z39.48-1992.

rutgersuniversitypress.org

Dedicated
to the memory of

MENACHEM KIPNIS
who died in the Warsaw Ghetto in 1942,
to his wife and artistic partner,

ZIMRE ZELIGFELD
who was killed at Treblinka in 1942,

and to

THE THOUSANDS OF MEN AND WOMEN
from the real city of Chelm
who were killed during the Holocaust

Contents

Note on the Text

Many words in Yiddish, particularly when they refer to the Jewish calendar, ritual, literature, or liturgy, are drawn from Hebrew. Throughout the translation, these words are not translated into English but appear in Yiddish transliteration with parenthetical definitions if understanding these allusions is essential to understanding the story. In other instances, when understanding these terms is not essential to understanding the story, they are explicated in endnotes. The transliteration of these terms follows the Yiddish pronunciation, even if they look different from their usual transliteration from the Hebrew (*Shabbos* instead of *Shabbat*, for instance). In addition to the parenthetical definitions and the endnotes, a glossary for all these terms can be found at the end of the book.

The captions provided for the photographs are drawn primarily from what accompanies them in YIVO's electronic photo archive, *People of a Thousand Towns*. Having seen all these pictures in the archives, I can assert that generally these captions are synopses of what appears on the back of the photographs themselves. The backs of the photographs are remarkable palimpsests of archival notations over many years of cataloging, and in some cases they even include notations by the photographer himself. When the photographs appear in the archive as clips from the newspaper, I was able to provide the full original captions, in both English and Yiddish, and these are discussed in the epilogue. Generally speaking, however, since this is not a critical analysis of these photographs or the history of their captions, I did not seek to decipher the backs of the photographs that appear in *People of a Thousand Towns* on my own. Rather, I relied on their published captions from the website when I used those images. In the few instances in which the Yiddish and the English are differentiated on the website, I reproduce that, but this occurs inconsistently and may therefore appear as inconsistent in the captions that appear in this volume. A handful of images that have been reproduced are not in *People of a Thousand Towns* and can only be found as physical copies in the archive. In captioning those images, I provided my own translations of the pertinent descriptions on the backs of the photographs. Thus, the captions are credited in two ways. The captions drawn from the electronic archive are attributed: People of a Thousand Towns, YIVO Institute for Jewish Research. The captions drawn from the photographs themselves and summarized by me appear with the attribution: YIVO Institute for Jewish Research.

Menachem Kipnis

Introduction

Post-European Images and Post-Shtetl Stories

Sheila E. Jelen

Born in Ushomyr of what is now Ukraine into a family of cantors, but orphaned as a young child, Menachem Kipnis (1878–1942) distinguished himself as a talented musical performer when at eight years of age he followed his older brother to Chornobyl and joined a synagogue choir. By eighteen, he was accompanying several cantors around Poland, Ukraine, and Lithuania as a soloist, and by twenty, he had become first tenor in the chorus of the Warsaw National Opera, a position he occupied for sixteen years. Much of Kipnis's adult life was spent traveling around Poland performing folk songs with his wife, Zimre Zeligfeld.[1] "When Kipnis teamed up with the younger Zeligfeld to perform Yiddish folk songs," writes Itzik Gottesman in his study of the Jewish folklorists of Poland, "they were among the most popular entertainment acts in Poland. . . . The most widely sung Yiddish songs today can be traced back to Kipnis's performance or publications of them."[2]

Kipnis's musical career expanded beyond the strictly performative when he began to publish essays on music, first in Hebrew and then in Yiddish, establishing himself, over time, as the expert on cantorial music in Warsaw.[3] "His recommendations," says Gottesman, "could make or break the career of a cantor."[4] Kipnis first became interested in photography in 1902 when he used photographs to illustrate his song transcriptions and musical notations. His photographic endeavors were internationalized when Kipnis was commissioned to send photographs of Jewish life in eastern Europe to the *Forverts* (Forward), the most widely circulated Yiddish daily newspaper in the United States. The popularity of his photographs in New York occurred at the same time that Kipnis was publishing a weekly column in the Warsaw Yiddish daily *Haynt* (Today). This column, titled "Fun der Kluger Shtot" (From the genius city), featured Chelm stories—folk stories about a city of fools—that Kipnis collected, edited, and introduced to a broader public.[5] According to Ruth von Bernuth in her history of Chelm stories, between July 1922 and March 1923, in *Haynt*, a total of sixty-seven stories appeared, at least one every Friday.[6] Kipnis published three books during his lifetime: two collections of Yiddish folk songs (1918 and 1925) and one adaptation of his Chelm tales (*Khelmer mayses*, 1930).[7] The Chelm tales that were published as a book in 1930 with ninety-two stories (the largest collection of these stories ever published) differed in many instances from the *Haynt* stories, in two ways. First, in *Haynt*, Kipnis identified those who contributed stories, sending them from "the field." Second, Kipnis framed the *Haynt* stories as if he were a correspondent, going out to the field himself (that is, to the real city of Chelm) and sending stories back from there. Both of these devices are absent from the book.[8]

Kipnis's work as an ethnomusicologist, singer, photographer, and folklorist unfolded at the height of Jewish folkloristic activity in Europe between the world wars. The ethnographic expedition of S. Ansky (1863–1920) throughout the Pale of Settlement from 1911 to 1914 anticipated a broad interest in the collection of folklore across Europe and inspired that work among Jews, both in Europe and in the United States.[9] In general, this movement was compelled by an awareness of the widespread modernization, evidenced in the embrace of secular and political ideologies, that had come to define Jewish migration from small town to big city, from Europe to the United States and elsewhere, and from Jewish houses of study to universities (when quotas permitted Jewish matriculation). Jews like Kipnis found avenues for expressing their Jewishness outside of a religious setting, as indicated by Kipnis's own shift from a career as a cantor to one as a performer of Jewish folk music. His own career change to a Jewish culture venue followed the trend among many intellectuals and activists of his day who had left the world of traditional Judaism but found themselves reengaging with it through culture instead of ritual. Ansky, for example, coined the term "ethnopoetics" to indicate the value of using Jewish traditional art forms in modern Jewish arts—literary, musical, and visual—as a means of preserving the culture of Judaism without having to punctiliously follow religious traditions.[10] The impetus behind much collecting of folklore was the sense of obligation to hold onto those things that constituted Jewish "ethnicity," that is, the cultural practices that would keep Judaism alive without the religious dogmas that had for so long defined it. The pre-Holocaust period, therefore, saw a reinvention of Judaism among Jews, within the context of ethnography and folklore. The thinking was that as long as Jewish identity could be redefined along the lines of Jewish culture, Judaism would survive.

Kipnis died of a stroke in the Warsaw Ghetto in 1942. When Emanuel Ringelblum contacted Zeligfeld with a request that she donate her husband's folklore collections to the Oyneg Shabbos archive—the grassroots archive created in the Warsaw ghetto that was buried in milk cans during the mass deportations of the Warsaw Jews to Treblinka—she refused.[11] Zeligfeld had hoped to publish Kipnis's materials after the war and was unsure whether she would ever see them again if she donated them to Oyneg Shabbos. Sadly, Zeligfeld was murdered in Treblinka, and nothing remains of Kipnis's collections aside from the books, photographs, and essays that were published. According to Itzik Gottesman, "when Menachem Kipnis died in the Warsaw ghetto in the spring of 1942, his contemporary, ghetto diarist Chaim Kaplan, wrote that Kipnis's importance to Polish Jews was second only to that of Sholem Aleichem, and that 'even the uncultured knew his name and enjoyed his folksy songs and satire.'"[12]

This volume brings together Kipnis's nonmusical work, focusing for the first time on the photographs he sent to New York for publication in the American Yiddish press during the 1920s and 1930s; these photos are set alongside the Chelm stories that he published in the Warsaw Yiddish press throughout the 1920s and in a single volume in 1930. Kipnis is best known as an ethnomusicologist, and a significant amount of research has been dedicated to the Jewish folk music he published before his death.[13] Less attention, however, has been paid to Kipnis's literary and photographic contributions to the endeavors of the *zamlers*, the folklore collectors in interwar Poland.

I became interested in Menachem Kipnis's photographs about sixteen years ago when I was researching the *Forverts* arts section in the YIVO Institute for Jewish Research's archive for my 2020 book *Salvage Poetics: Post-Holocaust American Jewish Folk Ethnographies*.[14] An archivist approached me and asked if I wanted to put together an anthology of Menachem Kipnis's photographs that might resemble a volume of photographs by Alter Kacyzne (1885–1941), another photographic correspondent for the *Forverts* who died during the Holocaust. *Poyln: Jewish Life in the Old Country* was initiated by Sulamita Kacyzne Reale, his daughter, and was edited by Marek Web, YIVO's chief archivist for nearly fifty years.[15] Because Kipnis had no children or survivors, the YIVO librarians were concerned that his oeuvre would not receive the same consideration as did Kacyzne's and his work would be lost. It would be a shame, I was told, for Kipnis's photographs to be buried in the archives forever. I knew nothing about Kipnis at the time, but I looked through the boxes of photographs that were handed to me and promised the librarian that I would consider such a project when I had the time. Nine years passed, and my family moved to Kentucky, where I joined a *leyn krayz* (a Yiddish reading circle) facilitated by my colleague Raphael Finkel, a computer scientist and Yiddishist. While considering which texts to read together, we came across Kipnis's collection of Chelm stories. I suggested to

Rafi that we read Kipnis's collection, and in the process of doing so, I realized (as one always does after one completes the writing of a book) that I should have included Kipnis in *Salvage Poetics*. Why? In that book, I focus on several photographers who weave narratives around their photographs, creating a bridge, through image, between pre-Holocaust eastern European Jewry and post-Holocaust American Jewry. Confronting the decline in Jewish literacy among American Jews, these photographers drew on the universal language of the image to commemorate, explicate, and in many cases reframe eastern European Jewry for Americans. Thinking about Kipnis's Chelm stories a decade after my encounter with his photographs, within the context of *Salvage Poetics*, I realized that his Chelm stories and his photographs had much to say to one another when considering their international span, their Yiddish-speaking big-city audiences, and their afterlife in the postwar era. It was my good fortune to have worked with the YIVO photographic archive and its archivist, Vital Zajka, on several earlier projects, including *Salvage Poetics*, and he was instrumental in helping me revisit and collect Kipnis's photographs, which, in part, are available online in the YIVO photographic database *People of a Thousand Towns*. Zajka also encouraged me to visit YIVO in New York to look in the archive for images that had not yet been digitized, some of which are featured here. Furthermore, Raphael Finkel, with whom I first read Kipnis's Chelm stories in the Yiddish original, agreed to translate them for this volume. All the translations included here are his. Raphael's fascination with the Yiddish language, his precision as a translator, and his sensitivity as a student and teacher of Yiddish culture have served this project beautifully.

Post-European Images

Founded in 1897, the Yiddish socialist *Forverts* newspaper, whose daily circulation at the height of its popularity during World War I reached two hundred thousand, launched its arts section in 1923—the first Yiddish daily in the world to publish a weekly illustrated supplement, according to Lucjan Dobroszycki and Barbara Kirshenblatt-Gimblett.[16] Originally a pastiche of loosely connected images, over time this section became more and more coherent, telling sustained stories on designated themes about contemporary Jewish life around the world exclusively through photographs and their captions. Among the most popular series of spreads were the ones comprising photographs sent in by "contributors in the field" who transported the *Forverts* readership back to eastern Europe with titles such as "Jewish Trades in Vilna," "Three Typical East European Jewish Couples of the Older Generation," "Odd Jewish Types in Europe," and "Jewish

Poverty in Poland." Kirshenblatt-Gimblet and Dobroszycki write the following in their overview of the arts section: "Sensationalism, pathos, and humor emanated from these pages to engage the readers, many of whom were themselves often contributors. The captions were impressionistic—'Some shanty!—A ghetto street in Opatov, Poland'—and rhetorical—'Abraham Donde, a war victim for whom assistance is asked of Vilna and Kovno townsmen.' Indeed, the pages of Old World photographs published by the *Forverts* were designed to assure immigrants newly arrived in the United States of the wisdom of their choice and to encourage them to assist the Jews who had remained in Eastern Europe."[17] Kipnis was one of the "contributors in the field" who took photographs of eastern European Jews and sent them to New York for publication in the *Forverts*. His photographer's eye became an important part of the rhetorical and ideological relationship established in the early part of the twentieth century between American Jews of eastern European origins and eastern European Jews still living in the "Old Country"; these photographs played a pivotal role in the construction of a sense of American Jewish identity as "post-European," or an identity based on the idea of the American Jewish community as the product of Jewish migration to North America from Europe, with all its unique linguistic, culinary, and affective relics.

I base my formulation of the term "post-European" to describe American, Yiddish-reading Jewry during the interwar years on Marianne Hirsch's well-known coinage "postmemory." According to Hirsch, who created the term to refer to the experience of children of Holocaust survivors, "postmemory" is "the relationship of the second generation to powerful, often traumatic, experiences that preceded their births but were nevertheless transmitted to them so deeply as to seem to constitute memories in their own right."[18] The term thereby ties the war experiences of their parents to their own lives in the present, creating connection over time. Other theorists of the second generation have labeled this experience in many different ways, including "absent memory," "inherited memory," and "prosthetic memory."[19] What "postmemory" accomplishes conceptually, however, that other terms do not is that it implies continuity. As Hirsch puts it, "The 'post' in 'postmemory' signals more than a temporal delay and more than a location in an aftermath. Postmodern, for example, inscribes both a critical distance and a profound interrelation with the modern; postcolonial does not mean the end of the colonial but its troubling continuity."[20] In keeping with this invocation of "postmemory" as a gesture, simultaneously, toward continuity as well as rupture, the vast majority of American Jewry during the interwar period was what I would term "post-European." With its implications about the continuity of Europe as a place in the collective identity of American Jews, the term "post-European" captures the primacy of "place" in the American Jewish

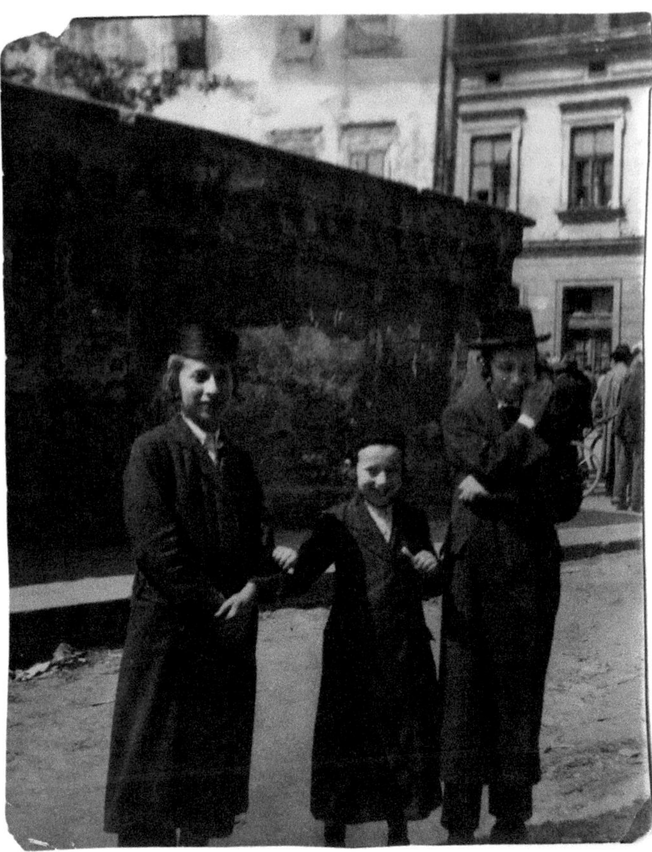

Pub. August 2, 1925. Cracow. [Yiddish] Three Hasidic boys posing on the street. [English] Pious youths in Krakow. (Youth at left was later filmed in Cracow by Earl Morse, an American Jewish tourist.) (People of a Thousand Towns, YIVO Institute for Jewish Research)

OPPOSITE: Film clips from Earl Morse film, 1935 (YIVO Institute for Jewish Research)

imagination regarding eastern European Jewish life. Kipnis's photographs, which were published in the United States in the *Forverts* from the 1920s to the 1930s and were subsequently anthologized, framed, and narrated in films and books, were all identified primarily by the names of places. Indeed, the captions for the photographs in their original publication in the *Forverts* most often named a place before providing other identifying features; the place names were reproduced in most of the photos' subsequent appearances, making the naming of place central to the story they tell.

To illustrate the way in which an emphasis on place in the captioning and framing of photographs of eastern European Jews creates a "post-European" ethos, let us look at one example. On August 25, 1925, the *Forverts* printed a photograph taken by Menachem Kipnis. It features three boys in Hasidic garb, the youngest between the older two. The caption in English reads, "Pious Youths of Krakow." In YIVO's "People of a Thousand Towns" database, the caption for this photograph is parenthetically expanded postwar with the following note: "(Youth at left was later filmed in Cracow by Earl Morse, an American Jewish tourist)."

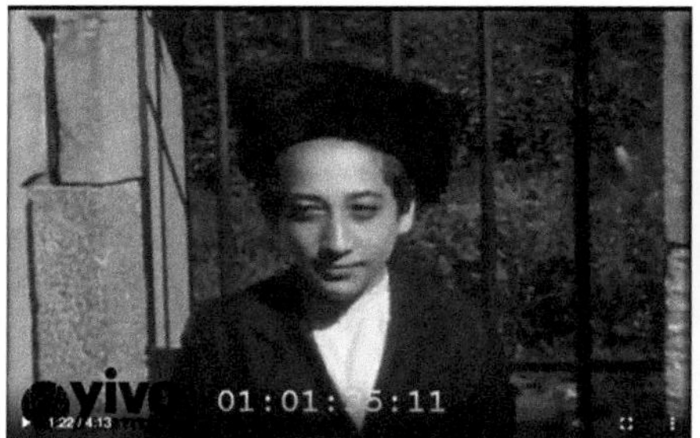
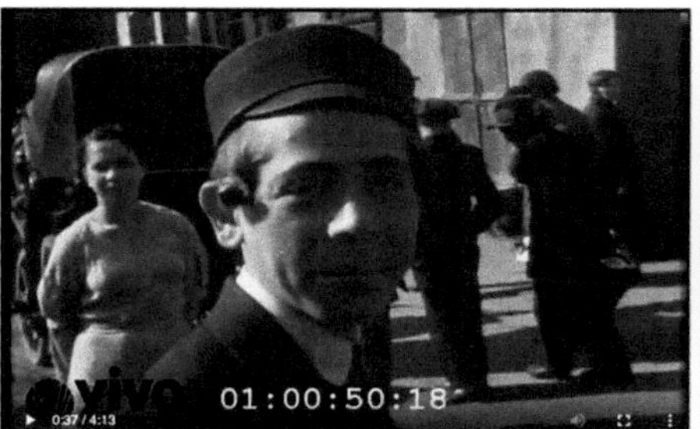

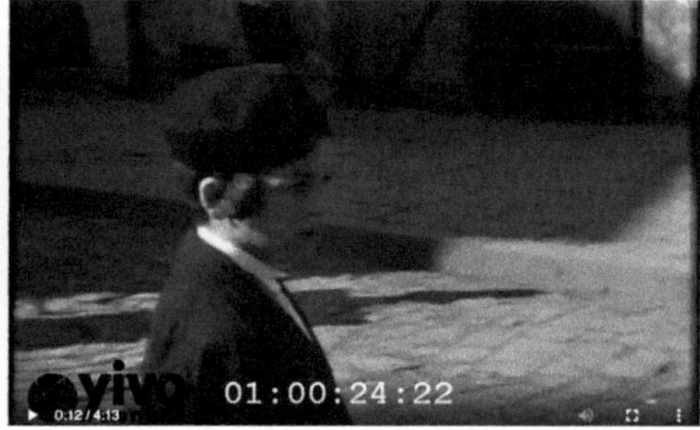

The Earl Morse clip dates to 1935.[21] In viewing it, I was hard-pressed to recognize any of the boys featured therein as one of the boys in the Kipnis photograph. What most intrigues me about the stated connection between the fleeting subject of an amateur film taken by an American Jewish tourist and a photograph commissioned by and published in the *Forverts* is the confidence with which the YIVO archivist asserts the identification of one subject with the other. It seems to me that the film and the photograph came together in the imagination of the YIVO archivist as an expression of the desire to reassess the subject of the initial photograph. The generic caption—"Pious Youths of Krakow"—is rendered specific only by its place name, with its human subjects presented as merely illustrative. The archivist's purported identification of the same boy in the later film and connecting it to this photograph grants the anonymous human subject a semblance of a particular identity, even if the boy's name is unknown.

There seems, in this footnote to the photograph, to be a struggle for subject. What is the focus of this photograph? In the original caption, the city of Cracow emerges as the answer, and the implication is that the post-European American Jewish audience of the *Forverts* does not seek to learn about the identity of the boys in the photograph. Rather, the important identifier for the photograph resides in the place where it was taken. In the archivist's addition to the caption on the YIVO archive's database, however, we encounter a different sensibility, one that seeks to link the boys in the photograph less with a place than with individual identities. Perhaps this is a post-Holocaust compulsion, wherein the sense of loss is best articulated through an identification not of places of the past but of individuals from the past who have been lost to us. The "post-European" sensibility that was so alive in the interwar American Jewish generation has shifted, I would argue, since the Holocaust. As evidenced by the archivist's departure from an exclusively place-oriented focus, today I would identify a different impulse in the viewing and identification of pre-Holocaust eastern European photographs of Jews. The contemporary impulse is one of "salvage," a concept to which we will shortly return.

Post-Shtetl Stories

Kipnis's role as a mediator between the worlds of eastern European Jewry in the "Old Country" and in the United States through the publication of his "post-European" photographs in the 1920s was not limited, however, to his work for the *Forverts*. While he was sending photographs of eastern European Jews to New York, he was also collecting, adapting, and publishing Chelm stories, folktales about a Jewish city of fools, in the Yiddish press in Warsaw, specifically in *Haynt*, a Yiddish daily published in Warsaw from 1906 to 1939 that at its peak in 1913 had 150,000 copies in circulation. Chaim Finkelstein, the last editor of the paper before the Holocaust, wrote about the newspaper's mission in his chronicle of the history of *Haynt*: "*Haynt*'s slogan was to tell the truth, the whole truth, about the Jewish predicament. *Haynt* was constantly speaking up for Jewish interests, ceaselessly calling for rights for Jews. . . . Was *Haynt* right, to demand civil rights so persistently for Jews? After all, our civil rights had been guaranteed, along with other national minorities, both in the post–World War One treaty and in the Polish constitution. Was it a good tactic, *Haynt*'s general policy of fierce opposition to the government, stubbornly demanding equal rights for Jews together with the Jewish parliamentary leaders?"[22]

Where did Chelm stories—short vignettes centered around the limitations of the human intellect, the blindness of unquestioning faith, and the love that keeps community members bound to one another despite their shortcomings—fit into this vision for Jewish journalism in interwar Poland? What role did Kipnis, through his publication and popularization of Chelm stories in the pages of *Haynt*, play in this vision? Again, I would draw our attention to the important role of place within the construction of modern Jewish consciousness, in both Europe and the United States during the interwar period. Despite having termed American Jewry during those years as "post-European," I would also invoke the term "post-shtetl" as we consider the dramatic popularity of Kipnis's Chelm stories in the Warsaw Yiddish press during those same years. As before, the term "post" implies both continuity and rupture, an awareness of the influence of the past on the present and of the close proximity between dramatically different ways of life, sometimes within the space of a single generation, as was the case for much of the Warsaw readership of *Haynt*.

Dan Miron, in his discussion of the literary representation of the shtetl, points out that the "shtetl" as it has been passed down through the Yiddish literature of the turn of the twentieth century was never meant to be a representation of reality.[23] Indeed, there was no such thing as a totally insular Jewish community, even though "the shtetl" was presented as such in modern Yiddish literary works. Rather, the literary "shtetl" was a construct meant to convey the perceived insularity of Jewish orthodoxy and Jewish tradition within the eastern European landscape. The literary "shtetl" was thus fair game for biting as well as friendly satire, a catalyst for self-reflection primarily among Jews who had left behind the world of traditional Judaism or the small town. Chelm stories are the ultimate type of "shtetl" fiction within Miron's conceptualization, because they are explicitly satirical, explicitly self-enclosed, and explicitly fictional. The narrative pretext for Chelm stories is so absurd that there is no mistaking them for reality. "Outsiders," such as the stories' readers are meant to be, have a hard time grasping the backward logic of Chelmites' lives, and therein lies the stories' humor. How, for example, do you ensure that your synagogue is built on a hill? You move the hill to the synagogue. How do you ensure that you can see the moon even on a cloudy night? You capture it in a barrel of water on a clear night. And so on.

The shtetl as a character in its own right is, by most reckonings, at the heart of modern Jewish, and specifically American, conceptions of pre-Holocaust eastern European Jewish life. A Yiddish diminutive for the word *shtot* (city), the *shtetl* became the rhetorical center of perceptions of traditional Jewish culture as early as the late nineteenth century in the writings of S. J. Abramowitz (Mendele Moykher Sforim, 1836–1917), who was considered, in standard modern Jewish literary historiographies, the "grandfather" of both Modern Hebrew and Yiddish literatures.[24] Known for his role in the modernization of ancient Hebrew, Abramowitz also was among the first to use Yiddish in a modern literary context, one that captured the rhythms of the "Jewish street" instead of simply being used to translate literature from other languages or prayers from Hebrew. The notion of the "Jewish street" is key to the notion of the "post-shtetl" because in the rhetoric of turn-of-the-twentieth-century Jewish modernization in Europe, the need to create a literature that would imitate and thereby reflect Jewish daily life was equated with being attentive to the "Jewish street." What constituted the Jewish street? The way people spoke; the way they ate; the way they interfaced with each other, with non-Jews, with their own history, with the sacred texts, with Jewish traditions, with modernity. The literature of the "Jewish street" became a shtetl literature, one that explored Jewish life through the lens of old languages put to new uses and through the provocations and possibilities of modernity.

The literature of the shtetl has been explored from many different valuable critical perspectives.[25] Here it might be interesting to consider how the modern notion of the shtetl articulates itself in the Chelm literature that Kipnis published in Warsaw. For Polish Jewish readers of *Haynt*, the draw of these stories was, to my mind, the same draw exerted by the works of Mendele; they were stories of the "Jewish street." But with several decades between the rise of modern Yiddish literature and the wide popularization of Chelm stories by Kipnis in the pages of *Haynt*, the Chelm stories provided a greater sense of distance for their readers. The Chelm stories published in Warsaw by Kipnis were populated by anonymous types, not by named characters, with all the actors fulfilling a social role and acting accordingly—a rabbi, a woman, a sexton, a shoemaker, a stranger, and so on. These "types" who fancied themselves quite brilliant were actually quite ridiculous and provided the opportunity for entertainment without any sort of uncomfortable personal identification. This depiction of a classic shtetl in Chelm required no deep personal commitment on the part of these Polish Jews, who were largely only one or two generations away from the *shtetlach* depicted in the classic stories of writers like Mendele.

Ruth von Bernuth points out in her history of the Chelm stories that Chelm's being associated with foolish Jews did not originate in the Jewish community at all.[26] She argues that the phenomenon of identifying a real locale with a population of fools can be traced back to an early-modern German source, *Das Schildburgerbuch* of 1598. Chelm and its precursors, she says, "have functioned for more than three centuries as an ironic model of Jewish society, both utopia and dystopia, an imaginary place onto which changing questions about Jewish identity, community, and history have repeatedly been projected."[27] Within the context of our discussion of post-European and post-shtetl works, what better candidate than Chelm stories might one find for a European artifact that is already attuned to modernity and can be adapted for a modern Jewish audience as it interrogates itself during the significant cultural upheaval of the interwar years? Kipnis and his Polish readers certainly thought so, it seems, because his weekly publications created a veritable Chelm boom in the 1920s.

What role did "place" play in Kipnis's conception of Chelm and his presentation of Chelm to readers of *Haynt* and beyond? Kipnis writes the following in his prologue to *Chelmer mayses*:

> Every people has its "clever town."
>
> Every land has its town about which they tell comical,
> silly, and laughable stories.
>
> We Jews have Chelm.
>
> Chelm, with its stories, is renowned throughout the world
> by the name of "Chelm Stories," "Chelm fools."
>
> They also make jokes and say that the Chelmites are no
> longer called "Chelm fools" but rather "Chelm foolers,"
> because they themselves are clever, but they fool everyone else.

> It's a fact, however, that, wherever Jews settle, they know about Chelm and Chelm stories.
>
> Chelm is so popular among Jewish people that wherever there is a comical and absurdly silly story, it's given a Chelm pedigree: "It's a Chelm story."
>
> "It happened in Chelm" is what they say when they hear a laughable story that makes no sense and whose entire point is its silliness.
>
> In this edited collection, which I bring to the public, I have tried, as far as I have been able, to give a selection of those Chelm stories that bear the stamp of folklore, the style and particular form that true Chelm stories follow.[28]

Beginning with an allusion to an actual city, Kipnis employs the classic folkloristic rhetoric, claiming for Jews what every other nation, according to him, is able to claim for itself: a "smart city" filled with fools. Like so many other Jewish artists and writers early in the twentieth century, he wanted to be able to classify Jews as a "nation" and to localize the experience not necessarily through Zionism but by calling for a unified literary locale, a series of texts that Jews could turn to in order to demonstrate their modern national identity.[29]

Kipnis's participation in this modern literary movement, therefore, is evident in his textualization of what were previously oral narratives, by canonizing these folktales through publication. In his prologue, Kipnis then goes on to rehearse the popular Yiddish idioms about absurd situations that grew out of familiarity with Chelm tales, "that would only happen in Chelm," positing social unity through language. He concludes by reminding his readers that he maintained the folkloristic form of these stories to the best of his ability, in text. The transformation into text of a folk form for popular consumption instead of for scholarly documentation, as several of his peers did, distinguishes his project in a significant way. For Kipnis, his Chelm stories were a constant work in progress, stories that he published first in the paper, then as an anthology, with editorial changes throughout, and his goal was always to engage a popular audience.

Salvage Poetics

This volume brings together, for the first time, Kipnis's interwar photographs of eastern European Jews, published in the New York Yiddish press, and his Chelm stories, published during the same years in the Polish press. This is not a critical analysis of the relationship between the two but an attempt to showcase them alongside one another as an example of what I have termed elsewhere "salvage poetics."[30] The term "salvage poetics" describes a phenomenon in modern Jewish culture wherein Yiddish fiction is offered in English translation and pre-Holocaust documentary photographs of eastern European Jewish life are reframed and adapted to create a sense of the world destroyed in the Holocaust. Certain photographs, certain works of literature, however, are better suited to be redeployed in post-Holocaust contexts than are others. Those works are in direct dialogue with Jewish modernity; they acknowledge the decline of Jewish traditions but also exemplify how the very vehicles of cultural modernity, fiction and photography, serve as a commentary on Jewish modernity itself when they are used to represent traditional Jewish life. The "post-European" effect of Kipnis's *Forverts* photographs and the "post-shtetl" effect of his Chelm stories in *Haynt*, I believe, work together when juxtaposed with one another to help us better understand how post-Holocaust audiences in North America might seek to reconstruct pre-Holocaust eastern European Jewish life. This volume, therefore, is meant to illustrate this dynamic by inviting its readers to consider the two genres in Kipnis's oeuvre side by side as part of a complex process of reconstructing the world of eastern European Jewry destroyed in the Holocaust.

In designing this book, I was torn between separating the photographs from the Chelm stories or interspersing them. I worried that if I interspersed them, readers would think that the photographs were placed as illustrations of the Chelm stories. Because the photographs are of real people, most of whose identities have been lost to time because of their original captioning in the *Forverts* on the basis of place rather than their names, I did not want to continue the tradition of depersonalizing them even further by implying that they can be said to illustrate satirical fiction. However, for purposes of reading the photographs and the stories side by side, I have decided to intersperse them while keeping in mind, and encouraging my readers to keep in mind, the principle articulated by the journalist and novelist James Agee in *Let Us Now Praise Famous Men*, the 1941 volume he coauthored with the photographer Walker Evans, documenting the lives of tenant farmers. In describing the relationship between photograph and text in the introduction to this book, Agee writes, "The photographs are not illustrative. They and the text are coequal, mutually independent, and fully collaborative."[31] What does it mean to be "coequal, mutually independent, and fully collaborative" within the context of the juxtaposition between Kipnis's photographs and his Chelm stories here? Neither genre is subsidiary to the other—one does not illustrate the other.

Each genre appeared independently in its own moment and can maintain its own independent identity even when situated side by side with the other one. Finally, each one, when understood within the context of salvage poetics as two sides of a dynamic engagement between photography and Yiddish fiction in reconstructions of pre-Holocaust eastern European Jewish life, might exist as fully collaborative without diminishing the independence, coequality, or integrity of either one.

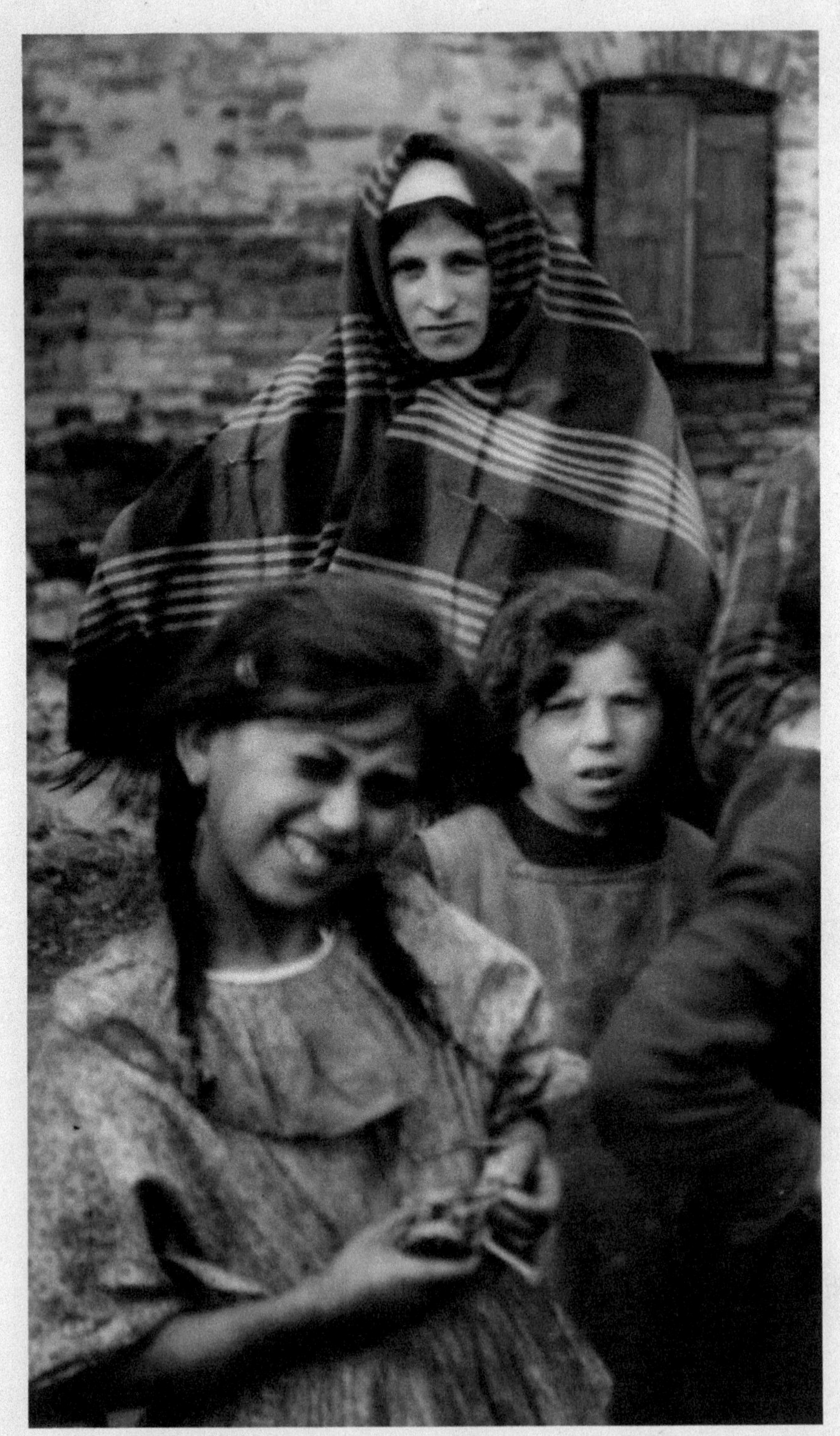

Chelm Stories

Collected and Edited

Menachem Kipnis
SZ. CUKIER, WARSAW, 1930

Every people has its "clever town."

Every land has its town about which they tell comical, silly, and laughable stories.

We Jews have Chelm.

Chelm, with its stories, is renowned throughout the world by the name of "Chelm Stories," "Chelm fools."

They also make jokes and say that the Chelmites are no longer called "Chelm fools" but rather "Chelm foolers," because they themselves are clever, but they fool everyone else.

It's a fact, however, that, wherever Jews settle, they know about Chelm and Chelm stories.

Chelm is so popular among Jewish people that wherever there is a comical and absurdly silly story, it's given a Chelm pedigree: "It's a Chelm story."

"It happened in Chelm" is what they say when they hear a laughable story that makes no sense and whose entire point is its silliness.

In this edited collection, which I bring to the public, I have tried, as far as I have been able, to give a selection of those Chelm stories that bear the stamp of folklore, the style and particular form that true Chelm stories follow.

OPPOSITE: 1920–1930s, Ryki. A cluster of Jewish women and girls pose "in conversation" for the photographer outdoors, near a river. (People of a Thousand Towns, YIVO Institute for Jewish Research)

From a Folk Legend

When God created the world and started to make habitations, he sent forth an angel with two sacks of souls. One sack was full of clever souls, and the other was full of truly silly ones.

Sweeping over the globe of the Earth, he sowed from above souls on the ground below, handful after handful. One handful clever, one handful silly, and that's how he divided the world equally, so that no town would get a larger share of clever or silly souls than another.

Flying over the place where Chelm now stands, an accident happened to the angel: his bag of silly souls was torn open on the tip of the hill, and all the silly souls poured out into one spot.

Soon thereafter, Chelm grew there.

The Hill They Shoved out of Town

The Chelm Jews once realized that the tall hill in the middle of the town was of no practical value. It wasted space and obscured the sun by day and the moon by night, keeping them from reciting the New Moon blessing.

What could they do?

They held a meeting, pondered for three days and three nights, and concluded that there was no other solution than to push the hill out of town.

And that's what happened.

In the morning, quite early, all the Chelm householders went out to the hill and started to push it with all their might.

They pushed and pushed for several hours without interruption, until they were tired and perspiring from the effort.

So they took off their long overcoats and pushed anew.

Meanwhile, as the householders were completely occupied with pushing the hill, thieves came and grabbed their overcoats.

When the householders looked around later and saw that the overcoats were missing, it was a cause for great rejoicing.

"Unbelievable!" they applauded, clapping their hands in joy, "we've pushed the hill so far that we can no longer see our overcoats!"

The Moon Caught in a Barrel

That the Chelm sages were strong enough to push the big hill out of the town: that makes sense, but to bring the moon down from the sky: that's beyond belief. Still, Chelm managed the feat.

How did the Chelmites grab the moon, and why was it necessary?

The event did not happen, God forbid, due to any rebellion of Chelm against the Master of the Universe but simply to earn some money.

Chelm was at that time in a very precarious position. The people were poor, and the town expenses were quite large; they needed to fund the marriages of the three young women whose father, the Rabbi, had died. They needed a fence for the cemetery and a warming device for the *mikve* [ritual bath]. The worst of all was the Polish landowner of Chelm, who made new rules every day to demand funds and taxes.

People went around without a clue where to get enough money for these enormous obligations.

They held a meeting, pondered for three days and three nights, and concluded that Chelm had to find a source of income that would never run out, something that would be unique to Chelm, so the whole world would have to come to Chelm and pay dearly for it.

Where do you find such a thing?

They held another meeting, and the sages of Chelm thought and furrowed their brows long and wide until they came up with:

"We need to catch the moon."

They needed to grab the moon from the sky and place it in the synagogue. Now that there would be no moon anywhere, all the Jews in the world would have to come to Chelm to recite the New Moon Blessing, and that would bring in a fine income.

But how do you catch the moon?

They held another meeting, pondered and pondered seven days and seven nights.

One thought was to tie together all the ladders in town to make one long ladder, lean it against the old synagogue, and let the *shammes* [sexton] climb up and drag down the moon.

But people were afraid, because he was a luckless fellow and might fall down and be killed. Then the town would face a new obligation to provide for his wife and children. So they thought of sending the Shabbos goy[1] instead.

But there was an outcry:

Sending a non-Jew to get the moon? He'd render it impure! And what if he does bring it down and then steals it away for the non-Jews!

In short, they pondered and pondered and concluded:

We should set up a barrel of water near the synagogue, and when the moon climbs into the barrel, we should quickly close it in with a thick sack, and voilà!

No sooner said than done.

About midnight it happened that the moon was traveling clear and peaceful in the middle of the sky, oblivious to danger, when the town elders set up a barrel of water in the synagogue courtyard. As soon as the moon was mirrored in the water, they quickly covered it with a thick sack, tied it tightly, and brought it into the synagogue. Chelm was certain that the moon was missing from the skies across the whole world, and all the Jews would have to come to Chelm to recite the blessing over the new moon.

Next lunar month, someone came and said that he had seen people reciting the New Moon Blessing in Trisk.[2] For such a lie, he got a beating. What do you mean? The moon is in a barrel tied with a sack in the synagogue. How can it be in Trisk?

Later, someone came from Ludmir and from Kovel and mentioned seeing people reciting the New Moon Blessing there, too. Nobody believed them. "Only our enemies would say such a thing!" they comforted themselves.

Only when they realized that nobody was coming to Chelm did they untie the barrel and discover that the moon was indeed gone. All of Chelm fell to the ground in terror.

"Miracle of miracles!" all of Chelm nodded, "we sealed it so tightly and it still got away! There must be no way on earth to keep it!"

The Teacher and the Billy Goat

It once happened that a *melamed* [children's teacher] in Chelm had a sick wife, so he went to a nearby town to buy a nanny goat.

Leading the goat by a rope on the way back to Chelm, the melamed passed an inn. He thought to himself that since he was now the owner of a goat, thank God, he ought to have a little drink.

He led the goat into the stall and went into the inn for a little whiskey.

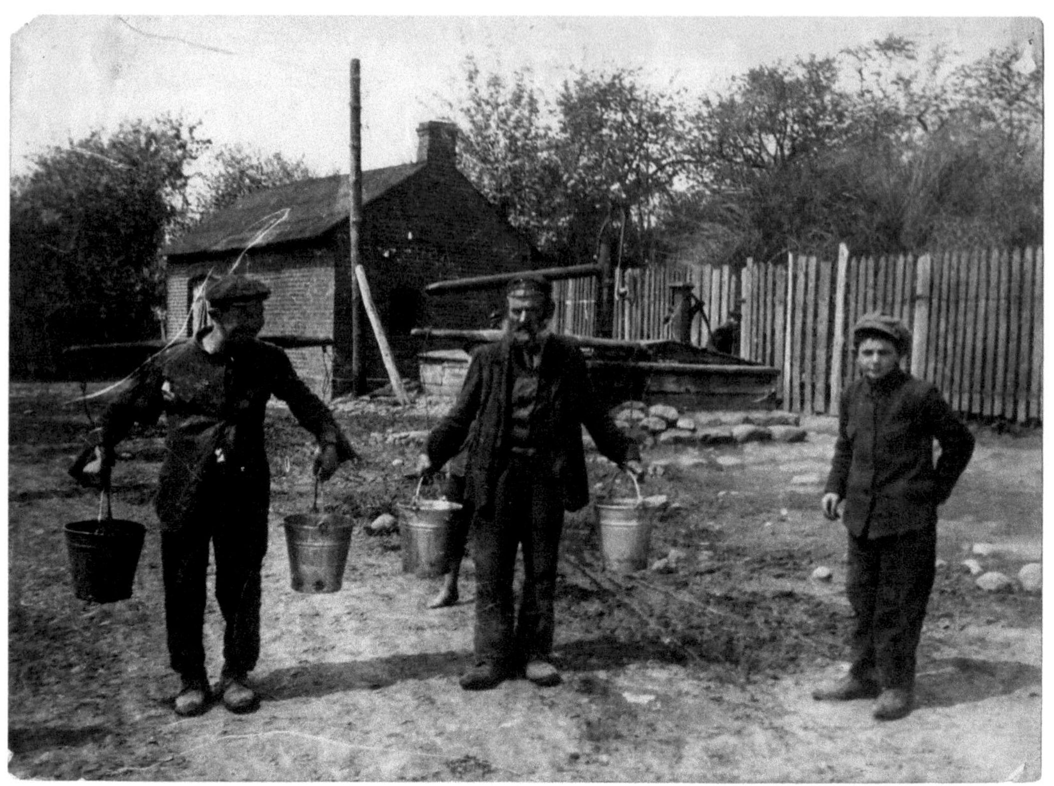

Pub. July 30, 1933. Lyuboml. Posing in a yard with yoke and pails: A Jewish water carrier of Lyuboml, a little town. (People of a Thousand Towns, YIVO Institute for Jewish Research)

The innkeeper recognized that the melamed was from Chelm and thought, "Let's play a little joke on him." He went into the stall, took out the nanny goat, and put a billy goat in its place.

The melamed took a glass of whiskey and had a snack, then returned to the stall and departed, leading the billy goat by the rope.

When he arrived home, the household rejoiced at the good fortune: Not too shabby, to own one's own nanny goat! His wife started to milk the goat. Curses and laments! It won't milk!

"You simpleton, someone has fooled you," she railed at him. "They gave you a billy goat instead of a nanny goat!"

Realizing the truth of the matter, he grabbed the goat early in the morning and marched back to town to get his money back.

Passing the same inn, he thought to himself: Since he wasn't feeling all that happy, he should first have a small drink to strengthen himself. He led the billy goat into the stall and went into the inn to have a drink. He told the innkeeper the whole story, that they had sold him a nanny goat, but it turned out to be a billy goat, so he was bringing the goat back to the town.

The innkeeper went out and replaced the billy goat with the nanny goat.

The melamed drank up his whiskey, took the goat, and went off with it to the town. There he raised such an outcry that all the townsfolk came running.

"What's the matter?"

"Explain this! Why shouldn't I scream, when instead of selling me a nanny goat, they pawned a billy goat off on me!" He threw himself at the fellow who had sold him the goat. "Here, take it back, the billy goat!"

"What a fool you are! What billy goat? Where billy goat?" They started to laugh at him. "It's clearly a nanny goat, not a billy!"

"What are you trying to put over on me, that it's a nanny. It's clearly a billy," he kept shouting.

In short, the seller shouted that it was a nanny, and the melamed that it was a billy.

"A billy!"

"A nanny!"

"A billy!"

"A nanny!"

He refused to leave until they would give him a letter written by the Rabbi himself attesting to it being a nanny goat. Otherwise, he wouldn't believe them. That's what he demanded.

All three went off to the Rabbi: the seller, the Chelm melamed, and the goat itself.

The town Rabbi was also not particularly knowledgeable in such matters; he wasn't sure whether it was a nanny or a billy, so he called in his wife. She examined the goat from all sides and established that it was a nanny, so the Rabbi gave the melamed a signed letter attesting that it was a nanny, not a billy.

The melamed took the goat and the Rabbi's letter and set off for home.

Passing the inn once more, he thought to himself, "Now that with God's help the goat is surely a nanny and not a billy, and I have a letter from the Rabbi attesting to that fact, it's finally right to have a small drink." So he led the goat into the stall and went into the inn for a drink.

The innkeeper went out and again replaced the nanny with the billy.

The melamed drank up his small whiskey and set out with his merchandise for Chelm.

When he arrived, he attacked his wife with curses: "How in the world can a Jewish woman not recognize a nanny goat? It was a nanny, and it remains a nanny. Now go milk it!"

His wife took a bucket and tried to milk it. It wouldn't milk.

"You should have eighty black years, you calamity!" she answered with curses. "It's a billy goat like before!"

"What do you mean, a billy? I have a letter from the Rabbi himself saying it's a nanny. Milk it, I tell you, woman, milk it!"

She started to milk it harder, but the goat started kicking.

The melamed grabbed the goat by the head, but the goat gave him such a shove with its horns that he rolled over several times. He grabbed it by the tail, but the goat jumped and

OPPOSITE: A man holds his goat around the neck with one hand. He holds a switch in the other. (From the Photographic Archives, YIVO Institute for Jewish Research)

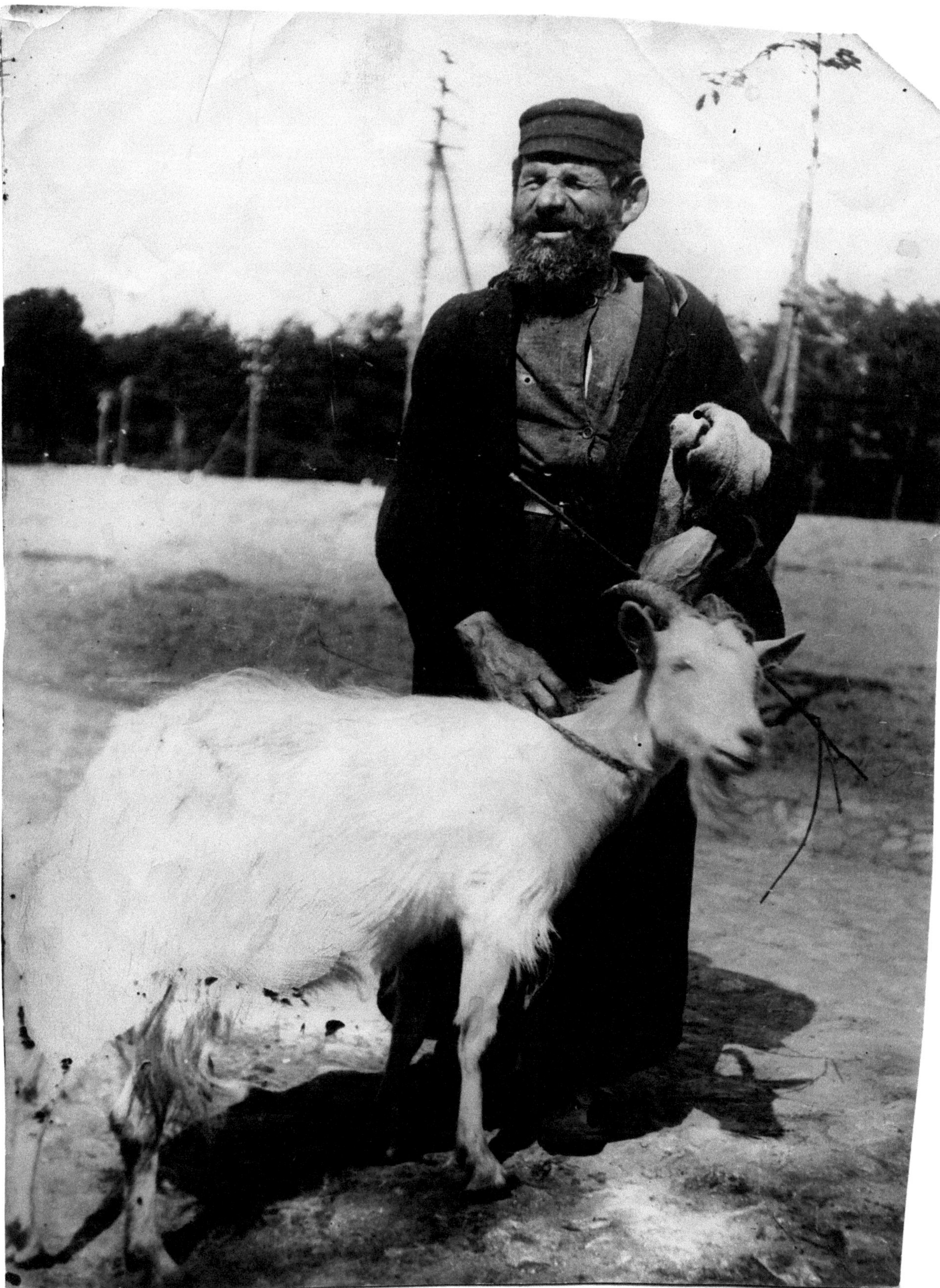

pranced and started to run off, dragging the melamed, all the while hitting him right in the face with its hind legs.

The goat ran like this through the Chelm streets, and the melamed dragged after it, holding the tail and crying,

"Help! People! Help!"

All of Chelm ran up, but they didn't know how to rescue the melamed, until a stranger happened by and shouted,

"Why are you screaming, Chelmite? Let the tail go, and the goat will stop dragging you along!"

So he let go of the tail, and the goat ran off.

When the melamed got up from the ground, opened his eyes, and came to, he had no words to thank the stranger for his advice that had saved him from a certain death. He never stopped admiring the clever people who inhabit God's earth.[3]

The Cat Incident

A stranger once came traveling to Chelm. He noticed that in preparing the dinner table, people set a knife, a spoon, and several switches of a broom. He asked why the switches were on the table.

They answered that because there were many small animals in Chelm, called mice, as soon as you sat down at the table, they would come crawling out and would steal the food from your mouth. So along with the knife and spoon, they would also set a switch to beat off the mice.

"You can't get rid of the mice?" the stranger wondered.

"How, then?"

"What do you mean, 'how'?" he questioned the Chelmites. "With a cat!"

Chelm had never seen a cat before.

They asked him:

"What sort of an animal is a cat?"

He explained that it is a destroyer that cleans out the mice.

"We would give you whatever you want in order to get such a beast," they begged.

"I can bring you one," the stranger answered gleefully.

They paid him a wealth of money, and he brought them a cat.

Things started to liven up in town. The cat immediately threw itself into the fray against the small pests, and in short order cleaned them out to the point that people could eat without a switch of broom on the table.

But then the cat began to create real trouble in town. You couldn't put a piece of meat down anywhere, or butter, or sour cream, or anything. It eagerly gobbled them all up.

"A dangerous beast!" they all cried. We need to get rid of it.

"How then can we get rid of it?"

They held a big meeting and concluded that they should take the cat, carry it up to the attic, and remove the ladder. The cat would have to stay up there.

That's what they did.

The next day they saw that the cat was still around.

They held another meeting and concluded that since the cat was able to come down from the attic without a ladder, it must be a reincarnation of a *dybbuk* [wandering soul] that was in need of *tikkun* [spiritual repair].

What sort of repair could they provide?

Again they held a meeting and concluded that they should bring it into the synagogue on the Sabbath and give it the third *aliya* [the most prestigious Torah honor].

That's what they did.

On the Sabbath, they carried it with great pomp into the synagogue, seated it next to the Rabbi at the eastern wall [the most prestigious seat], and awaited the Torah reading.

As soon as the reader called out with customary formality, "Let Mr. Cat arise for the third *aliya*!" the cat jumped up in fright onto the reading desk, from the desk to the lectern, from there up to the women's balcony, out the window, and away.

Everyone could clearly see that it was a wild beast that might trample people and had to be killed.

"How then can we kill it?"

They pondered for seven days and seven nights and concluded that they should fling it from a high roof.

They took it and flung it from a high roof, but it ended up on its four feet, no worse for the fall.

Now the community was really afraid.

The cat was certainly, God defend us, a curse.

They held a new meeting and concluded that since it landed on its feet after being flung down, they should tie it to the shammes and throw them down together.

That's what they did. The shammes was killed, and the cat ran off.

Now they realized that the cat was a misfortune that could, God forbid, destroy the whole of Chelm. They held a new meeting and concluded that they should throw the cat into the river.

They threw it into the river.

It crawled out.

They held another meeting and concluded that since it crawled out of the river, they should tie it to the *gabbai* [a synagogue functionary] and throw it into the river along with the gabbai, so it wouldn't be able to escape.

That's what they did.

The gabbai drowned, but the cat crawled out.

Now they realized that the cat was a destroyer that could, God forbid, demolish the whole world.

They brought a wagonload of straw into the synagogue yard, threw the cat into the straw, and set it alight.

The synagogue roof caught fire, and the fire spread to a second roof, from there to a third. The fire crossed over to the next street, from there to the next, then up the hill, until it encompassed the stores. The entire town went up in flames.

All that was left was coals and embers. The town was in ruins. The cat strolled on the remains peacefully and calmly, as if it weren't at all involved.

The Four Historic Decrees

Once there was a melamed in Chelm who had a yen for cheese blintzes on the holiday of Shavuos.[4]

He knew that on Shavuos, people ate cheese blintzes in all proper households, and the evil inclination made him want to taste this delicacy himself.

But he was a pauper without a penny to his name. He held a meeting with his wife and concluded that it was out of the question this year, but, God willing, next year on Shavuos, there must be blintzes, come hell or high water.

But it was going to cost a king's ransom: flour, eggs, butter, cheese, cinnamon, sugar; and he had no money.

The two of them, the melamed and his wife, worked out a plan: Every day of the year they would save one *groshn* [small amount of money] from breakfast. During the year they would collect enough money to cover the cost of cheese blintzes, with even a bit left over.

Decided and accomplished.

The next day they started implementing the plan. They owned a big chest they had gotten as a wedding present. They closed it securely, made a slot in the top, and every morning they dropped in the groshns they saved.

The melamed, though, soon had a thought:

Given that he was a melamed and worked hard to teach the small children and needed to fortify himself, it was too hard to spare a groshn from his breakfast. It would be enough if only his wife would save a groshn.

The melamed's wife, on the other hand, also considered:

Given that she was a weak woman, with a small child still at the breast, she shouldn't damage her health. It would suffice for her husband alone to put in a groshn every day.

That's how they fooled each other for a full year.

Right before Shavuos at the end of the year, they opened the box to take out the groshns they had collected.

When they saw that the box was empty, there ensued a commotion. The melamed attacked his wife, claiming that she had deceived him. For her part, she attacked him with the complaint that he had deceived her. They continued to curse and fight next to the open box, until they started tugging at each other's noses. In the middle of the fight, they tumbled into the box, and the heavy lid fell to and sealed them in.

In the closed box, the fight reached a new frenzy. Without letup, each punched and kicked the other. The box, which was wheeled, started moving around the room. The house had no threshold, and the door was open, so the box ended up outside. Now the melamed lived on Synagogue Street, which led downhill to the old synagogue. The box started to roll downhill and then ran full speed into the synagogue.

The congregation happened to be in the middle of prayer. Seeing a box suddenly come in and move back and forth from one end of the synagogue to the other, everyone took fright. People ran up from all directions.

"Spirits!"

"An evil one!"

"A reincarnation!"

"A dybbuk!"

"Asmodeus!"

"We should go unearth graves [as a protective remedy]!"

Meanwhile, the box moved back and forth from one end of the synagogue to the other.

The Rabbi took his walking stick, stood at the lectern, and shouted at the box:

"Dybbuk! I command you to return to your rest, to the place you came from!"

The box didn't obey him.

The Rabbi commanded that shofars [ram's horns] be blown [as part of an exorcism ceremony].

The box kept moving back and forth across the synagogue.

The Rabbi now saw that it was a dangerous spirit, may God

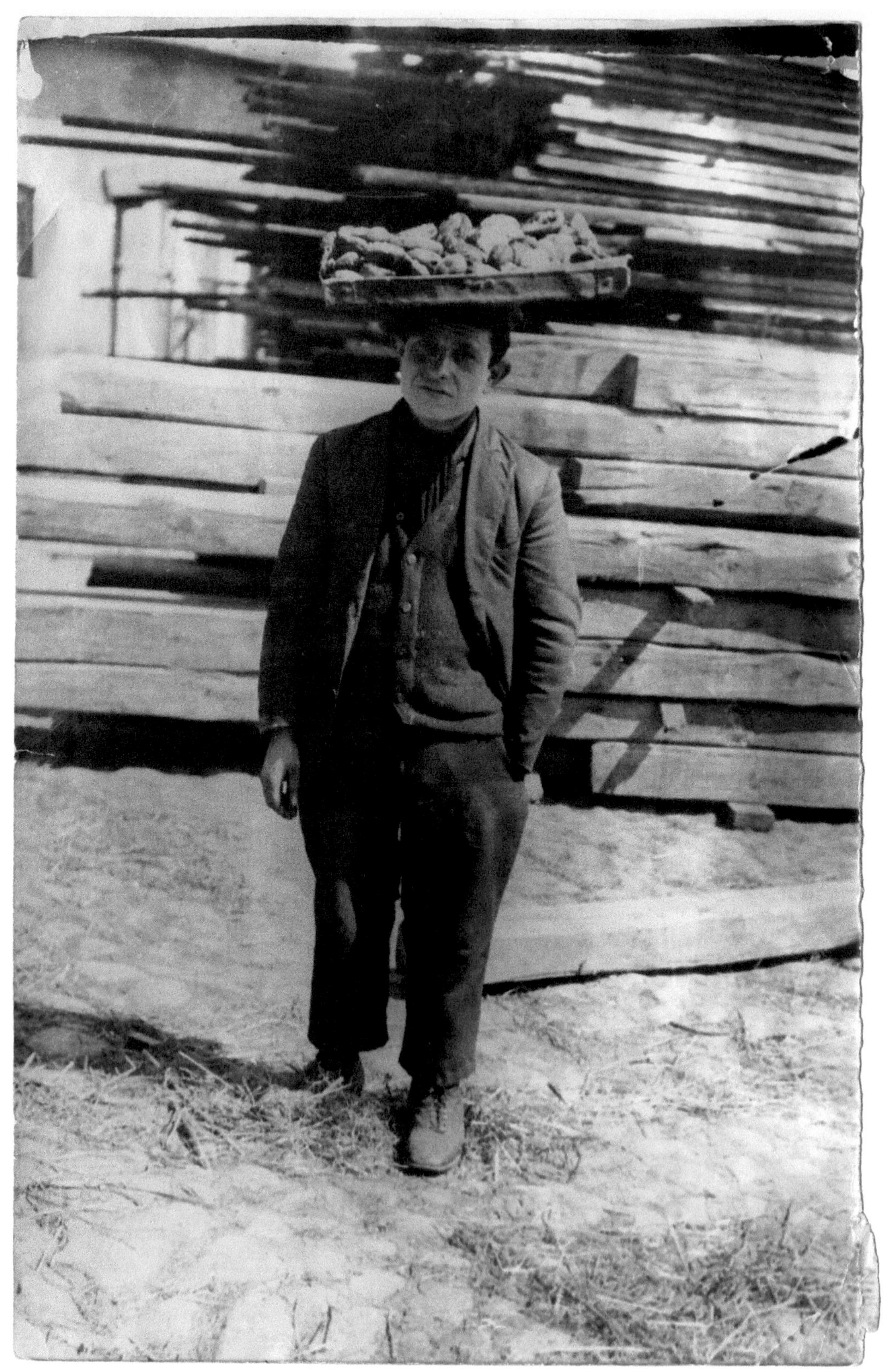

protect us, which could, God forbid, destroy the world. He ordered that the box be demolished.

But who would dare to approach the box?

They decided to draw lots. The shammes of the *khevre kadishe* [burial society] was selected.

A lot is a lot; it must be God's will and must be obeyed. The shammes recited the whole *Viduy* [confessional prayer before death] three times and proceeded to break open the box.

Fear and trembling fell on all of Chelm. The town was certain that a wild demon would spring forth from the box and reduce all of Chelm to rubble. They became even more terrified and astonished when they saw the melamed and his wife appear from the box.

After the melamed recounted how he and his wife ended up in the box, the Rabbi ordered the entire town to recite *Goymel* [prayer on surviving a life-threatening situation].

In order to prevent such a calamity from happening throughout the generations, they held a meeting and published four enactments: Henceforth and forever, no box should have wheels, no house should ever lack a threshold, no melamed should ever live on Synagogue Street, and no melamed should ever have a yen for blintzes on Shavuos.

These four decrees were duly inscribed in the town register as a perpetual reminder.

Yom Kippur in the Month of Tammuz

Once a merchant came to Chelm to sell wax. He set up a cart among the stores, but nobody was buying.

He stood by his cart for several days, but no customers showed up.

OPPOSITE: Types from Grozhibov, an important Jewish street in Warsaw. (From the Photographic Archives, YIVO Institute for Jewish Research)

This fellow happened to be clever and came up with an idea for getting rid of his entire stock. He went up and down the streets calling:

"Jews, prepare for the Day of Judgement!"

"Jews, the Day of Judgment is at hand!"

Hearing "Day of Judgment," Chelm was seized with trembling.

"What sort of judgment day?" they asked on all sides.

"What do you mean, what sort?" the merchant looked at them. "The day after tomorrow is, of course, Yom Kippur!"

When they heard "Yom Kippur," Chelm was terrified. How could Yom Kippur be the day after tomorrow, since Tisha B'Av[5] [a summer fast almost two months before Yom Kippur in the fall] hadn't yet occurred?

They ran and brought the town calendar and showed the merchant in black and white that the world was still in Tammuz [a summer month]. First you have to have Tisha B'Av [the ninth of the next month, Av], and what happened to Slikhes [penitential prayers during Elul, the month after Av] and Rosh Hashanah [the start of Tishrei, the following month]?

"You've made a mistake!" the merchant answered. "Your calendar is simply wrong!"

"What do you mean, a mistake?"

"A mistake, and that's all!" the merchant said, unwavering. "A human being can make a mistake. All the more so a calendar."

"If so," Chelm worried, "our Shavuos wasn't Shavuos, and on Peysach [Passover] we must have eaten leaven!"

Chelm was distraught. When they looked at the sky, it seemed that the sun should be a bit higher in Tammuz. Some began to perceive colder weather in their bones. An autumnal wind was blowing in Chelm. The merchant kept crying in the streets: "Jews, prepare for the day of judgment: The day after tomorrow is Yom Kippur!"[6]

In short, they mustn't let the mistake continue. It was too late for Rosh Hashanah, but at least they could observe Yom Kippur.

The town was in an uproar. The people assumed the attitude of the Days of Awe, recited Slikhes, engaged in repentance and good deeds.

The merchant went back to his buggy and wax. People needed to make wax candles, but nobody had prepared wax, so everyone raced to the merchant. He quickly raised the price and in one day was sold out.

Having sold all his wax, he went to the synagogue and announced that he was a fine cantor and happened to be in town. If they would pay him well, he would lead the Yom Kippur prayers, from Kol Nidre [opening prayer on the eve of the holiday] through Musef [afternoon prayer] and Neile [sundown prayer] as well.

The town grabbed the opportunity with delight. It must be that God Himself had sent him.

On Kol Nidre eve, when all of Chelm was in the synagogue and the houses of study, the merchant's partner showed up.

He saw with amazement a town in fear and trembling, empty streets, closed stores. Nobody was about. The light of tall wax candles shone from the houses. But it's just an ordinary Thursday. "What could have happened?" he wondered.

From a few children he found out that it was Yom Kippur and that everyone was in synagogue.

Confused, he went off to the synagogue. He went up to the eastern wall and took a look: His partner was standing at the reader's desk.

What was happening? Suddenly Yom Kippur, and his partner, who had never been a cantor, standing at the reader's desk. Something was fishy.

The "cantor" at the reader's desk noticed his partner and gave him a wink, indicating that he should be silent. He then began singing with the well-known melody of the Enkas Mesaldecho [prayer from the Neilah service at the conclusion of Yom Kippur],[7] and the congregation, thinking it was a new prayer, repeated it line for line:

> [The text is in rhymed Hebrew]
> I arrived in town, and they are all fools.
> I told them that today is Yom Kippur.
> I sold the wax for a high price.
> They also gave me 400 zloty,
> Half for you and half for me.
> Here today,
> Gone tomorrow: "then he ran off."
> Awesome and holy! [a standard poetic ending]

These stories have several variants.[8] Some tell that the events involved the well-known prankster Efraim Greydiger,[9] and the poem that he sang didn't end with "awesome and holy" but "God sitting on the throne of mercy" [the start of a well-known liturgical poem recited during Kol Nidre].

The Headless Rabbi

A stranger once traveled through Chelm past the synagogue courtyard and noticed that the shammes was standing and chopping a knotty block of wood. He was chopping and chopping but couldn't split it.

The stranger asked how long he had been chopping. The shammes answered that he had been struggling for three days but couldn't split the wood.

"You Chelmite!" the stranger laughed. "You have to set a

wedge into the block of wood. You hammer it, and one, two, three: the block is split."

The shammes couldn't grasp the idea at once.

"What are you saying? You set a 'wedge.' What sort of thing is that?"

The stranger explained again the idea of a wedge. He took a piece of wood, chopped one edge sharp and the other broad and flat, gave it to the shammes, and went off.

The shammes took the wedge, set it on the block with the flat side down and the sharp edge up, and gave it a blow with all his strength. The wedge flew up into his face and put out one of his eyes.

He started screaming, and all of Chelm ran up.

Seeing that the shammes had an eye put out, and having heard the whole story of the stranger and the wedge he had made and that the wedge had put out his eye, nobody had any doubt that the stranger was Satan himself and the wedge was a dangerous wrecking ball that could destroy all of Chelm.

What do you do with such an object?

They held a meeting and concluded that since the wedge was a destructive force that could, God forbid, destroy all of Chelm, they had to weaken its strength. The only way to do that would be to throw it into the synagogue.

With great trembling, all of Chelm pushed the wedge with long sticks from one place to another, until they had pushed it to the synagogue. They tossed it into the synagogue, locked door and window, and then went home relieved.

The next day they wanted to know what was happening to the object. They didn't know what to do: They were afraid to peek into a window, because it might put out their eye. To open the door would be a great risk, because it might run out and destroy all of Chelm.

They held a meeting, pondered and pondered, and concluded that they should go up to the attic, make a hole in the ceiling, and dangle the gabbai on a rope so he could see what the object was doing.

That's what they did.

They made a hole in the attic, tied the gabbai to a rope, and dangled him headfirst down into the synagogue.

He banged his head against the lectern and let out a terrified yelp.

As soon as he started shouting, they realized that the wedge was attacking him. They dragged him back up barely alive.

The next day they wanted to see once more what the object was up to. They held another meeting and concluded that looking through a window was a risk, opening the door was dangerous, because the wedge might run out and destroy all of Chelm. And the gabbai had already tried to enter from the attic. There was no other plan than tunneling under the synagogue and looking through a hole in the floor to see what the object was doing.

That's what they did. They tunneled under the synagogue, made a hole in the floor, and sent the Rabbi himself to peek inside.

The Rabbi crawled under the synagogue, stuck his head in the hole in the floor, glanced with fear at the wedge, and then wanted to draw his head back. But the hole in the floor was small, and he wasn't able to draw his head back so quickly. He became terrified and started screaming. As soon as he started shouting, they realized that the wedge was doing its work, so they started to pull the Rabbi by his feet with such force that they ripped off his head.

The town was in confusion. How can it be that the Rabbi had his head ripped off! Such a thing has never been heard of!

The Chelm householders comforted themselves:

"Maybe the Rabbi never had a head."

Who else but the synagogue shammes would know for certain if the Rabbi had a head or not?

They went to ask the shammes. He answered that since the Rabbi always sat covered with his tallis [prayer shawl] over his head day and night as he was studying, he didn't know whether the Rabbi had a head or not.

They went to ask the bathhouse attendant. After all, the Rabbi would go every Friday to the bathhouse, so he would know if the Rabbi had a head.

The bathhouse attendant answered that the Rabbi would always climb to the highest bench where the steam would rise over the shoulders, so he couldn't see if the Rabbi had a head.

They went to ask the Rabbi's wife. Who would know better than she if he had a head?

The Rabbi's wife answered that since the Rabbi would come home late at night from the *beys medresh* [house of study], and it was pitch black, she couldn't tell if he had a head or not.

They went from house to house to ask if anyone could ascertain whether the Rabbi had a head or not. Finally, a woman came and recounted that yesterday she had been to the Rabbi to ask a ritual question. He had shouted at her, "Let me alone! I have no head for your question!"

Now everyone was convinced that the Rabbi had never had a head, so they were relieved.[10]

They tell this story with variants. Some say that it wasn't a wedge but completely different: It was a synagogue that they built in Chelm without a door. They held a meeting to ponder how to get into the synagogue and concluded that they should make the entrance underground. They made a hole in the floor, and that's where the misfortune occurred. The Rabbi was in a hurry and wanted to inspect the synagogue, so he poked his head in but couldn't draw it back. All of Chelm ran up and tugged and tugged until they ripped off his head.

Again, others say that the story involved salt. The story goes that salt was once very expensive. Chelm thought the matter over. Why should we buy salt and pay so much, when we could sow salt, have our own for cheap and even sell it to others?

Chelm started sowing all the fields with salt. Wild animals came out of the forest at night and licked up the salt. So Chelm went to war against the beasts. Many

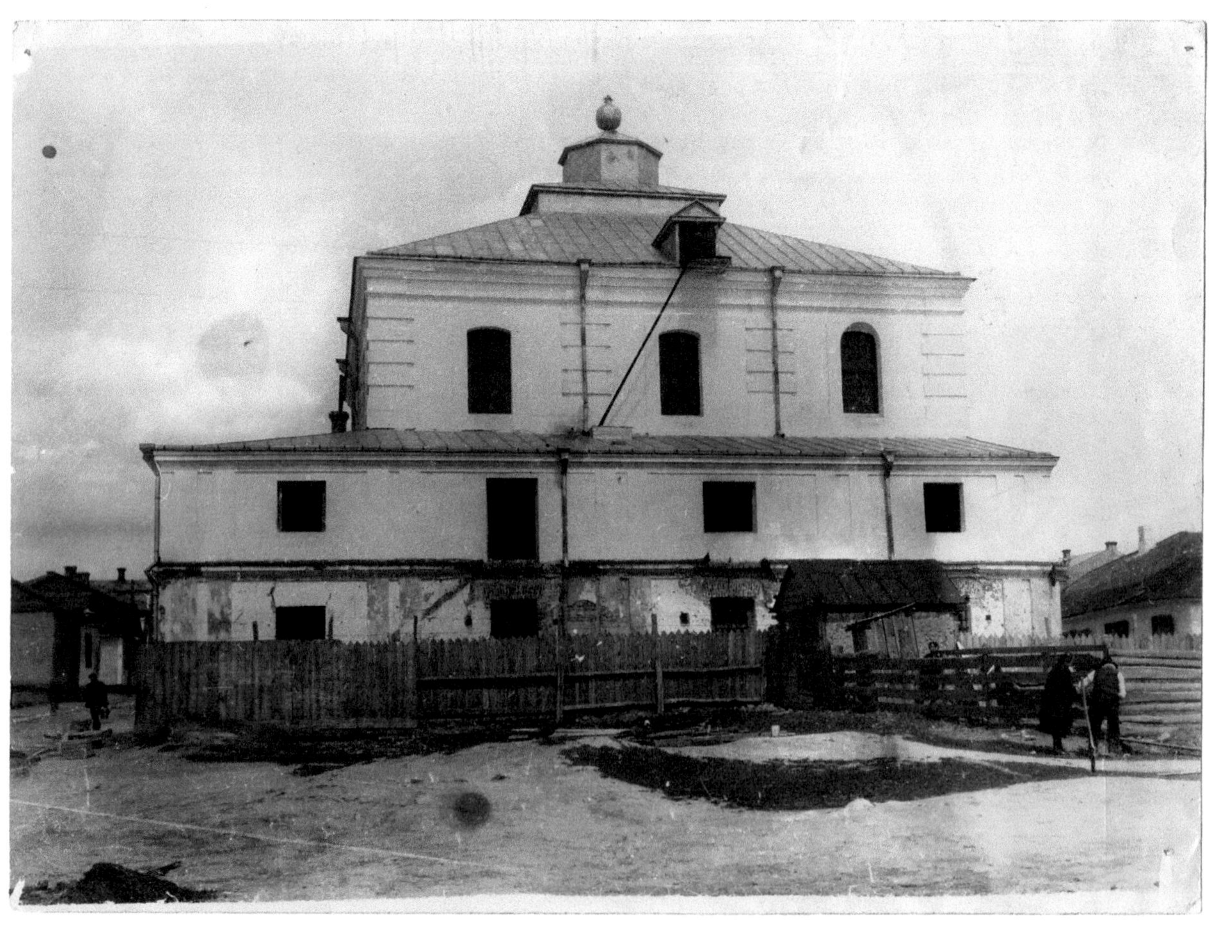

casualties fell on the field of battle, including the Rabbi. They found among the dead a corpse without a head but didn't know if that was the Rabbi. But did the Rabbi have a head or not? And then the story continues about how they asked everyone.

According to one version nobody could tell for certain if the Rabbi had a head, so they concluded that they should wait until someone saw him in a dream and reported whether he had a head or was headless.

According to another version, Chelm brought in outside experts who studied the Rabbi's writings and came to the conclusion, based on those writings, that he certainly had no head.

How Chelm Lost All Its Bedding

Once the bathhouse in Chelm burned down.

There was no money to build a new bathhouse, so everyone went about scratching. Everyone was red and raw from itching and scratching.

How can you manage without a sweat bath? Everyone would, God forbid, die of the itching and scratching.

They held a meeting, pondered for three days and three nights, and concluded that given that the town was poor, they should send forth three highly respected householders into the wide world to collect donations for a bathhouse.

No sooner said than done.

The three most respected and clever householders set out. Jews are "the merciful, children of the merciful," so when they heard that Chelm needed donations for a sweat bath, everyone contributed, both small and large. For months the three emissaries traveled from town to town, until they had collected enough money to build a new bathhouse.

OPPOSITE: Pub. November 7, 1924. Lutsk. The exterior of the fortress synagogue, built during the seventeenth century on the site of an older wooden synagogue. It was constructed in the form of a fortress to help defend against the invasions of the Cossacks and Tatars. (People of a Thousand Towns, YIVO Institute for Jewish Research)

When it was time to return to Chelm, they had a question: What should we do with the money? There were gangs of thieves and forest brigands around Chelm who might attack and make off with all the money they had collected.

They held a meeting, pondered and pondered, and concluded that carrying the money would be dangerous. Because the forest brigands outside of Chelm might attack them, they should convert all the money into merchandise and send it to Chelm by wagon.

But they had a new worry: What would happen if the thieves and forest brigands attacked the wagons? They would grab the merchandise, and Chelm would again remain without a bathhouse.

They held another meeting, pondered for three days and three nights, and concluded that carrying the money was very dangerous: The thieves and brigands who infest the forests around Chelm might attack them and take the money. So they should buy merchandise with the money they had collected and send it to Chelm by wagon. But there is then the concern that brigands might attack the wagons and take the merchandise. So the best, most certain plan would be to buy feathers with the entire sum of money and send the feathers with the wind to Chelm and thereby be safe from robbers and brigands.

That's what they did.

They bought feathers with the entire sum of money, waited for an auspicious time when the wind was blowing in the direction of Chelm, and sent the feathers flying. Calm and satisfied, they returned home to Chelm.

When they arrived in Chelm, they were greeted with great honor, and the town was delighted that finally there would be money to build a new sweat bath, and people would have an end to scratching.

"Where is the money?" they were asked.

The three emissaries told how, being afraid that brigands

might attack them and take the money, they decided to buy merchandise and send it to Chelm, where they could sell the merchandise and build the bathhouse. But since sending merchandise by wagon also posed a risk of robbery, they bought feathers and sent them to Chelm by wind, so they were entirely safe from brigands and robbers.

In Chelm "joy and gladness" reigned.[11] Feathers are no laughing matter! It's a safe form of merchandise that can easily be sold, and it's also of use already.

"Where then are the feathers?"

They waited one day, two days, three days. All of Chelm was occupied in going to the outskirts of Chelm to meet the feathers. But they neither saw nor heard them.

"Obviously, they are delayed on the way," they comforted themselves. "A person can be delayed; all the more so feathers."

More days passed, and the feathers had still not arrived.

Chelm held an enormous meeting, pondered three days and three nights,[12] and concluded that in order to protect the money from brigands, the emissaries had acted properly in buying feathers and sending them safely on the wind. But the feathers hadn't arrived? It's simple:

They lost their way.

These feathers had never been to Chelm, so they didn't know the way, and, poor things, they are wandering about somewhere not knowing how to fly to the town.[13]

What can we do?

They held another meeting, pondered for another three days and nights, and concluded that since the feathers had lost their way and couldn't find the way to Chelm, they should send Chelm feathers out to meet them and show them the way to Chelm.

And that's what they did.

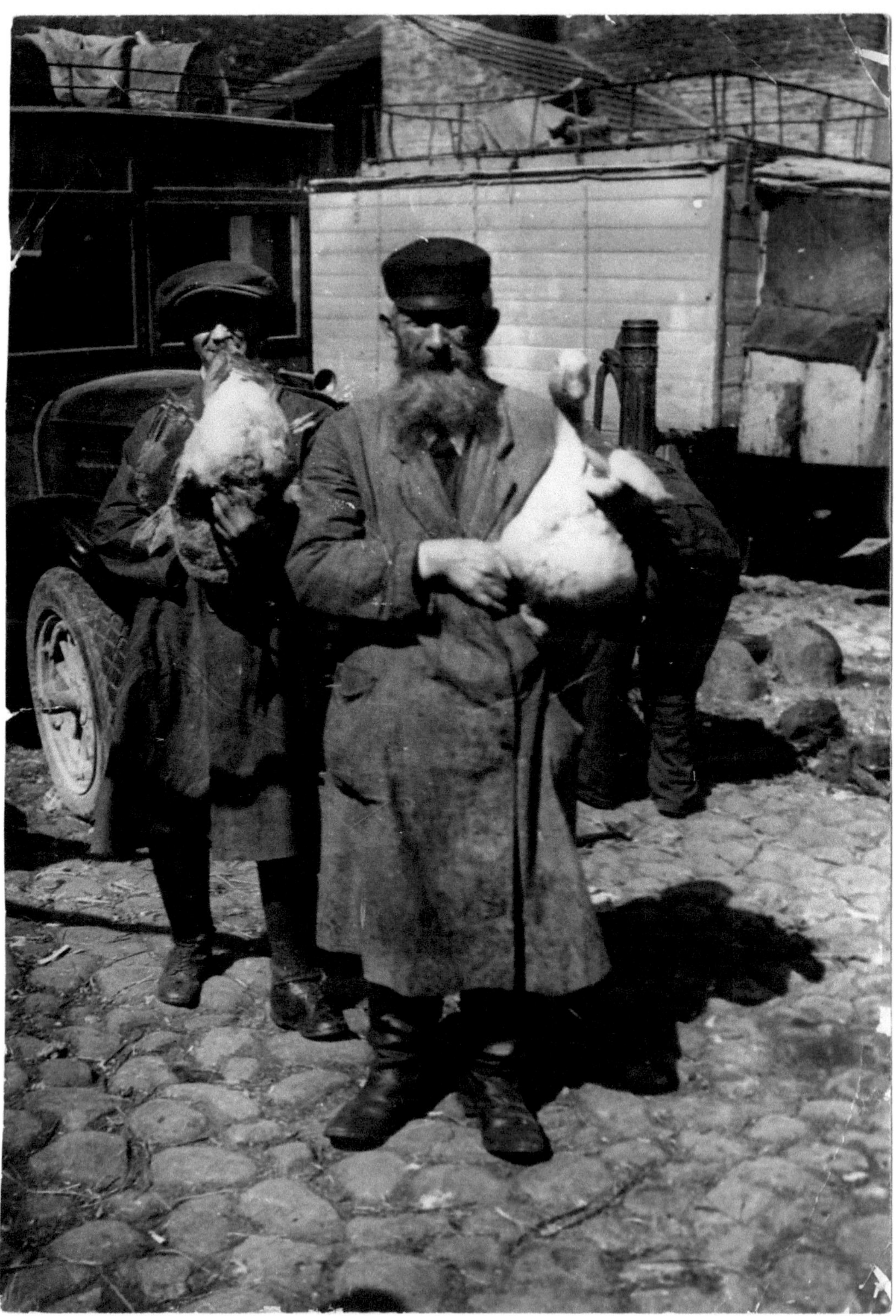

All of Chelm brought out their bedding to the outskirts of town, opened the seams of the pillows, and let the feathers loose in the wind to find the lost feathers and bring them into town.

That's how Chelm ended up without a sweat bath and without bedding.

Whom Did the Chelm Rabbi Greet with "Good Sabbath"?

Three Chelm Jews were eating on the Sabbath in the middle of the marketplace, warming themselves in the sun. The Rabbi passed by and said to them, "Good Shabbos" [Good Sabbath].

A dispute arose among the three. Each of them said that the "Good Shabbos" was for him and not the others. They fought over this until they decided to go to the Rabbi and ask which of them the Rabbi greeted with "Good Shabbos."[14]

When they came to the Rabbi, he answered that the "Good Shabbos" was for whoever was the biggest fool of the three.

They left the Rabbi and again started fighting, because each of them said that he was the biggest fool and that the Rabbi had directed the "Good Shabbos" only to him.

They fought for a long time, none of them willing to give in to the others, until they decided to go again to the Rabbi and ask which of them was the biggest fool.

When they came to the Rabbi, he asked each of them to tell him what sort of foolishness they had committed, and then he would tell them which was the biggest fool.

The first started his story:

"When I got married, I received a large dowry and a fur hat, a gift from my father-in-law, with the condition that I must never touch the fur hat with my hands. If I violated the condition, I would lose the dowry. My wife used to

OPPOSITE: He has transported his geese from the provinces to Warsaw to bring them to market. (From the Photographic Archives, YIVO Institute for Jewish Research)

dress me in the hat and later take it off, so I never touched it with my hands.

"One Shabbos, right in the middle of winter, the snow and frost were severe. I went with my fur hat to the synagogue, but a strong wind came and blew the hat off my head into the snow.

"What could I do, since I wasn't supposed to touch the hat with my hands?

"I lay down in the snow and started to kick and burrow into the snow under the hat until I had managed to place my head under the hat. That's how I got it back on my head. So, Rabbi, what do you think?"

"You are certainly a big fool! But we still need to hear what the next one says. Maybe he's even a greater fool."

The second started telling about his foolishness:

"When I got married, I received a large dowry. Right after the wedding I bought a cart and horse and went with the money to Ludmir to the big market. There I bought a large consignment of coverings, rugs, and carpets. I started to pack it all on the wagon. But it wouldn't fit. I had too much merchandise for such a small wagon. What could I do?

"I dreamed up a plan. I struck my horse with a few good slaps and ordered it to take the loaded goods by itself to Chelm, and I loaded the remaining rugs and carpets on a second wagon, which I rented, and I traveled with it to Chelm.

"When I arrived in Chelm, I expected that my horse and cart that I sent ahead with the merchandise would already be home. But that's not what happened. No horse, no cart, no merchandise. Thieves had stolen it all, and that's how I lost all the dowry. What do you think, Rabbi? Am I not a bigger fool?"

"You are certainly a big fool!" the Rabbi agreed. "But we still need to hear from the third fellow. Maybe he's a bigger fool than both of you."

The third started telling his story:

"When I got married, I also received a large dowry. I soon opened a tavern, sold whiskey to the peasants, and made a living.

"The tavern had a street door, which we would lock every night before going to sleep.

"Once, when I and my wife, Genendl, were already warmly covered in bed, I remembered that I hadn't locked the door.[15] I told my wife to go lock the door. She said that it was cold, so I should go lock the door. I said to her that I had locked the door yesterday; today it was her turn to lock the door. She began to shout that yesterday she had locked the door, so it was my turn today. I shouted back, 'Liar!' She retorted, 'Fumbler! Good for nothing! Fool!' This went on until we had enough of fighting, and we decided that we should both be silent. Whichever one made the first noise would have to go lock the door.

"We lay in bed and were silent.

"Suddenly a soldier opened the door and shouted in Russian, 'Give me vodka!'

"We remained silent.

"'Give me vodka!'

"We let out not a sound.

"The soldier saw that we weren't answering him. He went to the barrel, drew a glass of whiskey, and drank it down.

"We remained silent.

"He drank down another glass, and we remained silent.

"He got completely drunk, started to dance, jumping and pounding his fists on the table. We remained silent.

"The soldier thought about it, came over to my bed, and started tickling me in my beard.

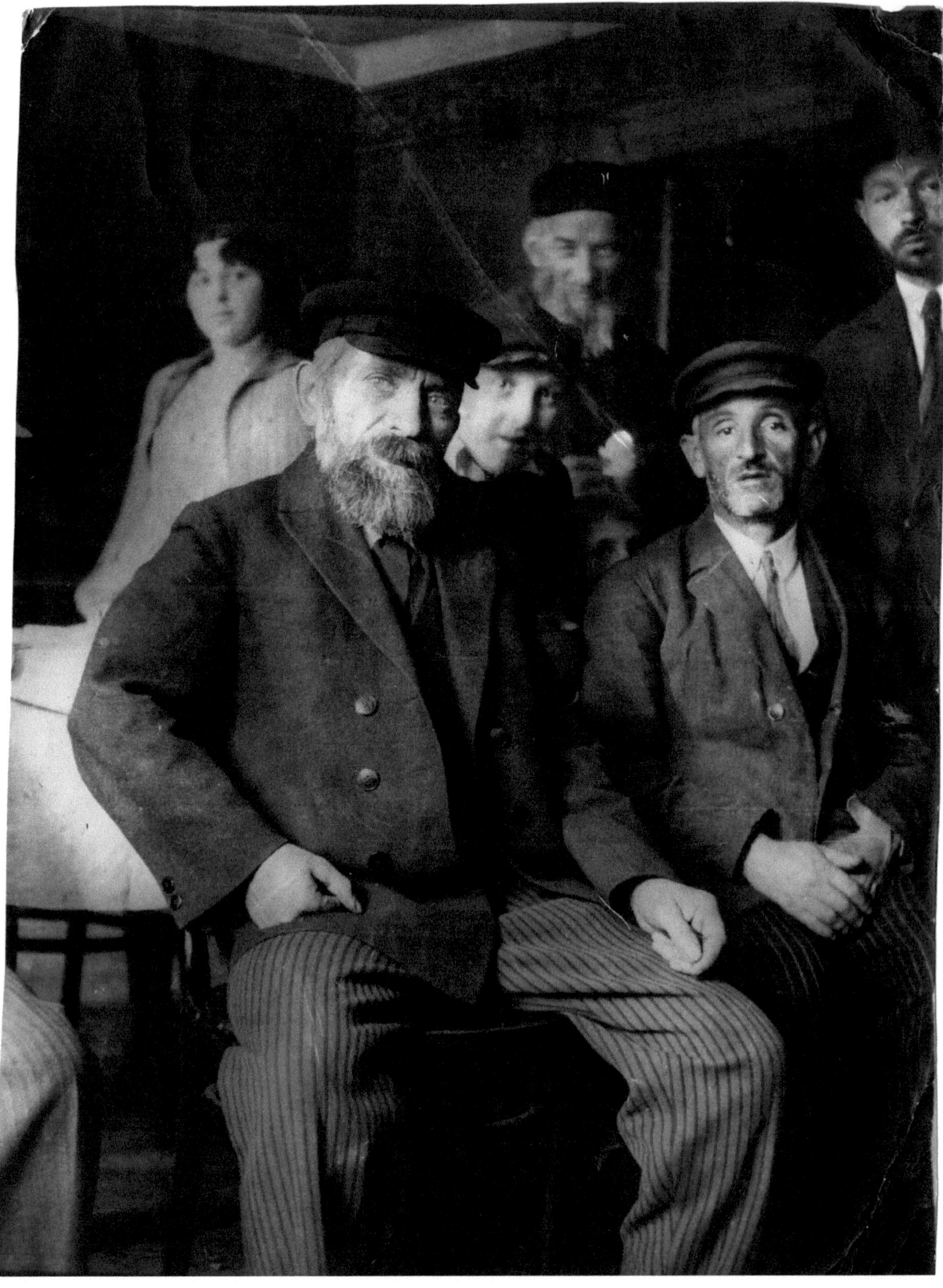

"I thought I wouldn't be able to, but I remained silent.

"He took the yarmulke from my head, filled it with stinking water from the chamber pot, and put it back on my head.

"I couldn't take it anymore. I called out with a suffocated voice:

"'*Gevald*![16] It stinks! I could get cholera!'

"'Aha! You spoke first!' my Genendl exclaimed from her bed. 'So you go, fumbler, and lock the door!' So, Rabbi, what do you think of that?"

"You are certainly the biggest fool!" the Rabbi said. You stood for it so long and didn't say a word; you should have managed just a bit longer and not given in to your wife!"

The third fellow left the Rabbi's study happy, especially because it must have been to him that the Rabbi had wished a "Good Shabbos."[17]

You Have to Know How to Speak to a Rabbi

Three Chelmer Jews were walking on Tisha B'Av in the marketplace. One was sick, the second was old, and the third suffered from a hernia.[18]

Because they were suffering from the fast, they decided to go to the Rabbi's study to get permission to eat.

The sick one went in first.

"Rabbi," he said, "I'm sick. May I eat?"

"If you are sick, you may eat," the Rabbi answered, "but don't be insolent. You should know how to speak to a Rabbi: When you tell a Rabbi that you are sick, you should add "it shouldn't happen to you."

When he came out, the old Jew asked him what the Rabbi had said. He recounted to him that he had told him to eat, but you have to know how to speak to a Rabbi.

OPPOSITE: Nathan Bialystoker with his family. An innkeeper. (From the Photographic Archives, YIVO Institute for Jewish Research)

"How, then?"

"When you tell something to the Rabbi, you should add "it shouldn't happen to you."

The old Jew went in to the Rabbi's study and asked,

"Rabbi, I am, it shouldn't happen to you, old.
May I eat?"

"If you are old and can't manage the fast, you may eat. But don't be insolent. When you tell a Rabbi that you are old, you don't say 'it shouldn't happen to you.' You say 'may it be upon you and your children.'"

The old Jew went out. The one with a hernia asked him what the Rabbi had said. He recounted to him that he told him to eat, but he had upbraided him that he didn't know how to speak with a Rabbi.

"How should you speak, then?"

"When you speak with a Rabbi, you should say 'may it be upon you and your children.'"

The man with the hernia went in and asked,

"Rabbi, I suffer, may it be upon you and your children, from a hernia. May I eat?"[19]

Pills for the Holy Spirit

The well-known prankster Efraim Greydiger once came to Chelm.[20] He wanted to collect money for a charity, but the Chelmites were unwilling to contribute. He arrived at a plan: He went out of town, collected goat turds, coated them with confectioner's sugar, and set up a table in the middle of the marketplace. He started calling out:

"Jews: Pills for the holy spirit! An amazing bargain at a fair price. Whoever eats a single pill acquires the holy spirit."

When they heard "pills for the holy spirit," all of Chelm came at a run: men, women, boys, and even girls.

"How much do the pills cost?" the crowd was eager to know.

"Ten groshns apiece. But with a condition: When you buy a pill, you mustn't eat it at once. You have to wait a day to taste the pill. If you eat it at once, it will have no effect."

All of Chelm started buying the pills. A poor person would buy one pill for ten groshns. Someone with a bit of money would buy several pills, and a rich person could afford a full plate of pills, for himself, for his wife, and for his children as well. Within an hour Efraim Greydiger had sold all the pills and accumulated a lot of money.

That night, as he was leaving town, a woman ran up with a lament.

"What's the matter?"

She was delayed. She hadn't been in Chelm, and now she had found out about the bargain that all of Chelm had bought. All the women had gotten pills for the holy spirit, but she alone would remain, God forbid, without holy spirit. She asked him to have pity on her and sell her at least one pill so she would also know of the taste.

"How can I help it, madam," he responded. "I don't have any more!"

But the woman wouldn't let him alone. She fainted, she cried with bitter tears, she asked him to have pity on her.

He couldn't bear to see her great pain. He looked and looked until he found somewhere one dried-out pill. He said to her:

"It's your lucky day, madam. I have found for you the very last pill that I had kept for myself. But the price is forty groshns. But for this price, you can taste the pill immediately, although the entire town has to wait until tomorrow."

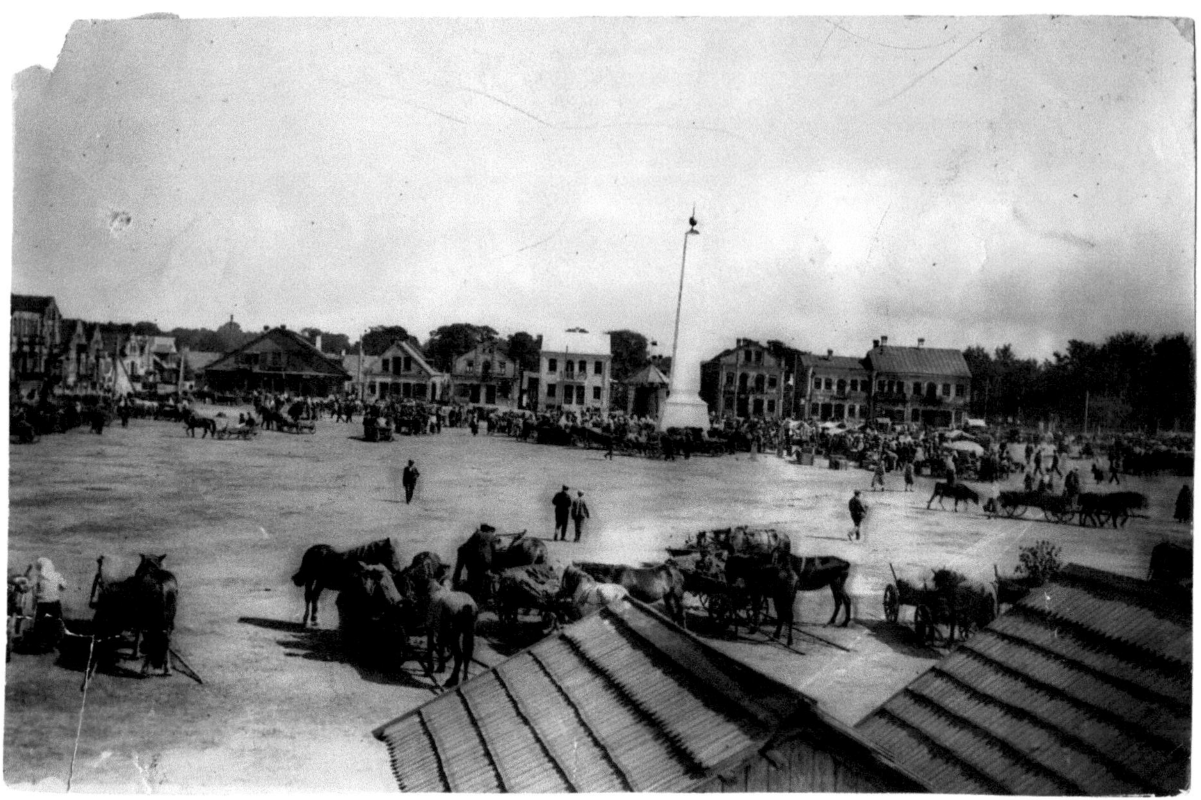

She had no choice. She gave him forty groshns and immediately put the pill in her mouth.

"*Gevald*!" she let out a squeal. "It's a goat turd!"

"Now you see, madam, that it is truly worth forty groshns! You realize that it is a goat turd, but all of Chelm will only find that out tomorrow." He laughed and was on his way.

Chelm Truth

The citizens of Chelm once noticed that there was no truth to be found. The whole world had truth, but Chelm alone was missing it. What can one do, because you can't live without truth?

They held a meeting, pondered and pondered, and concluded that they needed to send for truth out in the world.

"Where should we look?"

"In Lithuania!"[21]

They hired a fellow with a horse and cart and sent him to buy truth.

The closest Lithuanian town was Brest. So the fellow with the horse and cart set off on the path to Brest.

Having traveled all day, he stopped for the night at an inn, led his horse into a stall, and went in to the inn.

"Welcome! Where do you come from, and where are you headed?" the innkeeper greeted him.

"I come from Chelm, and I'm headed to Brest. They sent me to buy truth," the fellow explained.

"Truth?" the innkeeper hummed. He quickly realized who he was dealing with.

Now the innkeeper was a clever fellow. He said to the Chelmite, "I can sell you truth!"

"How much does your truth cost, and in what form do you sell it?" the Chelmite asked. He figured that God had sent him truth while he was on the way.

"I sell truth by the cask. One cask costs no less than five hundred *kerbls* [another name for a ruble]."[22]

"Five hundred? That's too expensive; I didn't bring that much," the Chelmite answered. "I'll go back to Chelm and present the case to the community. If they give me the money, I'll return and buy the merchandise."

The next day the fellow traveled back to Chelm and explained to the community that on his way to Brest, he chanced upon an inn where he could buy truth, but it would cost five hundred kerbls for a cask.

OPPOSITE: Pub. March 7, 1926. Lukow. "The eyes and ears of a whole town are turned to it . . ." The town crier. The liberty bell on what looks like a telegraph pole rings out good news, bad news, fire alarms and it even announces when the town bath is ready for customers. (People of a Thousand Towns, YIVO Institute for Jewish Research)

They held a meeting and concluded that five hundred kerbls was really a lot of money, but since they simply couldn't survive without truth and since they might not find any in Brest itself, or it might be more expensive there, they would pay the five hundred kerbls. The fellow with the cart set out again to the inn to buy truth.

When he arrived at the inn and handed over the five hundred kerbls, the innkeeper took a cask and filled it with the kind of "merchandise" that, no matter what language you speak, even the Holy Tongue, lets out a stench. He sealed it tightly and placed it on the cart. The fellow carried it back right to Chelm.

Outside town, all of Chelm came to meet him, along with the mayor and the most honorable citizens, to greet him as befits truth itself.

The fellow brought the cask to the mayor's yard. There the crowd grew even bigger.

With great care, the mayor and the onlookers removed the cask from the cart and placed it in the middle of the yard. Then they drilled a hole in the cask. The mayor approached and took a sniff.

"Yuck! It stinks!" he cried out and held his nose.

The second gabbai came up and put his nose to the hole.

"True!" and with a sour face he waved his hands.

The third gabbai came up and also cried out,

"True!"

Likewise the fourth and the fifth gabbai. Everyone who took a sniff cried out, "True!"

That's why to this day in Chelm they say that the truth stinks.

The "Morning Watch" Society

Once a plague broke out in Chelm. Children departed from the world, let it not happen today. The situation was terrible.

They held a meeting in order to get some advice and determine what sort of action the town should undertake to halt the plague.

They pondered and pondered and concluded that they should found a "morning watch" society. Jews should wake up every day before dawn, pray, and study Torah. That should halt the plague.

That's what they did.

But the Chelmites were deep sleepers and were unable to wake up.

So the situation was still terrible.

They held another meeting and concluded that there should certainly be a "morning watch" society, but since the people were deep sleepers and couldn't arouse themselves from sleep, they should hire a shammes to wake them up.

That's what they did.

The shammes came the next morning with a complaint. He was cold at night and was afraid that he might get so cold that he would die.

So the situation was still terrible.

They held another meeting and concluded that there should certainly be a "morning watch" society, but since the people couldn't wake themselves up, they should hire a shammes to wake them up. But then what? The shammes complained that he was cold at night and might even, God forbid, die of the cold. So they should dress him in a fur coat. He would be warm, not catch a cold, and, God forbid, not die.

That's what they did.

The town gabbai came up and interrupted the reading of the Torah with a complaint: Given that he himself wore a fur coat, nobody would be able to distinguish the gabbai from the shammes.

They held another meeting and concluded that there should certainly be a "morning watch" society, but since the people couldn't wake themselves up, they should hire a shammes to wake them up. But the shammes complained that he was cold at night and might even, God forbid, die of the cold. So they would buy him a fur coat so he wouldn't, God forbid, catch cold and die. But then what? The gabbai interrupted the reading of the Torah with a complaint that he also wore a fur coat, and nobody would be able to distinguish the gabbai from the shammes. So they should reverse the shammes's coat with the fur side out, and people would then be able to distinguish the gabbai from the shammes.

That's what they did.

But the next morning the shammes came up with a new complaint. Wearing the reversed coat, with the fur side out, he was attacked by dogs that thought that he was a wolf, and they bit him and ripped him to shreds.

So the situation was still terrible.

They held another meeting and concluded that there should certainly be a "morning watch" society, but since the people couldn't wake themselves up, they should hire a shammes to wake them up. But the shammes complained that he was cold at night and might even, God forbid, die of the cold. They would buy him a fur coat so he wouldn't, God forbid, catch cold and die. But then nobody would be able to distinguish the gabbai from the shammes. So they should reverse the shammes's coat with the fur side out, and people would then be able to distinguish the gabbai from the shammes. But at night the dogs thought he was a wolf and were attacking him. So they should buy a horse and seat the shammes on it. Now the dogs wouldn't think that he was a wolf, and they wouldn't bite him.

That's what they did.

But then the question arose: Where would they keep the horse?

They held another meeting and concluded that they should keep the horse in the women's balcony of the synagogue.

That's what they did.

The next day the women came to the synagogue. In terror they screamed that they were afraid to pray alongside a horse lest it kick them.

They held a meeting and concluded that since the women were afraid to pray alongside the horse, because it might kick, they should move the horse to the men's section of the synagogue.

That's what they did.

The next day, as they came into the synagogue, everyone shoved the horse away from his place, so the horse again had nowhere to stand.

They held a brand-new meeting and concluded that since nobody would let the horse stand in the synagogue near his place, they should place it at the reader's desk.

But it was still terrible. After all, where is the cantor to stand?

They held another meeting and concluded that the cantor should sit on the horse.[23]

But now it was really terrible. Since the cantor was sitting on the horse, how would he manage to back up three paces at the end of the standing prayer?

They finally held a great meeting and concluded that at the point when he was concluding the standing prayer, the gabbai

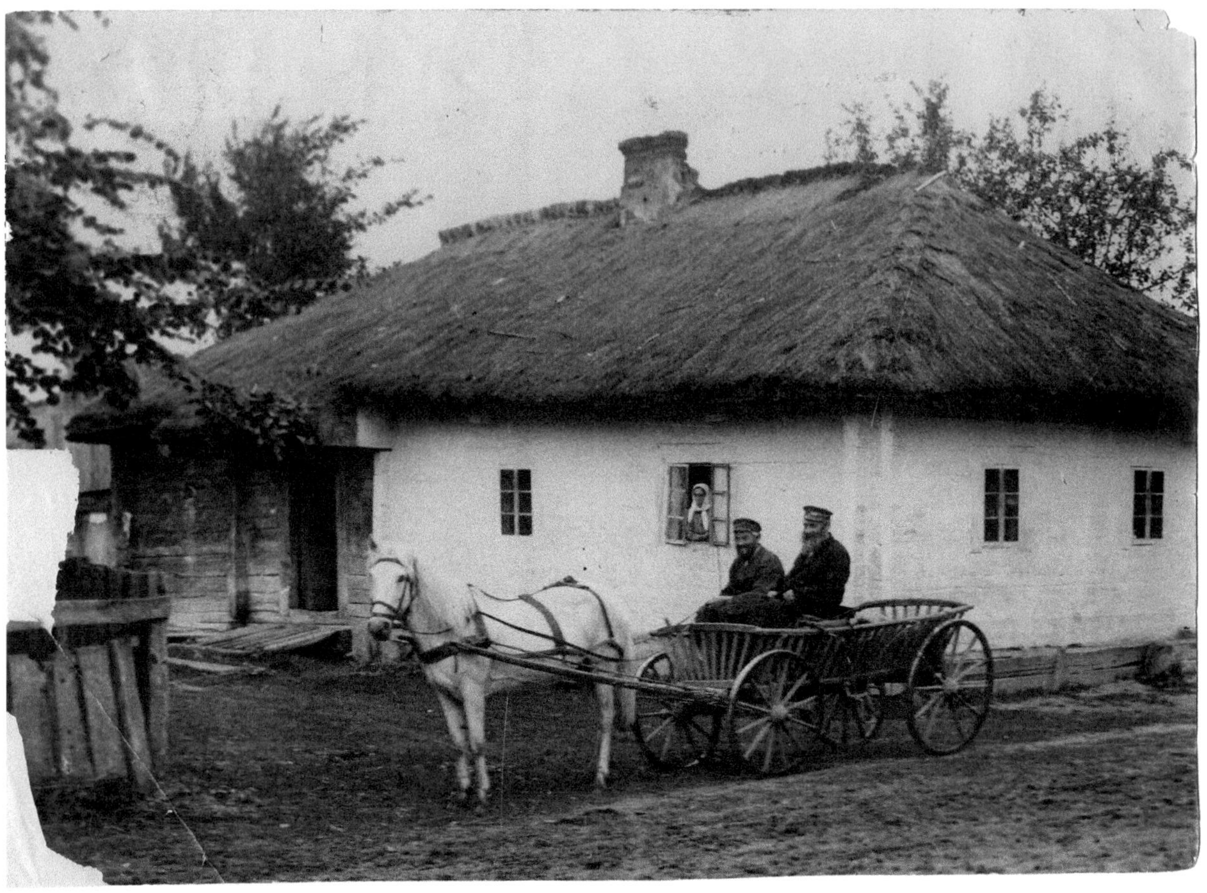

should tug the horse's tail, and it would back up.

That's exactly what they did.

So to this very day, when you see the Chelm gabbai pulling a horse by the tail, you know that they are about to conclude the standing prayer.

The Chelm Cripple

Once a Chelmite took a trip with a wagon to Warsaw. He held both hands stiffly in front of himself, with two fingers poking up.

"A cripple, poor thing," everyone commiserated, "a man with useless hands, may God protect us."

The man went to the wagon, settled on a price with the wagon driver. He couldn't move his hands, so he asked the driver to reach into his pocket to take out the money that they had agreed on.

"A pity," people nodded their heads. "He can't move his hands."

The traveler wanted to climb onto the wagon but was unable, so the wagon driver pushed and shoved until he had settled the traveler up on the wagon and seated him comfortably among the other passengers. They set out for Warsaw.

The cripple sat there with his useless hands and the stiff fingers and looked out at God's world on the way from Chelm to Warsaw. All the other passengers bemoaned the fact that God had punished someone by giving him useless hands.

After traveling a half day and all night, they had needed to help the cripple several times. Here he had to get down from the wagon, here they had to pull him back up. They really went all out for him. It's no small matter, to have two useless hardened hands and two fingers pointing up.

Only when they were approaching Warsaw did a woman, sitting on the wagon directly across from the traveler, ask:

"Tell me, uncle, has it been a long time since you suffered the misfortune?"

"What misfortune?" the Chelmite answered in a fright.

"The misfortune with your useless hands, that you are holding out with two fingers up."

"That's not uselessness," he answered. "That's a measure. Given that I'm traveling to Warsaw, my wife had me promise to bring her a pair of shoes. I took the measure of her feet, and that's precisely the distance between these fingers that I'm holding up. The shoes shouldn't be larger orsmaller even a hair's breadth. You don't know my wife. If I get it wrong, she'll kill me."

OPPOSITE: Pub. Oct. 4, 1925. Ushitsa, Ukraine. [English] Outside a cottage with a thatched roof: two men in traditional dress pose in a horse drawn telega (wagon); the woman posing in the window is the mother of well-known cantor Mordekhai Hirshman, who served in Vilna and the United States. [Yiddish] "If you don't have a Ford than a 'ferd' [horse] will do," joke the Jewish merchants of the Ukrainian village. The horse and wagon is their major partner. (People of a Thousand Towns, YIVO Institute for Jewish Research)

The Night Watch

The previous story, but quite different.

A blacksmith once arrived in Chelm. The town came out to see what sort of person he was. They saw that he was dark-haired and sooty. They reasoned:

The blacksmith is dark-haired, and such folk are gypsies, and gypsies are thieves, he might steal us blind.

They held a meeting and concluded that since the blacksmith might steal all the merchandise in town, the storekeepers should stay up all night and sleep by day, and everyone else should stay awake during the day and sleep by night, and the blacksmith wouldn't be able to steal.

That's what they did. The storekeepers stayed up at night and slept during the day.

But there was, of course, nobody to sell anything during the day.

So they held another meeting and concluded that since the storekeepers were sleeping all day, and nobody was available to sell merchandise in town, they should hire a watchman to stay up at night and sleep by day, so the storekeepers could sell their merchandise.

That's what they did.

The watchman came the next morning and said that it was cold at night, and he was afraid of catching cold and dying.

So the situation was still bad.

They held another meeting and considered the matter:

Given that the watchman was cold and might catch cold and die, what could they do so he wouldn't be cold, catch cold, and die?

They pondered and pondered and concluded that they should wrap him in a fur coat, so he wouldn't catch cold and die.

That's what they did.

The town gabbai came with a complaint.

He himself wore a fur coat. Now if the watchman was wearing a fur coat, too, nobody would be able to tell the difference between the gabbai and the watchman.

They held another meeting, pondered and pondered, and concluded that they should turn the watchman's coat inside out, with the fur side out, and people would then distinguish the watchman from the gabbai.

That's what they did.

Quite early the next day the watchman came at a run with his inside-out coat and a complaint. At night, wolves attacked him, thinking that he was a sheep, and tried to eat him.

They held a new meeting to ponder what to do, so the wolves wouldn't think that the watchman with the inside-out coat was a sheep and try to eat him.

They pondered and pondered and concluded that they should place the watchman with his inside-out coat on a horse. Then the wolves wouldn't think we was a sheep, and they wouldn't try to eat him.

That's what they did.

The next day the watchman came at a run once again with a complaint that the horse had carried him off at night and practically threw him into the ditch.

They held another meeting, pondered and pondered what to do to prevent the horse from carrying the watchman out of the town and into the ditches. They concluded that they should tie the horse to a pole, so the watchman would no longer be carried off out of town and into the ditch.

That's what they did.

There arose a controversy in town. Everyone wanted the horse with the watchman to be tied up near his store.

They held a new, enormous, meeting and pondered the matter from start to finish:

A blacksmith has come to town. He is sooty and dark-haired. Dark-haired people are gypsies. Gypsies are thieves. They are worried that the blacksmith might rob all the town's merchandise. The whole town should remain awake during the day and sleep at night, and the storekeepers should be up at night and sleep during the day. But then nobody was around to sell during the day. So they hired a watchman to sleep by day and stay awake at night, so the storekeepers could sleep at night and be up during the day and sell their merchandise. But the watchman complained that it was cold at night, and he might catch his death of cold. So they wrapped him in a fur coat to prevent his getting cold at night. The gabbai complained that he himself wore a fur coat, and people wouldn't be able to distinguish the gabbai from the watchman. They turned the watchman's coat inside out, so people once again could distinguish the gabbai from the watchman. But at night a wolf attacked the watchman, thinking him a sheep, and tried to eat him. So they put the watchman on a horse so the wolf would know that he was a watchman and not eat him. But the watchman was afraid the horse would carry him out of town into the ditch. So they decided to tie the horse to a pole. But there was a controversy, because every storekeeper wanted to have the horse tied near his shop. How could they resolve the controversy and satisfy everyone?

They pondered for seven days and seven nights and concluded that since the old bathhouse belonged to everyone, they should tie the horse with the watchman near the old bathhouse, and nobody would complain.

That's what they did.

They took the horse and tied it to a pole near the old bathhouse, seated the watchman on it, and that's how he protected all of Chelm from robbery.[24]

The next morning the watchman came and said that it appeared that thieves had been wandering about the shops.

They ran to see and found all the shops emptied of merchandise.

They attacked the watchman from all sides:

"Why didn't you catch the thieves?"

"Because I was sitting on a horse, and the horse was tied up near the old bathhouse," he answered.

"So why didn't you untie the horse?"

"Because I was afraid that it would drag me into the ditch," he answered.

"So why didn't you get off the horse?"

"Because my fur coat is inside out, and I was afraid that a wolf might think that I was a sheep and try to eat me."

"Then why didn't you turn the fur coat back to the normal side?"

"Because the town gabbai also wears a fur coat, and people need to distinguish between the gabbai and the watchman," he answered.

"They why didn't you simply take the coat off?" they asked him.

"Because I was afraid that I might catch my death of cold," he answered.

"Then why didn't you call out and wake us up to catch the thieves?"

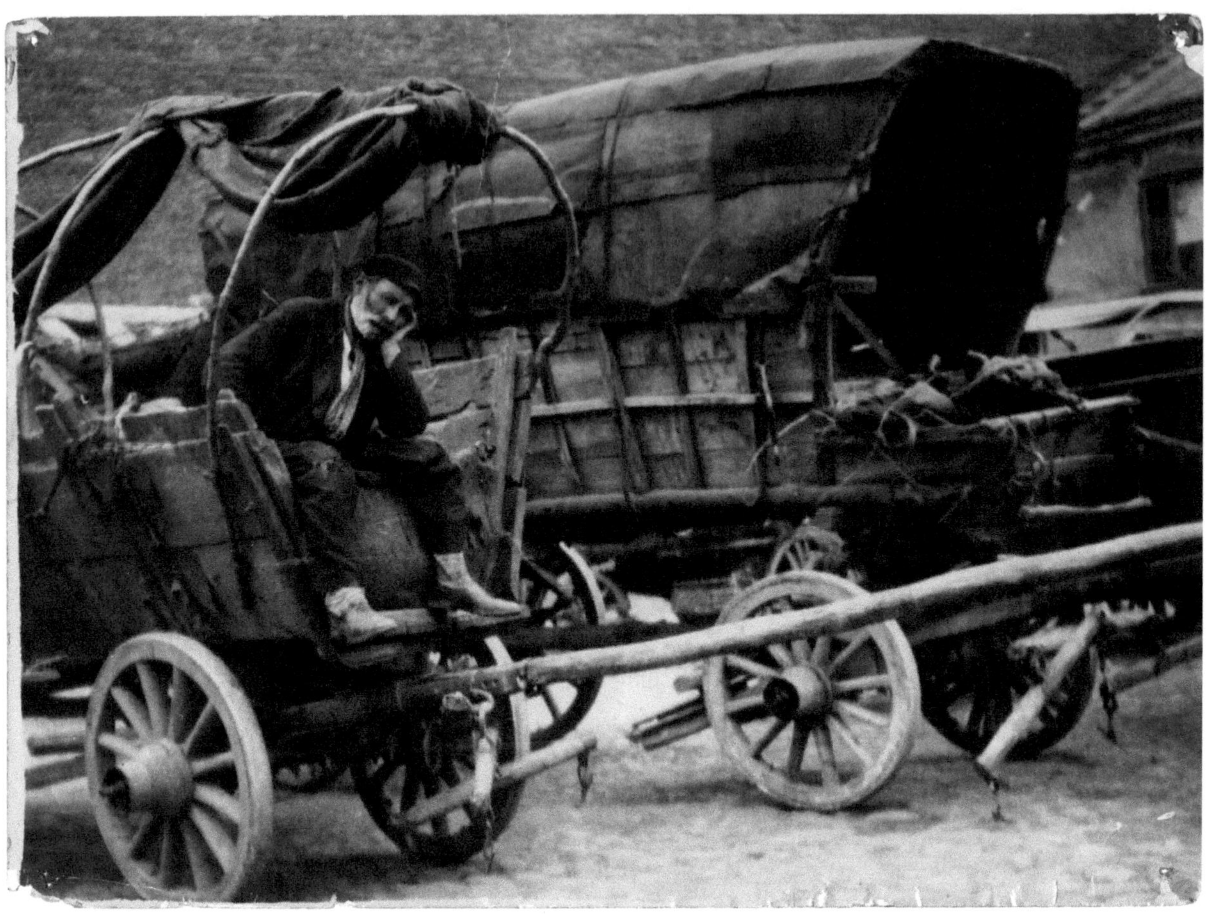

“Just listen to you! That’s why you hired me, to be up at night and sleep by day, so you could be up by day and sleep by night,” he answered.

Hearing such clever responses, all of Chelm applauded and called out,

“There’s no town as clever as Chelm anywhere!”

For his cleverness and quick-headedness they doubled his pay.

Interestingly, I have been assured that there actually was a pole near the old bathhouse until the [first world] war. The Germans came and used to tie their war horses to it every day until they uprooted it.[25]

The Rabbi Had a Calf

The Rabbi of Chelm suddenly became ill, and nobody knew what the matter was. They had him drink fish oil, they let blood, they applied cups, they exorcised an evil eye, but nothing helped.

All the Chelmites gathered for a meeting, pondered and pondered and tried to figure out what was wrong with the Rabbi. One suggested that he had a fever. Another said that it was hemorrhoids. A third one suggested that he had a pain in his belly. Since they couldn't figure out the nature of the disease, they concluded, by unanimous agreement, to bring the Rabbi to a big city to an expert healer to declare what was wrong with the Rabbi and what sort of cure to give him.

That's what they did.

They hired a wagon and seated the sick Rabbi together with a shammes to watch over him and to speak on his behalf with the healer.

When they arrived in the big city, the shammes told the healer that the Rabbi was sick and needed a cure.

The healer examined the Rabbi and said that they should bring the Rabbi to a village where the air was fresh, and he should live there, among the trees and grass and good pasture land.

The shammes returned with the Rabbi to Chelm and explained:

"The healer said that we should bring the Rabbi to a village, where there are trees and grass and good pasture land."

All of Chelm was astounded. What could this be?

If you apply cups to someone, it's a sign that his shoulders hurt. If you give someone fish oil to drink, it's a sign

OPPOSITE: No passengers, so this wagon driver is taking a nap. (From the Photographic Archive, YIVO Institute for Jewish Research)

that he has intestinal problems. If you exorcise an evil eye, it's a sign that his head hurts. But to bring someone where trees and grass grow—what sort of illness is that?

They held another large meeting, pondered three days and three nights, and still didn't know what was wrong with the Rabbi. Finally someone, the cleverest melamed in Chelm, spoke up:

"My masters, I know what the trouble is! Fields, grass, and pasture in a village: That's a treatment for a calf in the belly! I remember that when my cow was about to calve, they also told me that I should bring it out to a village where there were trees, fields, grass, and good pasture. That's a clear indication that the Rabbi is pregnant with a calf!"

Having heard this suggestion, all of Chelm was overcome by the immense wisdom that the clever melamed had evinced. They held another meeting, pondered for seven days and seven nights, and concluded that from that day forward they should send all the children in town to study only with that clever melamed, so that all Chelm children should grow into sages like him.[26] They also decided to send the Rabbi to a nearby village, where a Jewish tax collector resided and where there were trees, fields, and grass. The Rabbi would stay there until he would have the calf.

They hired a wagon, seated the Rabbi on it, seated the shammes at his right hand to watch over him until the hour would arrive, and sent them off to the village to the Jewish tax collector.

When they came to the village, the tax collector ran up and greeted the Rabbi with the greatest respect and wouldn't hear of taking any money. The great honor that Chelm had bestowed on him was enough, sending the Rabbi to him to have the calf, not to anyone else in some other village.

That's how the Rabbi strolled about all day in the village through the fields, among the trees, grass, and good pasture. He had plenty to eat at the tax collector's home. He became rounder and fatter by the day. The shammes watched over him and rejoiced to see that the Rabbi was getting so round. He awaited with impatience the time when the Rabbi would have his calf and he would be able to run back to Chelm with the good news.

One fine morning, the shammes woke up and looked around. A calf! A red calf resembling the Rabbi was lying on the ground and looking right at the Rabbi sleeping in his bed. It bleated yearningly: "meh, meh, meh."

The shammes understood that the Rabbi had had his calf. He quickly grabbed his undershirt, his shoes and socks, and ran to Chelm with joy:

"Mazel tov!" he called out in the streets. "People! The Rabbi had his calf!"

In Chelm there was "joy and gladness." It's no small matter to have lived to see a calf from the Rabbi himself! It was like a holiday in town. Everyone put on festive garments, greeted each other with "Mazel tov!" and started drinking whiskey and carrying on. They pronounced an official blessing on the Rabbi and the young calf, recently born, and it was like a carnival.

When the town had finished its celebration, the finest householders put on their holiday raiment and set out to the village to bring the Rabbi and his calf back "with drums and dancing."

When they got to the village, they saw the Rabbi, his face shining with pleasure, and the calf, bouncing about the room and mooing quite happily.

The Chelmites were in seventh heaven; their joy knew no bounds.

Before nightfall, the householders set first the Rabbi on the wagon and then, at his feet, the calf, and they ordered the driver to set forth. But suddenly the tax collector ran up and started to make a commotion.

"Why are you taking my calf?"

The Chelmites had a good laugh.

"What sort of nonsense are you prattling?"

But the tax collector wouldn't stop.

"Give me back my calf!" he cried.

"What calf?" they all looked at him.

"The calf that is lying on the wagon!"

"Stupid villager that you are!" they laughed at him. "That's the calf the Rabbi had!"

"What Rabbi?" the tax collector complained. "That's the calf my red cow just had, and the calf is mine!"

"Be off, you stupid youth!" the Chelmites screamed at him. "You want to take away this calf that our Rabbi had?" They started whipping the horse.

The tax collector made an enormous noise, and his wife ran out with their daughters. They held the horse by the head and prevented it from moving until they would get back their calf. There was pulling and shoving, until the entire village arrived at a run.

The Chelm householders saw that the situation was dire. The tax collector wouldn't give way, screaming that the calf was in fact his, that his red cow had had it. The Chelmites had a meeting on the wagon, pondered and pondered, and came up with a plan.

"The nature of a calf is always to follow its mother. We should put the Rabbi at one side and the cow at the other side, and let the calf down from the wagon. Whichever of the two the calf runs to is clearly the one that had it. If it runs to the Rabbi, it's the Rabbi's, and it belongs to Chelm and the entire Chelm community.

"Agreed!" called out the tax collector.

They brought the Rabbi down from the wagon and set him on the right side. The tax collector brought his cow from its

OPPOSITE: A man peddling his phonograph music for a few pennies. (From the Photographic Archive, YIVO Institute for Jewish Research)

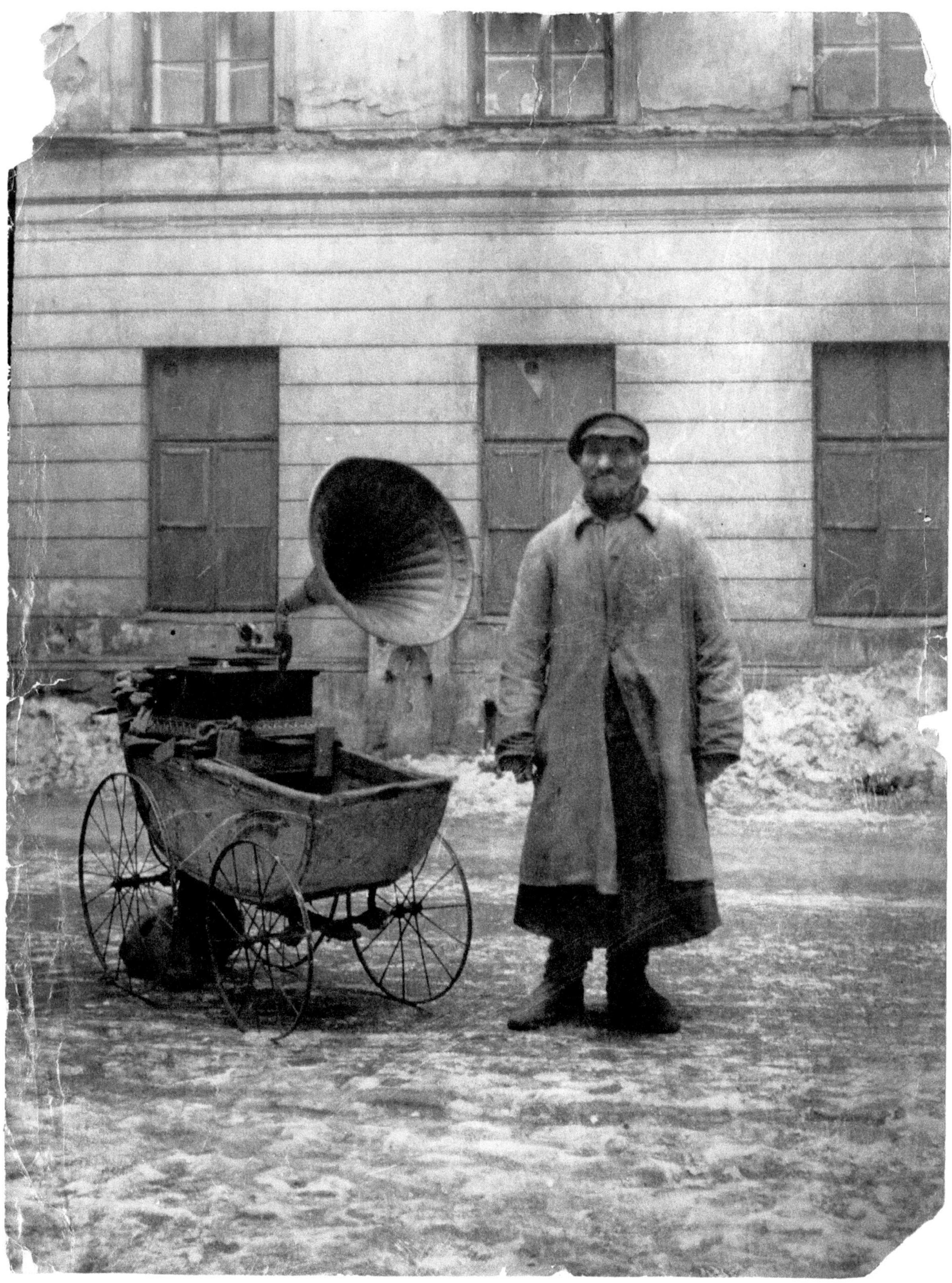

stall and set it on the left side. They took the calf down from the wagon with trembling hands, and they set it in the middle of the yard. They gave it a switch with a stick so it would run.

It lifted its tail, jumped a few times in the courtyard, made a somersault, and ran right to the Rabbi.

When everyone saw this, they clearly understood that the calf belonged to nobody but the Rabbi. Even the tax collector and his wife were also convinced that the Rabbi had had the calf, not their cow. Everyone got back on the wagon: the Rabbi, the calf, the householders, the tax collector, and his wife. They all set out for Chelm.

When they approached Chelm, the whole town came out with musicians, song, and dance. They brought them into the town in a great parade. People rejoiced, drank whiskey, and partied for seven days and seven nights. They didn't stop praising the wisdom of Chelm and the greatness of their Rabbi, who had honored the town in his old age with a red calf.

The Doctor Who Revived the Dead

Once a doctor arrived in Chelm. He was an expert on all illnesses and certainly no fool. He did have one flaw: He loved to read books. Anyone who came to see him found him reading a book.

Chelm noticed that their doctor was always reading books. They held a meeting to ponder the matter and concluded: Given that the doctor was forever reading books, it must be that he didn't know medicine. After all, if he knew medicine, he wouldn't need to be reading books. So they would no longer go to him to be cured but rather to another doctor.

When this doctor saw that the sick no longer came to him and realized the reason, he let it be known in the streets that the entire town, men, women, and children, should gather together in the middle of the marketplace. He would prove that not only was he a great doctor, who could heal all the sick, but he could also revive the dead. He would bring back the dead in full view of everyone.

When they heard this announcement, all the town gathered, young and old, in the middle of the marketplace. The doctor stood in the center and said:

“Well, name me a dead person, and I'll revive him.”

“A dead person? Which one should we give him?” the people began to consider.

“Let him revive Hershel Avremtses, that fine young man who died two years back, leaving a young wife and two small children.”

“I will revive him on the spot!” the doctor called out and made a gesture as if to start. But a woman soon rushed up and started to wail.

“Dear doctor, you are going to revive my husband? God forbid you should do that. When he revives and sees that I am remarried, it will be dreadful. I'm quite happy with my new husband; I love him and he loves me. I beg of you, doctor, have pity on my young years and don't revive him. Feel free, dear doctor, to revive anyone at all, just not my husband!”

“So whom then should I revive?” the doctor asked.

“Let the doctor bring back to life Yankl Porkhutke, an old man, who was quite wealthy!” someone called out.

“God forbid!” ran up the children and grandchildren, begging for mercy from the doctor. “You'll ruin us all! We have long since divided the inheritance. One got a house, another the business and merchandises, a third the mill. If he gets out of his grave, we'll have to give it all back. Be merciful, dear doctor, and don't destroy all these families!”

“So whom then should I revive?” the doctor called out. “I must revive someone!”

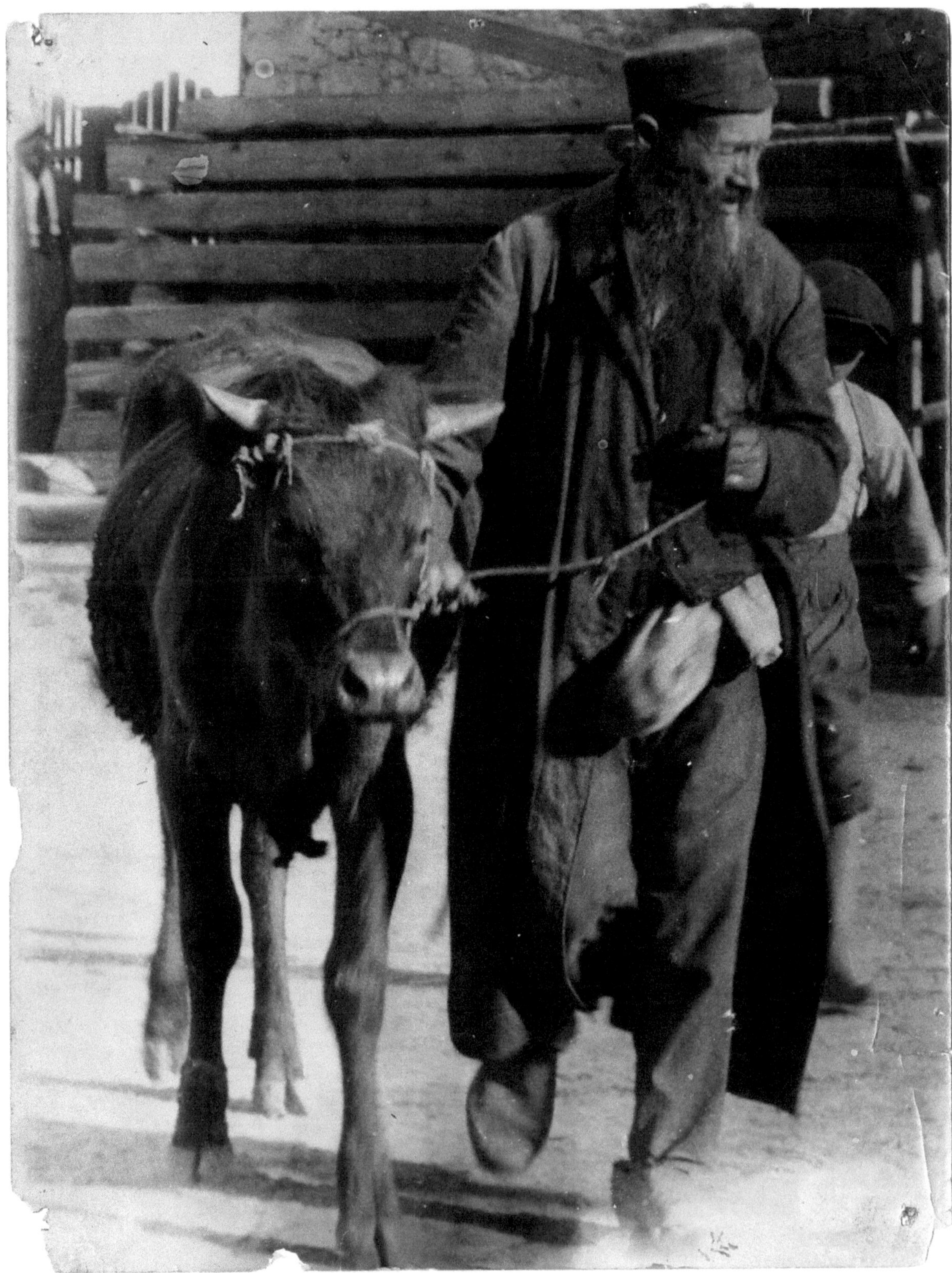

"Revive Feygele, the young woman who died a few weeks ago," called out someone.

"Feygele? I'll bring her back to life right away!" the doctor started his motions.

But her husband ran up with a pale, frightened face.

"Don't revive her, I beg off you, dear and beloved doctor! If you bring her back, I'll simply die. I have a new wife, a nice young woman, and I'm not hankering so much for my previous wife.

That's how the doctor repeatedly started to bring back another dead person, but every time someone ran up and begged, God forbid, that he do no such thing.

"Well, folks" the doctor finally called out. "Now you see by actual experience that I can bring the dead back to life. And if I can revive the dead, I can certainly heal the living sick!"

That's how all of Chelm saw with their own eyes that their doctor was the greatest doctor in the whole world. Everyone started returning to him for cures.

It turned out well for him.

And for us, even better![27]

The Beast That Wouldn't Milk

Once the Rabbi's wife took sick in Chelm, and the healers ordered her to drink milk.

The town took counsel: Given that buying milk every day costs a lot of money, it would be better to collect money from the community to buy a cow. She would drink the cow's milk, it would cost less, and it would be healthier for her.

That's what they did.

OPPOSITE: Pub. June 19, 1927. Pilawa. [English] On the road to the slaughterhouse. [Yiddish] Meat for the Sabbath. Yankl the butcher has purchased a calf for the Sabbath and is leading it to the slaughter. (People of a Thousand Towns, YIVO Institute for Jewish Research)

They collected money and sent the shammes of the synagogue to buy a cow for the Rabbi's wife.

Arriving at market, the shammes saw a peasant standing with a bull to sell. He asked the peasant how much he wanted for the cow. The peasant realized whom he was dealing with and named a price that was twice the value of the bull. The shammes paid the money and led the bull by its rope to the Rabbi.

All of Chelm came running to inspect the Rabbi's cow. They soon fell to thinking: Now that the Rabbi has a cow, it needs a stall. Where can we find money for a stall?

They held a meeting and concluded that since there was no money to buy boards for a stall, everyone should bring one floorboard, and that would suffice for a stall for the cow.

They all ripped up their floors and brought boards to the Rabbi's yard.

Now there was a new problem. They had the boards, but where would they get nails to pound into the boards? Nails also cost money!

They held another meeting, pondered and pondered, and concluded: Since there was no money for nails, everyone should hold his board in his hands.

That's what they did. They established a stall out of boards, put the cow inside, and the Rabbi's wife went to milk it.

When she began to feel for the udder, the bull gave her a kick with its rear foot right in the heart. She fell in a faint.

It took a long time before they were able to bring her to.

They started to consider: What can we do to prevent the cow from kicking so the Rabbi's wife wouldn't fall in a faint?

They held another meeting and concluded that since a peasant woman had always milked the cow, the Rabbi's wife should dress like one, so the cow would think that she was a peasant woman. Then it would let itself be milked without kicking.

So the Rabbi's wife dressed like a peasant woman and started to milk. The bull gave such a kick in her teeth that they barely got her out of the stall alive.

Awful! What can we do now?

They held another meeting, pondered and pondered, and concluded that since the cow would not under any circumstances let the Rabbi's wife milk it, the Rabbi himself should milk it. It would certainly show respect for the Rabbi and let itself be milked.

So the Rabbi went and started milking the cow. But as soon as he touched it, he got a shove that sent him and the pail flying all the way to the door.

So it was a real problem. It was unheard of that a cow wouldn't let itself be milked by the Rabbi himself.

So they held another meeting, pondered and pondered, and came up with this: Since a peasant had certainly milked the cow, the Rabbi should dress like a peasant, and it would let him milk it.

They took the Rabbi and dressed him in a peasant coat, a peasant cap, peasant boots on his feet.[28] They belted him with a red belt and sent him to milk the cow.

But as soon as he sat down on the ground and wanted to milk it, he received such a fierce blow below the belly that he lay there half dead.

"Well, you are an insolent thing!" the Chelm householders said angrily. "We have no alternative but to milk you by force!"

They got a rope and tied the Rabbi to the bull's tail. The Rabbi sat down again to milk it, and the whole community held the bull by the horns.

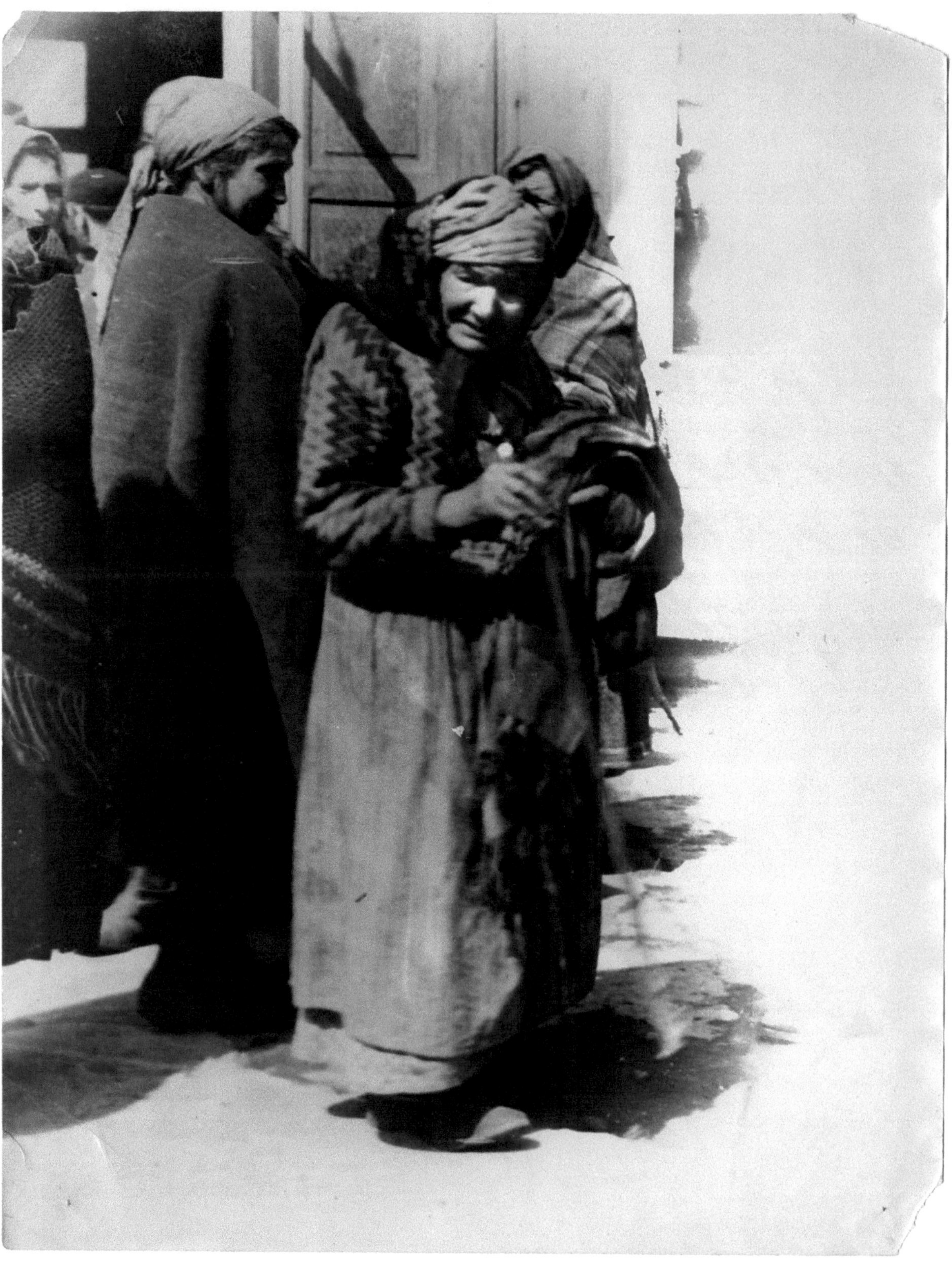

The bull saw that they were going to milk it by force. It started kicking with the feet, jumping and tugging, until it pulled away from the community's hands, ran out of the stall, and ran around Chelm. The Rabbi was dragged behind and started shouting:

"Help! Cut off its tail!"

That's how the bull dragged the Rabbi around all the streets of Chelm until he dragged him as far as Bukovina.

The Shofar Case

Boots were once unknown in Chelm. All the residents wore shoes, but they had never set eyes on a boot.

It happened once that a stranger passed through, a wealthy man in boots. Chelm was suffering from heavy mud. He stuck one boot in the thick mud and lost it altogether.

Before Passover, when the mud had dried out, they found the boot in the middle of the market, and everyone came running. Since nobody knew what sort of item it was, they held a great meeting, pondered and pondered about the boot, and they concluded that it must be a case for a shofar, and it must be heaven-sent.

They took the shofar that was lying without a case in the holy ark, placed it in the case, and with great ceremony brought it back to the synagogue and placed it in the ark.

It then happened that the rich stranger who had lost his boot arrived once more in Chelm. He went to pray on the Sabbath, and they honored him with the ceremonial ark opening.

When he opened the ark, he was amazed:

"How did my boot get here?" he cried.

"What boot? It's a shofar case!"

OPPOSITE: Old woman. (From the Photographic Archive, YIVO Institute for Jewish Research)

"What do you mean, a case? It's my boot!"

In short, the rich man insisted it was a boot that people wear on their feet and that he had lost in the heavy mud. The Chelmites insisted that he was trying to trick them out of their case, the treasure that the One Above had sent them. They were fighting and cursing. It even came to blows. Then the Chelm landowner heard the commotion and came at a run.

Both sides set out their complaints. The rich man swore by all possible oaths that it was a boot, and the Chelm householders swore that it was a case for a shofar and had been since the Creation.

The landowner heard both sides out and ruled that if the stranger would show a second boot, that would be a sign that the object was a boot for a foot, but if not, that would show that it was a case for a shofar.

Because the rich man had left his other boot at home and couldn't show the matching boot to the one lying in the Holy Ark, he had to leave Chelm in disgrace. It was clear to everyone that it had been a shofar case from ancient times and that it belonged to Chelm.

The Pest That Consumes the Grass

A horse rider once traveled past Chelm and stopped for the night on the field near the town.

At dawn he cut a bit of hay from the meadow with his sickle for his horse and then rode off, forgetting his sickle on the grass.

Chelm had never seen a sickle before.

In the morning as people went out from the town, they noticed that the meadow grass was strangely cut and that nearby was lying some sort of crooked object with teeth.

All of Chelm soon ran up, and fear grabbed them. One thing was clear: The crooked object with saw teeth was a

OPPOSITE: Pub. March 7, 1926. Otwock. Owning two goats is enough to make one man something of a boss. A Jewish citizen . . . goes for a walk with his two goats and offers them leaves to eat. But first he explains that a goat must not be a pig . . . and that they must give more milk. (People of a Thousand Towns, YIVO Institute for Jewish Research)

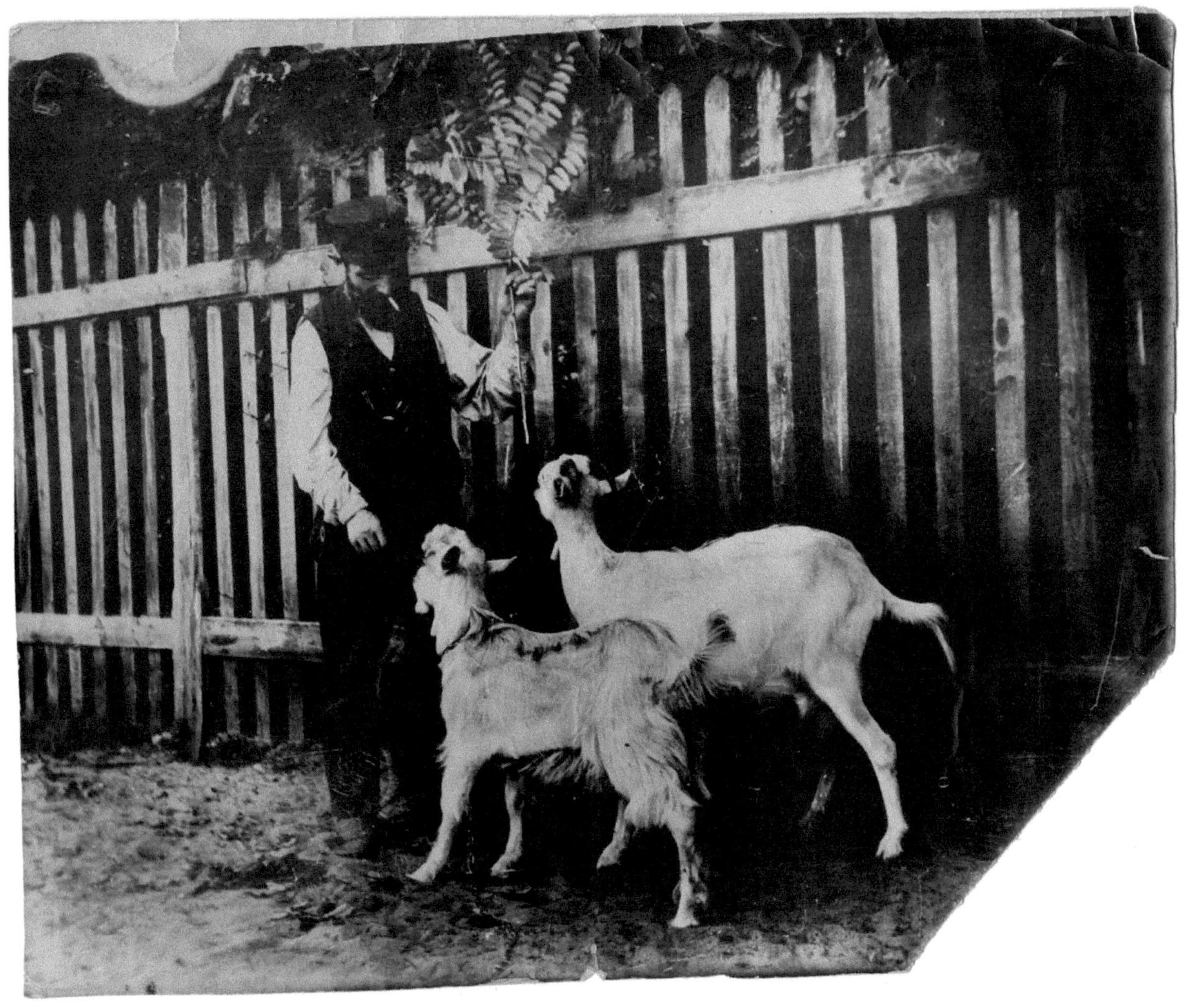

dangerous imp, a wild thing, a pest, that creeps over fields and eats up the grass.

Without delay, Chelm called a meeting and started to ponder: What should they do with the pest that had appeared near the town so that it wouldn't, God forbid, eat all the grass and leave nothing for the cows?

They pondered and pondered and concluded: a fence! They would surround the pest with a wooden fence to prevent it from moving.

That's what they did. They surrounded the scythe with a fence, which is still standing today.

The Chelm Firehouse

When they established the first firehouse in Chelm, they took all the equipment—barrels, pumps, and hoses—and theysurrounded it with a brick wall so that thieves couldn't steal anything. A fire broke out, so they ran to the firehouse to get the water barrels. But they couldn't get in. They had forgotten to make a door in the wall. What to do? They ran to hold a meeting, but before they could finish, all of Chelm had burned down.

Teaching an Unbeliever a Lesson

Once a rich Jewish German came to Chelm, an unbeliever who would intentionally go out on the Sabbath with his carriage to annoy the community with his public desecration of the Sabbath.

Chelm looked for ways to teach the rich unbeliever a lesson. They pondered and pondered and concluded that every Sabbath when the German unbeliever traveled by on the streets, several people would lie under the wheels. The carriage would fall over, and he would break his back.

How to Prevent Thieves

They set up the first furnace in the study hall. They were afraid that thieves might take it and sell it to a nobleman. So they held a meeting, pondered and pondered, and came up with a measure:

They would write with red ink on the furnace:

"[In Hebrew] This furnace belongs to the great study hall of the holy community of Chelm," so that if thieves stole it, the inscription would show where it came from.

In Case It Grows

When they built the first synagogue in Chelm, they left pieces of timber sticking out of every corner.

OPPOSITE: A Jewish artists union meeting in Warsaw. (From the Photographic Archives, YIVO Institute for Jewish Research)

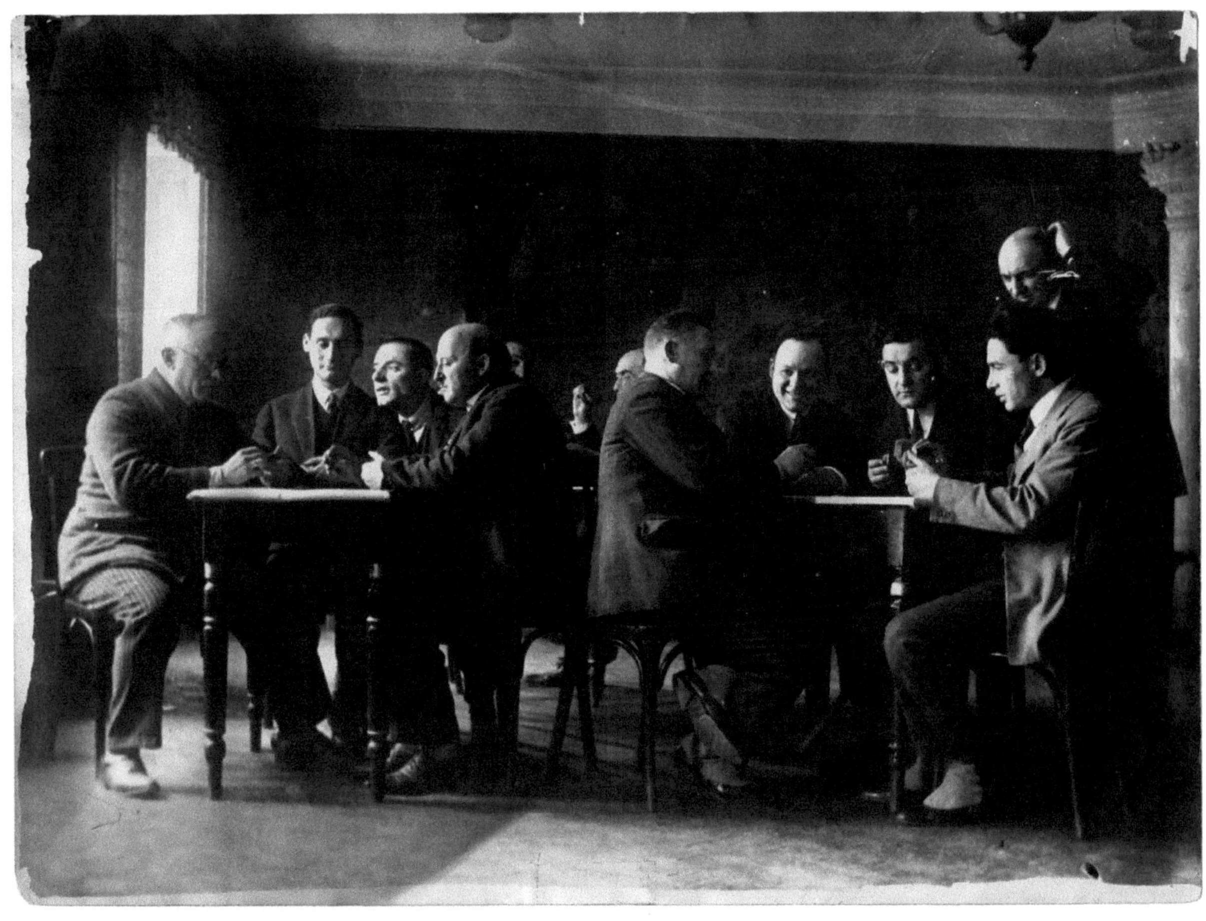

“What’s the purpose of these extra girders that poke out of all the sides of the synagogue?” passersby would ask.

“In case it grows,” answered the Chelmites. “If the synagogue should grow, we’ll have leftover girders to widen it.”

How the Old Shammes Awakened the Congregation for Psalms

Once Chelm suffered an enormous annoyance: The town shammes had grown old; his feet no longer served him, and he had no strength to go out at night from house to house to knock with his hammer on the shutters to awaken people for reciting Psalms.

That was clearly not good. So they held a meeting and concluded that since the shammes was old and had no strength to go at night knocking on every single shutter, they should bring all the shutters in town to one place near his house, and he would give a single blow of the hammer on all the shutters, and people would get up.

How They Chop Wood in Chelm

The Chelm shammes was chopping at a block of wood for several days but couldn't split it. A stranger passed by and laughed at him: How can one chop at a block of wood for several days and not split it? With a wedge he could split it in five minutes!

"So what is a 'wedge'?" the Chelmites wondered.

The stranger took a piece of wood, cut out a wedge, gave it to the shammes, and went on his way.

The shammes took it, set the wedge just so on the block, and gave it a blow with the axe. The wedge flew right into his face and split his nose.

He let out a cry, and a great crowd came running up. The shammes recounted that a stranger had given him a wedge, that he had given it a blow with this axe, and that it jumped into his face and split his nose.

Chelm immediately held a meeting and began to ponder the wedge from all sides. They pondered and pondered and concluded that a wedge is actually useful for splitting a block of wood. However, they should do exactly the opposite of what the shammes had done:

The shammes had struck with the wedge against the block, and it had split his nose. They ought to strike the wedge against the shammes's nose, and it would fly back and split the block.

Mighty Thieves

A Chelmite was once traveling to a small village.

Seating himself in Chelm on the wagon, he decided: Here, where the wagon is, there is no mud. Why should he wear galoshes on his boots? So he took off the galoshes and placed them on the ground under the wagon. Then he set forth.

When he arrived at the village, he bent under the wagon to collect his galoshes. But they weren't there!

"Oh, wow! Such mighty thieves they have in this town," he cried out. "I just arrived here in town, and already they've managed to steal my galoshes!"

What Can Happen in Chelm

It once happened in Chelm that when traveling to a wedding, they forgot to bring along the groom.

Sentencing the Fish

The community head of Chelm used to go himself to buy fish in honor of the Sabbath.

One Friday he bought a great live carp, stuck it down his shirt with its head down and with its tail sticking out.

On the way home the fish thrashed and slapped the headman across the face.

"Ha!" was the commotion in town. "Such disrespect has never been heard of. A fish that slaps the headman right in the middle of the marketplace is insolent and ought to be drowned!"

So that very day, Friday afternoon, the shammes took the fish and in the sight of everyone threw it into the river.

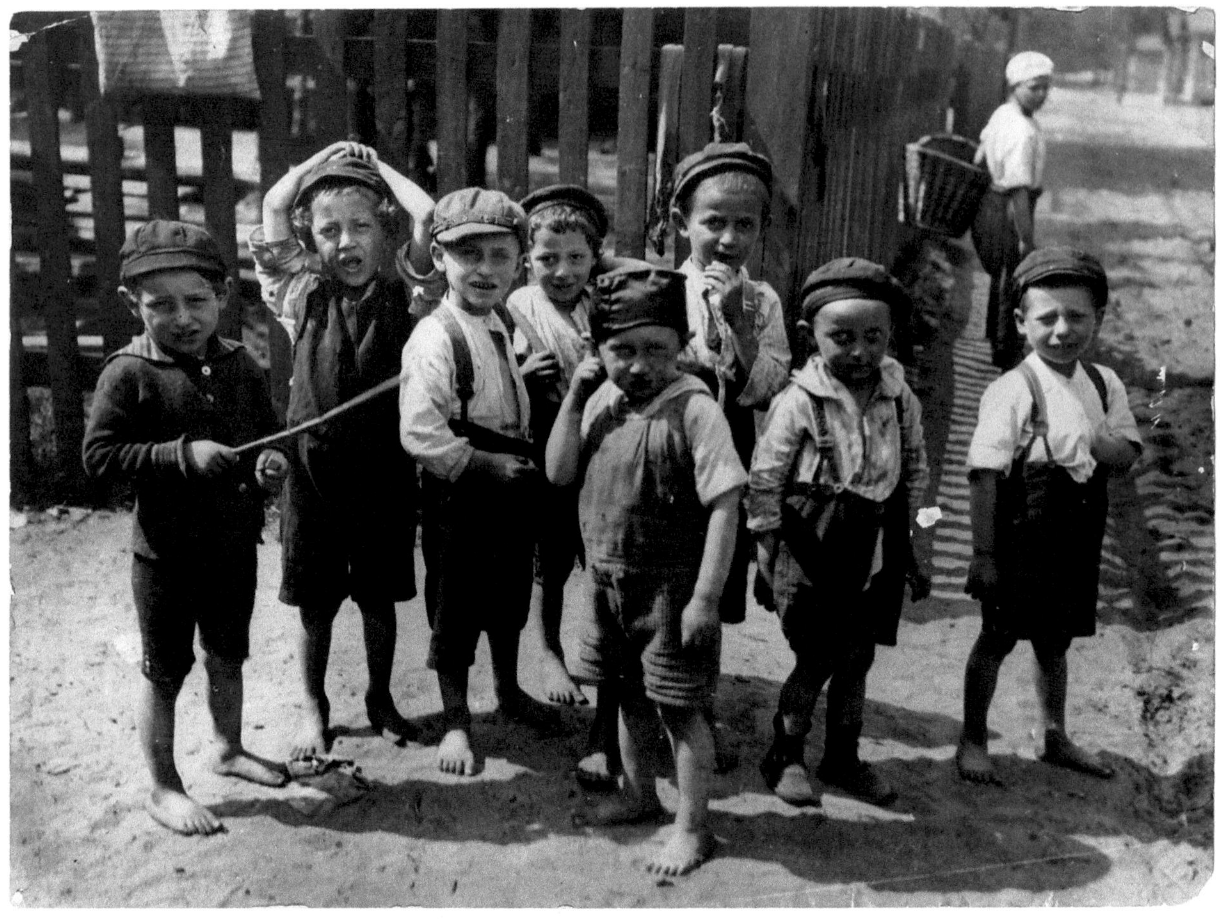

Confused Feet

A stranger once came to Chelm. He saw that in one house, several people were lying in a bed, worn out and exhausted, more dead than alive.

What had happened?

They told him that they had lain down Saturday after lunch to nap, and they had been lying there for three days and couldn't get up, because they had confused their feet and no one could find his own.

The stranger took off his belt and began to strike them all over.

Out of pain and hurt they all jumped out of their places and ran, each to a different corner. Afterward they couldn't thank the stranger enough that he had saved them from a certain death.

A Windowless Synagogue

Once they built a synagogue in Chelm. When it was finished, they noticed that it was dark inside. They had forgotten to build windows.

What to do? They held a meeting, pondered for seven days and seven nights, and came up with a clever idea. They should gather sacks, fill them with sunshine outside, and bring the light into the synagogue to brighten it up.

Calling in the Goat

A Chelmite once found himself in a quandary. He was holding a loaf of bread but didn't know which end to start.

He pondered and pondered. Meanwhile, he saw a goat through the window. He came up with a clever idea: to call the goat in and give it the loaf, and whatever end it would start, he would also start.

That's what he did.

A Crow for a Trial Period

A Chelmite once heard that crows live for two hundred years. He didn't believe that story, so he bought a crow for a trial period to convince himself that it was true.

They Didn't Consider the Return Journey

Forty years ago, when they built the rail line between Chelm and Brest, the Russian authorities let it be known that

OPPOSITE: pub. October 9, 1927. Falencia. [English] "Hail, Hail the gang's all here!" [Yiddish] Under the young green trees, little Moiyshes and Shloymes play. Falencia schoolboys who were running into the woods to play. (People of a Thousand Towns, YIVO Institute for Jewish Research)

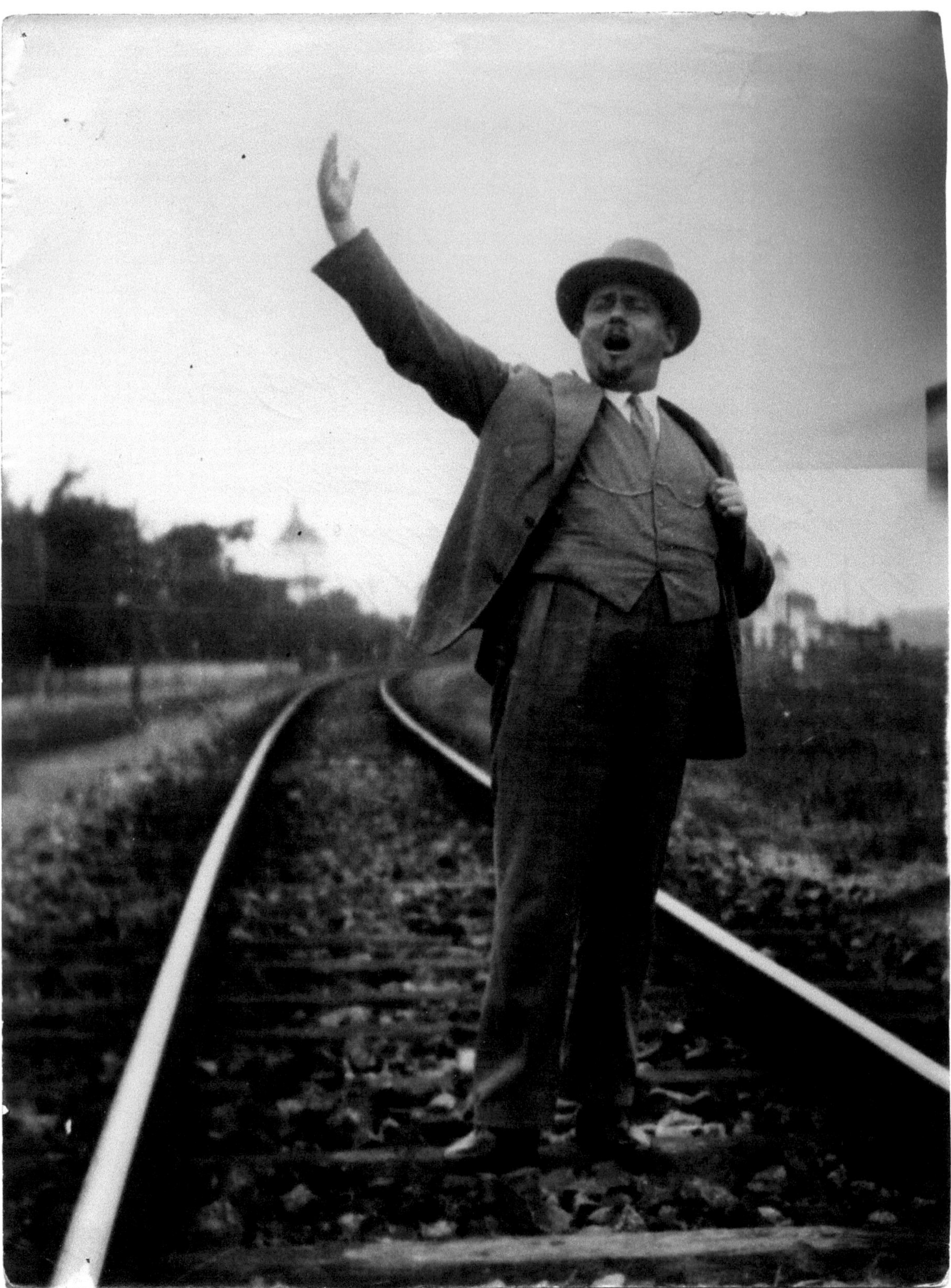

whoever wanted to travel on the first train could go to Brest for free.

Hearing that it was free, all of Chelm hurried to the train and traveled to Brest. When it was time to return, they were all told to buy tickets. There was an outcry. In their joy, Chelm had entirely forgotten about the return trip. Nobody had brought spending money, so they had to pawn all their cloaks and watches to raise enough money to travel back to Chelm.

In Chelm, a Nail Is a Nail

A Chelmite once came to Warsaw and spent the night in a guesthouse. There was a fly on the wall, which he thought was a nail. He took off his coat and hung it up. The fly flew away, and the coat fell to the ground.

"Warsaw so-called nails!" he complained, picking up his coat. "In Chelm a nail is a nail!"

Forgot His Head's Measure

A Chelmite went to the hat maker before Passover. He started to pat and search in his pockets, and then he turned to leave.

"What have you lost, uncle?" asked the hat maker.

"I was planning to buy a hat in honor of the holiday, but I've lost the measure of my head," answered the distressed Chelmite.

The Chelm Son-in-Law and the Drum

A villager married his daughter to a son-in-law from Chelm, and he supported him for several years. Then he gave him the dowry and told him to become a merchant and make his own way.

The Chelm son-in-law took the dowry and headed to Lublin to find a source of income.

OPPOSITE: Moshe Koussevitsky, Warsaw's chief cantor from the Tlamatsker synagogue, tests his voice standing on the train line from Otwock, a resort town near Warsaw. (From the Photographic Archive, YIVO Institute for Jewish Research)

Wandering through Lublin, he noticed that someone in a brass hat was standing around in a high tower and doing nothing. It seemed curious to him. He went up the tower and asked what he was doing, standing around and doing nothing.

The fellow with the brass hat answered:

"You see this drum standing here? If there should be a fire somewhere in the city, I beat on the drum, and the fire gets put out."

The Chelmite really liked this merchandise, so he began to bargain with the constable to buy the drum.

At first, the constable didn't even want to think of selling, but seeing with whom he was dealing, he gulled him out of the entire dowry and sold him the drum.

The Chelm son-in-law packed up the drum and set out for home. There he rented a shop and placed his bargain there.

His father-in-law came in and asked him what the merchandise might be. He told him that he couldn't show him; he was waiting for a fire.

"What do you mean, for a fire?"

"My father-in-law will soon see."

He sat for weeks in his shop waiting for a fire, but there was no fire. Unable to wait any longer, out of curiosity he went and set fire to his father-in-law's house.

When people saw the fire, they went running for water and started to put it out.

"Don't bother! Don't bother!" he called out. "I have a machine that will extinguish the fire itself." He unpacked the drum and beat it until the entire town burned down.

Sent to Learn Wisdom

Chelm once looked about and noticed that it was lacking Wisdom. One can't manage with one's own Wisdom; one has to get it from outside.

They held a meeting and selected the cleverest person in Chelm. They sent him to Lithuania, all the way to Vilna[29] to bring back the Wisdom.

When he arrived in Vilna, where should he go to learn Wisdom?

He headed straight for the great study hall.

When he arrived, the shammes came over and greeted him.

"Where are you from?"

"From Chelm!"

"Why would you come all the way from Chelm to Vilna?"

"I came, that is, the town sent me here, to learn Wisdom," the Chelmite answered.

"Wisdom? I will teach you Wisdom!" the shammes suggested.

"Fine!" the Chelmite grabbed at the opportunity.

"How much does your Wisdom cost?" he asked the shammes.

"If you give me five rubles, I'll give you Wisdom."

"Not expensive at all," thought the Chelmite. I should do it.

The Chelmite handed over five rubles, and the shammes asked him this riddle: "Tell me, Chelmite, what this might be: my father's son and my mother's son but not my brother?"

The Chelmite screwed up his eyes, pondered and pondered, but had no idea how to answer.

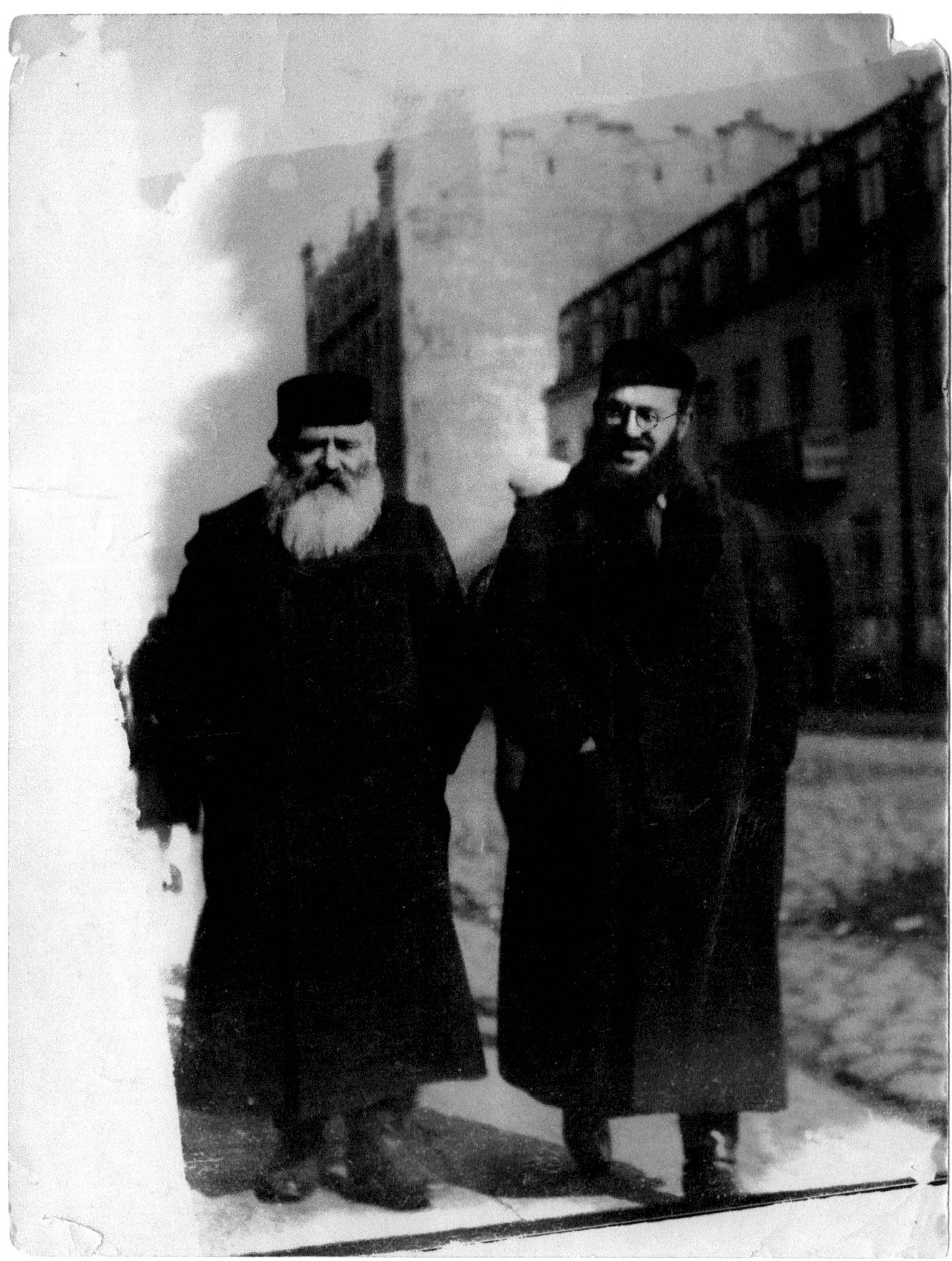

"Me myself!" shouted the shammes. "I am my father's son and my mother's son, but I'm not my brother!"

"Wow, that's great!" The Chelmite licked his lips over this enormous Wisdom and with joy set out for home.

When he arrived back in Chelm, he first collected the whole town in the synagogue courtyard to transmit the Wisdom that he had brought. He then asked everyone this question:

"Tell me, I ask you, who is this: My father's son and my mother's son but not my brother?"

Everyone stood awestruck and did not know what to answer.

"Fools!" he shouted. "It is, of course, the shammes of the Vilna study hall!"

The Cow in the Attic

The renowned prankster Efraim Greydiger once arrived in Chelm.

He passed a house and saw that they were dragging the cow up to the attic, but it didn't want to place a foot on the ladder.

"Why are you putting yourselves to all this trouble; why are you dragging the cow up to the attic?" Efraim Greydiger asked.

"Can't you see that it's exhausted?" answered the Chelmites in embarrassment. "It's been two days already that it hasn't tasted a single mouthful. There's hay in the attic, and we want to drag it up so it can eat."

"Such Chelmites that you are!" he exclaimed. "Is that the only way to do it? I have a good method, and you won't have to drag the cow up to the attic."

"Oh! Dearly beloved! God himself must have sent you," they addressed him. "What is your method?"

OPPOSITE: 1920s. Warsaw. Two men on Twarda Street, returning from the Nozyk synagogue. The photographer wrote, "Two Hassidim walking back from prayers." (People of a Thousand Towns, YIVO Institute for Jewish Research)

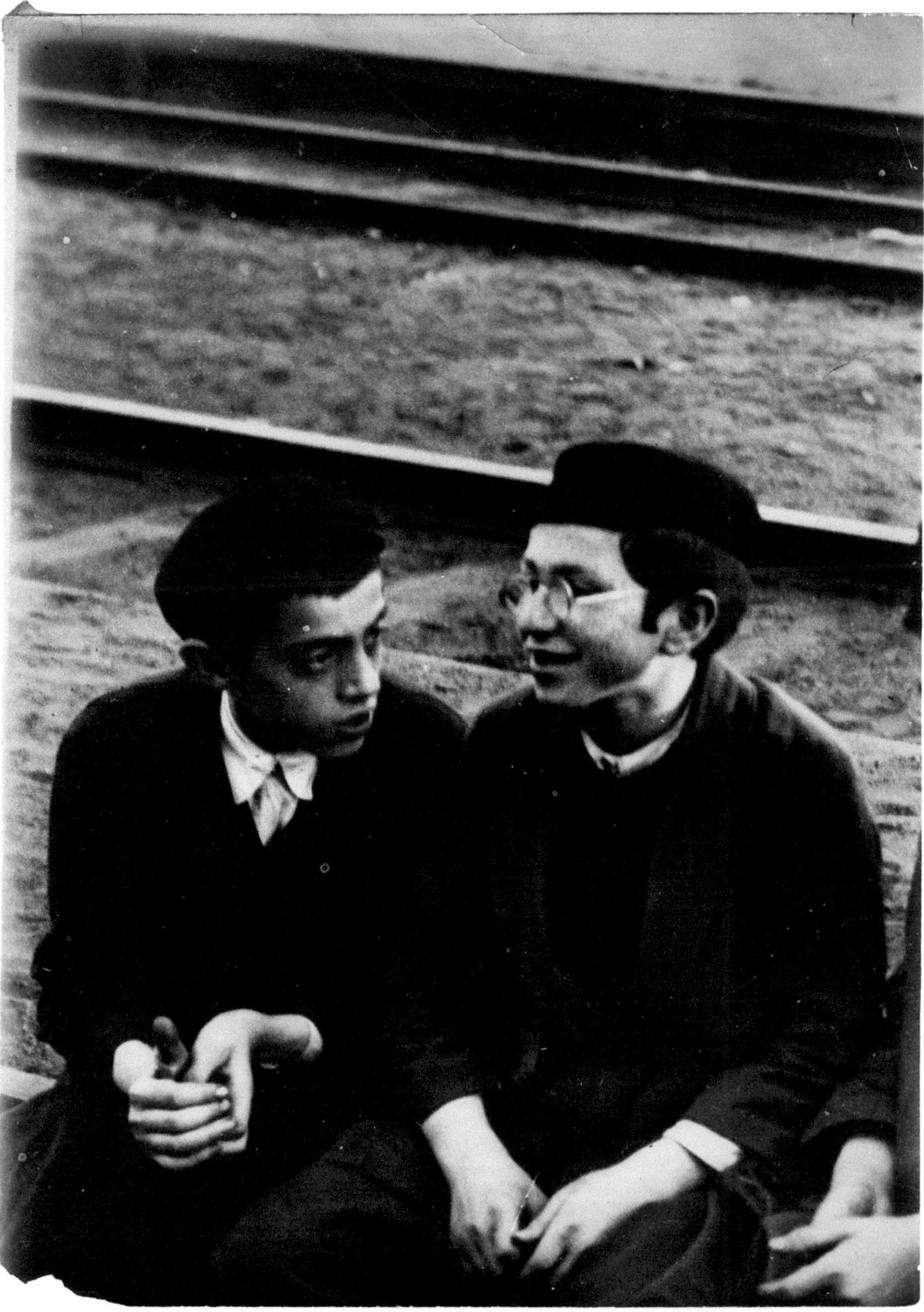

"If you feed me a nice lunch and give me a handout, I'll show you something."

The Chelmites had no choice; they fed him a fine lunch and gave him a gift, too. Now they wanted to see the method that he had to avoid dragging the cow up to the attic.

Efraim Greydiger calmly ate the lunch and made preparations as if to some enormous and difficult piece of work.

"Well, Chelmites, just hand me the ladder!" Efraim Greydiger said.

They gave him the ladder and eagerly viewed what he would do, this sage. He climbed up to the attic, grabbed a bundle of hay and tossed it down, calling:

"Chelmites, fools that you are! Why do you need to drag the cow to the hay in the attic, when you can toss the hay down to the cow on the ground?"

The Chelmites opened their eyes, and that's when they discovered how much wisdom the world still holds.

The Right Answer

A Chelmite was asked, "What would you do if you found thousands and thousands of rubles in the market and you knew who had lost them. Would you resist the temptation and return the money or not?"

The Chelmite didn't have to think for long. He answered: "If I knew that the money belongs to Rothschild, I am afraid I would not resist the temptation and I wouldn't have returned it. But if I knew that the thousands belong to the poor shammes of the old study hall, I would return it to the last cent."

OPPOSITE: Pub. 1920s–1930s. Falencia. Two Orthodox Jewish boys in conversation, seated outdoors near railroad tracks. (People of a Thousand Towns, YIVO Institute for Jewish Research)

The Alley Is Too Narrow

A man with a log on his wagon traveled into a narrow alley. Because the log was long and was lying across the wagon and the alley was too narrow, the log bumped against both sides of the alley, and he couldn't continue.

All of Chelm ran up, and they started to wrack their brains: "What can we do to help the wagon and log pass through the alley?" They pondered and pondered and concluded that the only solution would be to remove a row of houses on each side of the alley to allow the log to get past.

So that's what they did. But as they were taking down the houses, a Chelmite ran up with a shout:

"What are you doing, fools that you are! You could have cut the log in half, and it would pass right through!"

Nobody, however, even considered turning the log lengthwise.

A Proud Answer by the Chelm Rabbi

The Rabbi of Chelm once traveled from Chelm to Brisk.

Someone came up to him and asked where he came from.

"I'm a Chelmite," he answered.

"Tell me, I beg of you," the other responded. "They say that in Chelm there's a rabbi, a mighty scholar, really a delight, but a fool such as you rarely find."

"That's me!" the Rabbi answered proudly, pointing at himself.

The Finest Person in Chelm

A person from Warsaw and a Chelmite happened to meet.

"Sholem aleychem!"

"Aleychem sholem!"[30]

"It seems to me that you are a Chelmite?"

"Yes, a Chelmite. Born in Chelm and lived there all my life."

"Do you know everyone there?"

"Of course!"

"If so," the person from Warsaw continued, "can you tell me how Hershel is doing? The Hershel who limps?"

"Hershel who limps? I don't know him."

"How can it be that you don't know him. Everyone in Chelm knows him! He's completely blind in his left eye, and he can barely see with his right eye."

"Hershel, who limps and is blind in his left eye and can barely see with his right eye? No, I don't know him."

"How can that be? Man and beast know him! He has a hernia and has a scab on his head."

"Oh!" the Chelmite said, "Hershel, who limps, is blind in his left eye and can barely see with his right eye, has a hernia and a scab on his head. You think I don't know him? Of course I know him. Even the small children know him. He's the finest person in Chelm. He's far from being a nobody, is Hershel!"

The Chelm Fire Brigade and the City Shammes

Chelm came to realize that in the big cities they had found a remedy for conflagrations: a fire hose. So the town bought a hose with a spray nozzle and gave it to the shammes to keep.

The shammes inspected the hose and decided that it was a holy vessel that could be used to store other important items, such as horseradish for Passover, garlic, whitewash for the oven, and suchlike.

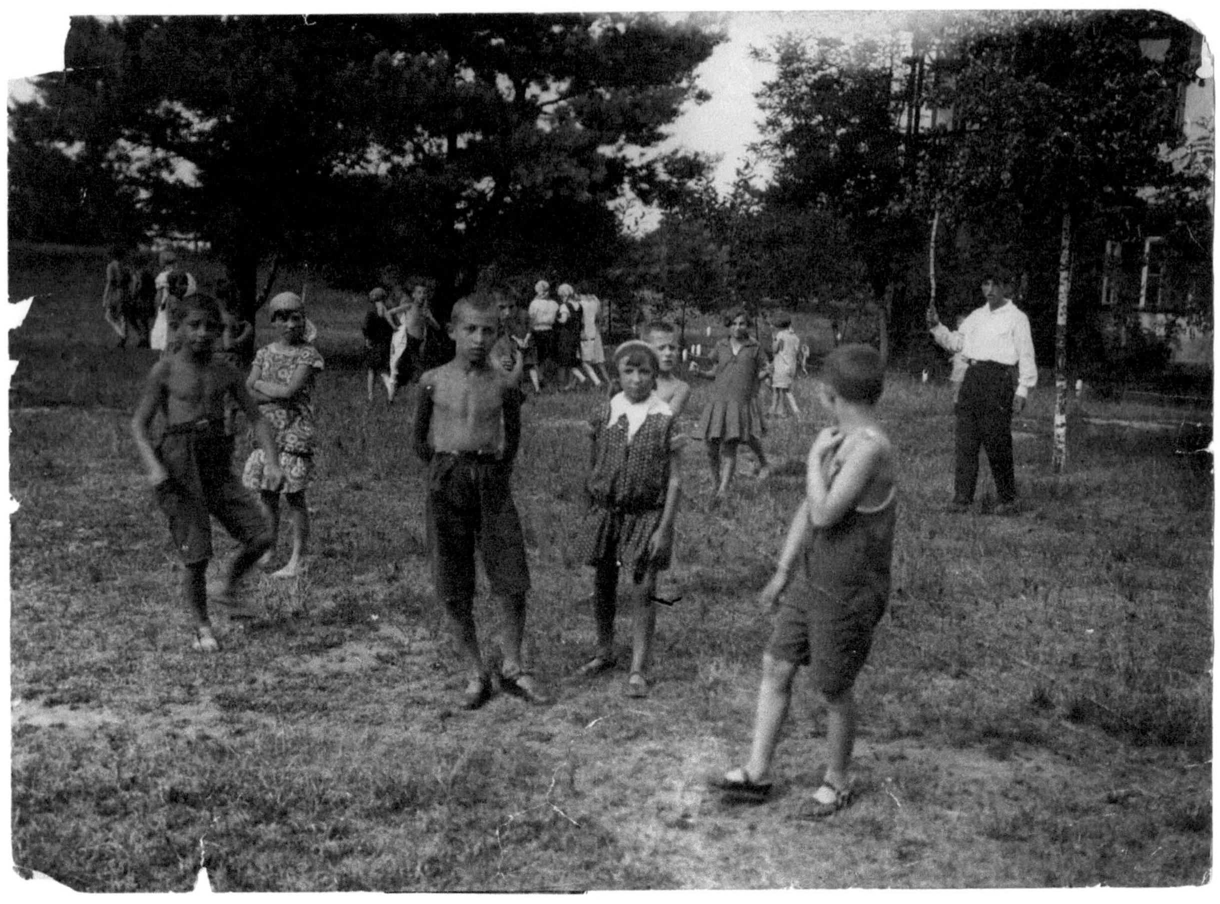

So it happened once that a fire broke out in Chelm, and folk ran to the shammes, grabbed the hose with its nozzle, dunked it in water, and started to spray, but nothing happened. They started investigating and found the hose full of important objects.

The next day the town came to a meeting: What can we do now with the hose?

The youngsters started to exclaim that from this day forth the shammes should no longer be the hose's guardian.

The elders objected and exclaimed that the shammes already had an established claim to the hose.

The insolent youngsters admitted that it was true that the shammes had an established claim on the hose and that they shouldn't take it away, but he should swear on a holy object that from now on he wouldn't use it to store any horseradish for Passover, any garlic [which is a charm against a plague], and no whitewash for the oven: nothing at all.

The elders objected:

Where then should the shammes keep such important objects?

They pondered and pondered for three days and three nights and arrived at a compromise. The right of possession of the hose remains in fact with the shammes, and he has the right to store all the important items he has in it. But he should swear by a holy object that from today and henceforth, before a fire breaks out, he would empty the hose.

He Knows Where to Search

A Chelmite stood outside the town and looked at the dry earth.

"What are you looking for?" asked someone passing by.

"I lost a ruble in the synagogue courtyard, so I'm looking for it."

"You Chelmite!" the other laughed. "If you lost it in the synagogue courtyard, what are you doing here?"

"Such a genius you are!" laughed the Chelmite right back at him. "There's a lot of mud in the synagogue courtyard, but here, it's dry. Where is it better to search?

How They Measured a Place in the Chelm Cemetery

In Chelm, the old cemetery was full, so they went to establish a place for a new cemetery. But they didn't know how big the cemetery should be. They wanted it to be neither too big nor too small, just the right size for Chelm.

OPPOSITE: In Medem Sanitorium, Warsaw. (From the Photographic Archive, YIVO Institute for Jewish Research)

They held a meeting, pondered three says and three nights, and came upon a good idea: All the men and women, along

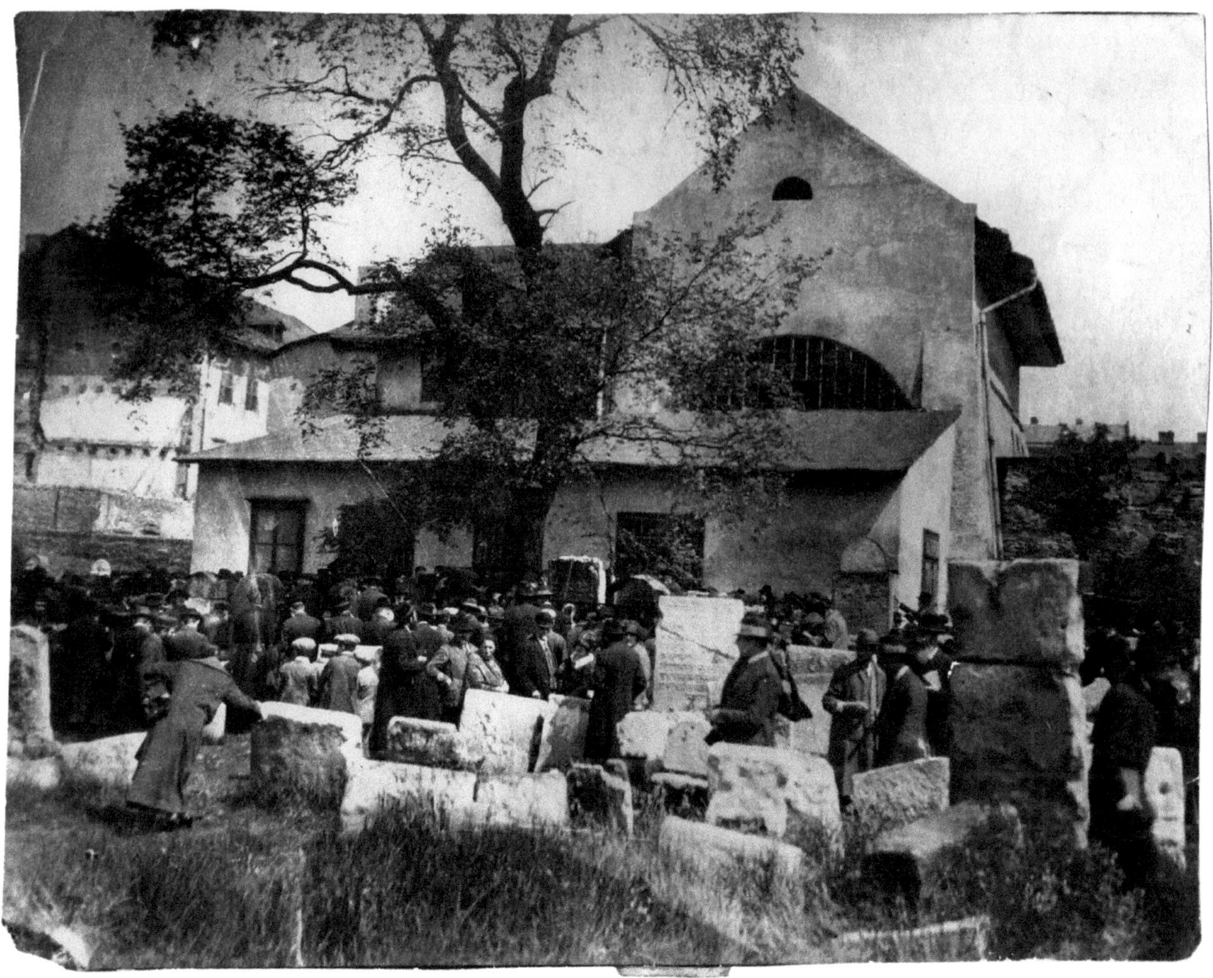

with the children, should lie on the ground outside the town, and they would be measured with a rope. However wide and long the plot they occupied, that's how big they would make the cemetery.

That's exactly what they did.

When all of Chelm, all the householders, along with wives, children, even babes in arms, were lying down on the ground outside the town, one next to the other in rows, they were measured with a rope to see how much area they occupied. That's how big they made the cemetery.

He Marveled at Warsaw

A Chelmite once wanted to see Warsaw.

The whole world shouts out: "Warsaw! Warsaw!" So you really need to see Warsaw.

So one day he got up quite early, took a stick in his hand with a sack of food for the way, and set out on foot to Warsaw.

When he had traveled half the way, he felt like sleeping. He was afraid that he would drift off, and when he awoke, he wouldn't know in which direction to continue. So he lay down with his feet facing Warsaw and his head toward Chelm. When he woke up, that would be his sign: Whichever way his feet are pointing, that's the way to Warsaw.

So he fell asleep.

A prankster happened by and saw that someone was laying on the ground, stretched out in the middle of the path, with his head toward Chelm and his feet toward Warsaw. He immediately knew that the sleeper was a Chelmite. He grabbed him by the feet and repositioned him the other way, head toward Warsaw and feet toward Chelm.

The Chelmite woke up, wiped his eyes, and looked to see which way his feet were facing. He continued on the indicated way.

He went that way half a day back toward Chelm, certain that he was traveling to Warsaw. At nightfall he arrived at the gates of the town.

"Such a lovely town, this Warsaw!" he marveled from a distance.

He went further, and he began to recognize the walls.

"Just like Chelm!" he said to himself.

OPPOSITE: 1920s–1930s. Cracow. Jews praying at the tombstone of REMA (Rabbi Moses Isserles) on legboymer (Lag b'Omer) on the anniversary of his death. REMA, who died in 1572, is buried near the synagogue in Cracow that bears his name. (People of a Thousand Towns, YIVO Institute for Jewish Research)

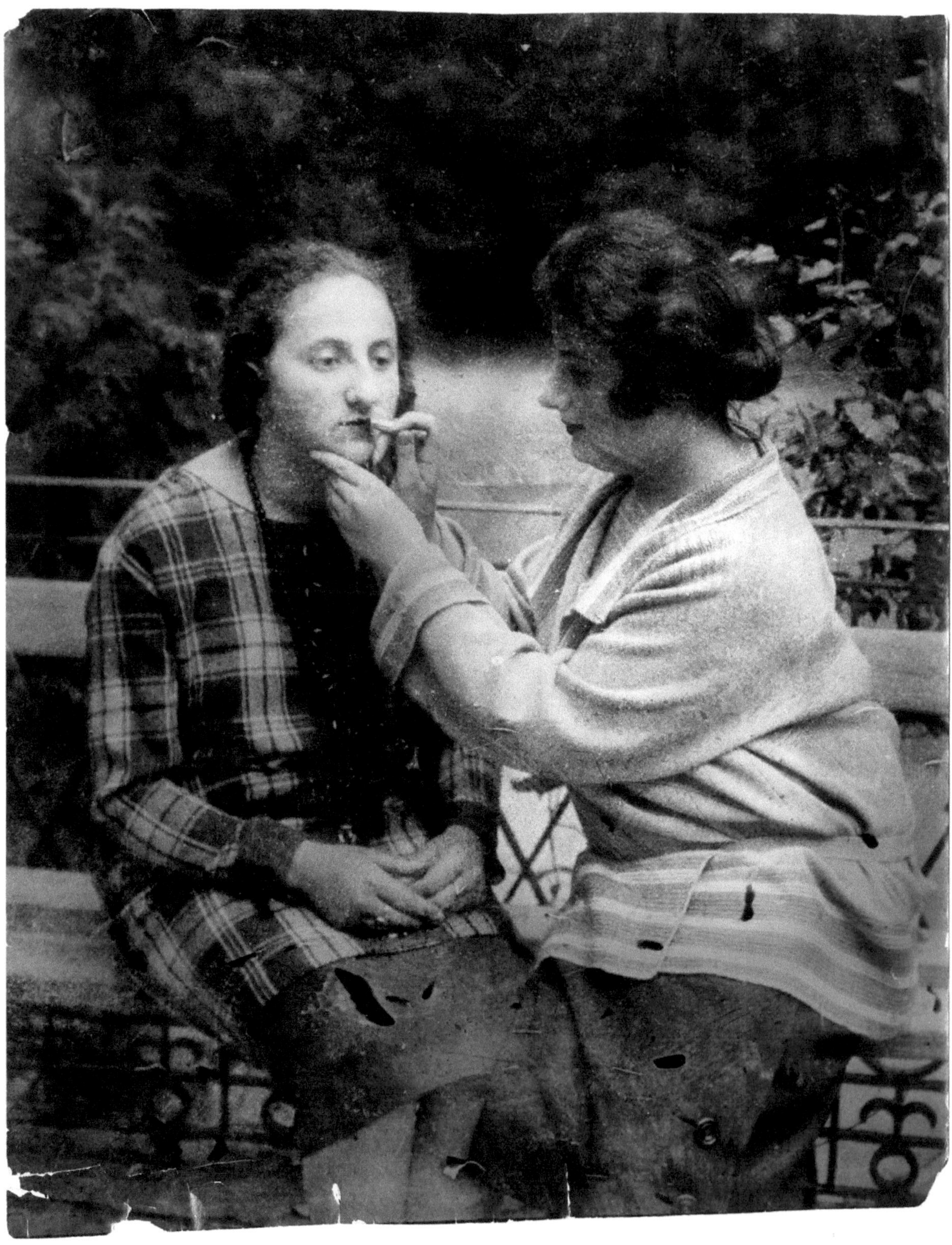

He came into the town. Well-known streets . . .

"Just like Chelm!" he kept marveling.

He walked on further and saw a synagogue.

"Exactly like in Chelm!"

He continued on. He saw houses with earthen benches and goats.

"Exactly like in Chelm! Not a hair different!"

He was already in his own street across from his own house.

"Exactly like in Chelm!"

Suddenly the door opened and out came his wife.

"Help! Jews!" he called out in fright with a yelp. "In Warsaw there's also a Zlate?"

How the Chelmites Prostrate Themselves

A Chelmite once asked someone how to prostrate oneself.[31]

"To prostrate oneself," the other explained, "you fall on the ground with your head stretched to the east and your feet to the west."

When it came time in the synagogue to prostrate oneself, the Chelmite stretched out on the ground exactly reversed, head to the west and feet to the east.

"You're reversed, uncle!" someone exclaimed.

When he heard "reversed," he rolled over with his belly up.

The Chelmite Czar and the Golden Shoes

Chelm once determined that it wasn't fitting for the Czar (the world recounts stories about the Chelm Czar, so it must

OPPOSITE: pub. August 22, 1926. Warsaw. [I Yiddish] The eyes black, the lips red but when there is nothing to do they make them even redder. [I English] Flappers are flappers, even in Warsaw, as these maids in the Saxon Park show. (People of a Thousand Towns, YIVO Institute for Jewish Research)

have had such an individual) to wear ordinary shoes like any creature of flesh and blood. Nobody would recognize him, and they wouldn't treat him with the proper respect. They held a huge meeting about this and concluded that they should provide the Czar with a pair of golden shoes.

So the Czar walked about in Chelm in golden shoes.

But Chelm was subject to deep mud. The mud coated the golden shoes, and once more, they couldn't recognize who was the Czar and who wasn't.

They held a second meeting and concluded that the Czar should wear golden shoes. But the mud? They should provide him another pair of shoes, this time of leather, but with holes in front. He should place the golden shoes inside the leather shoes. The gold would shine forth through the holes, and people would know who is the Czar and who is an ordinary person.

That's what they did. The Czar wore two pairs of shoes, the golden one inside and the leather ones with holes outside.

But Chelm suffered heavy rains, and the rainwater soaked through the holes. The Czar's feet were always sloshing in the shoes.

So they held another meeting and concluded that the Czar must wear golden shoes. But the mud? They should provide him another pair of shoes, this time of leather, but with holes in front. He should place the golden shoes inside the leather shoes. The gold would shine forth through the holes. But what then: Chelm suffers heavy rains, and the water soaks through the holes, so the Czar's feet are always sloshing in the shoes. There's a remedy for that: The holes should be stuffed with straw.

That's what they did. Every day the Czar would stroll about Chelm's streets in golden shoes, themselves inside leather shoes with holes in front, and the holes were stuffed with straw.

Everyone was able to see that this was the Czar, and they honored him with great respect.

OPPOSITE: A man wandering through the streets of Warsaw with a harp. For a few groschen of charity, people make requests. (From the Photographic Archive, YIVO Institute for Jewish Research)

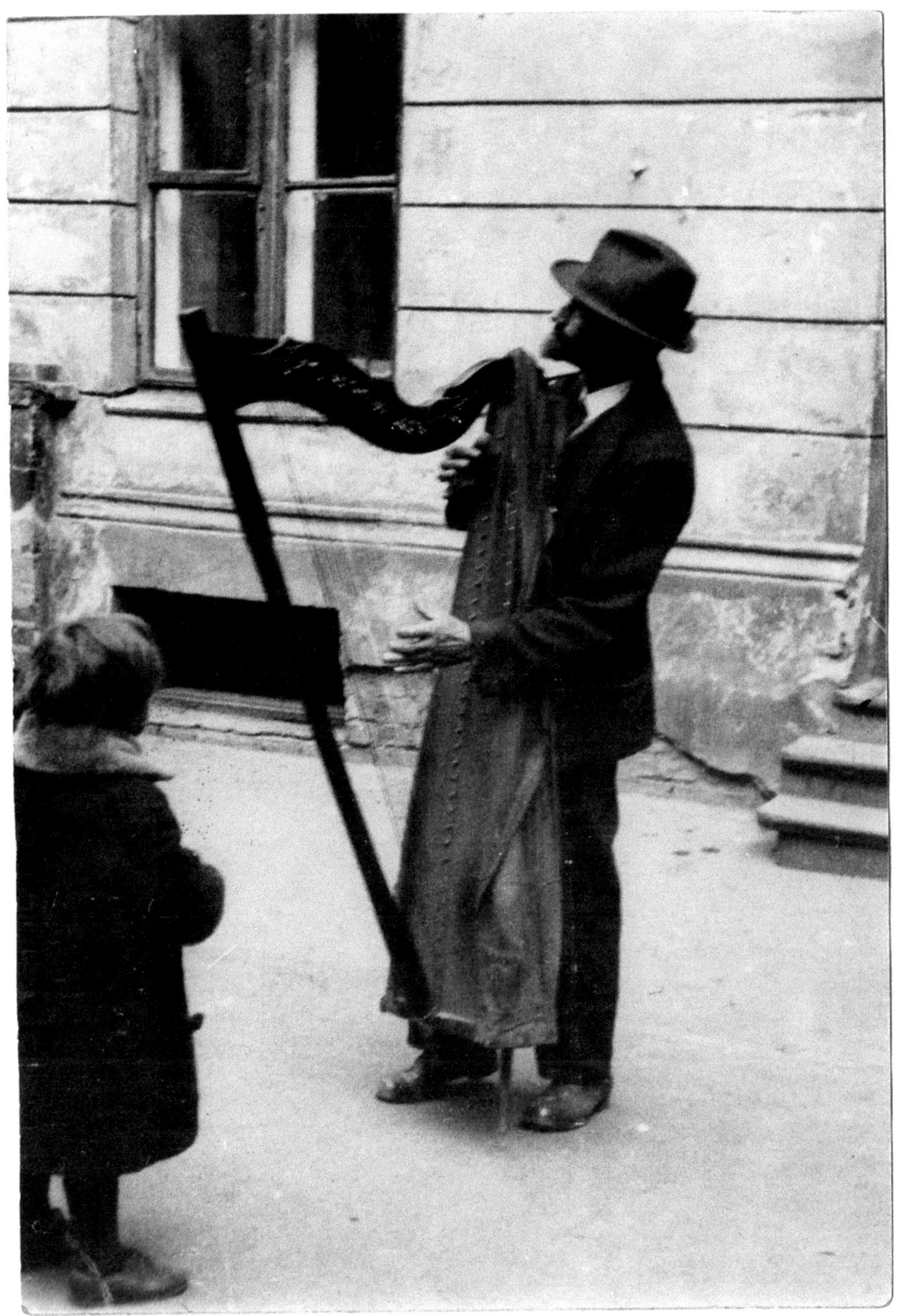

How They Dragged the Trees from the Top of the Mountain to Build the Town Synagogue

When they started to build the town synagogue in Chelm, they cut down trees on the large hill, and they wore themselves out bringing the trees downhill on their shoulders.

A stranger came by and laughed:

"Fools that you are! Why do you have to wear yourselves out carrying the wood down from the hill? Just let them roll down!"

"He's right!" They all opened their eyes, and with the last ounce of strength they dragged the wood back to the top of the hill and released it. The wood rolled down on its own, and all of Chelm saw what a clever world still existed outside of Chelm.

The Householders Carry the Shammes in Their Arms to Awaken the Congregation for Psalms

Once there was a snowless winter in Chelm. It was already past Purim,[32] but they hadn't seen any snow or any sled path. Since there was no sled path, the peasants weren't able to bring their goods into the town, so food was in great demand.

Suddenly, one night, the day before Passover, the snow began to fall.

It was gladness and joy in Chelm. Everyone stayed home in order to keep the snow pristine.

But that raised a problem in Chelm:

Certainly all the menfolk and women and children were able to stay home so as not to ruin the snow, but how could they manage with the shammes, who needed to set out before dawn to awaken the congregation to recite Psalms? He would be treading on the snow and ruining the sled path.

The Chelm sages came upon a plan. It was decided that to prevent the shammes from trampling the snow, he shouldn't go on foot to awaken the congregation for Psalms. Four householders should carry him.

Hanging a Tailor Instead of a Shoemaker

Once a Chelm shoemaker was sentenced to death; they were supposed to hang him.

The community went to the governor and interceded:

"We only have one shoemaker in Chelm, but we have two tailors. Instead of the condemned shoemaker, hang a tailor."

It Must Certainly Be in Krakow

A young Chelmite ran to the train.

"What are you running for, raising such a sweat?" they asked him.

"I'm traveling to Krakow."

"Why to Krakow, of all places?"

"You have to understand. Yesterday I lost a ring. Now Chelm is on a hill, but Krakow is in a valley. The ring must have rolled down to Krakow, so I'm traveling there to look for it."

The Floor of the Chelm Bathhouse

They built a bathhouse in Chelm. When they finished the entire building and were ready to lay the floor, Chelm faced a difficult question:

What sort of floor should they make?

They shouldn't lay unplaned boards, because the bare feet would catch on splinters sticking out of the wood. But if they lay smooth, planed wood, people would slip on them and break their skulls.

What to do?

They thought for three days and three nights and found a good idea:

They should plane the wood to make it smooth and then lay the smooth side face down.

He's Not a Scaredy-Cat

A young Chelmite boasted of his heroism, telling this story:

"Once in the middle of the night, I saw a thief creeping into my house. I kept quiet, because you have to realize that I am not easily frightened.

"The thief opened the armoire. I kept quiet.

"He rummaged among the clothes. I kept quiet. I'm not one of those who get scared.

"He tied the things in a bundle. I kept quiet.

"When I saw that he was opening the drawer to take out the money, I started shouting loudly:

'Kto tam khodoy po moey komodzye! [кто там ходой по моей комодзе: Who is walking on my chest of drawers!]'

"He grabbed the bundle and ran off as if the devil were after him."

How They Read the Megillah in Chelm

Beets used to grow around the Chelm synagogue. The Shabbos goy's goat came and pulled up a beet. The synagogue fell down and killed the goat.

Out of vengeance for his dead goat, the Shabbos goy decided to steal the synagogue's megillah.[33] He made a pair of trousers out of it.

When Purim came and they went to read the megillah, it was missing.

Where is the megillah?

They started looking for the megillah, searching and searching, until they found that the Shabbos goy had stolen it and made a pair of trousers from it.

So they took the Shabbos goy, laid him on the reading desk, and read off the megillah.

A Synagogue on Cotton

When they were building the first synagogue in Chelm, they started thinking: How can we keep the synagogue warm in winter?

They held a meeting, pondered and pondered, and concluded:

They should insulate the entire synagogue on the inside with cotton.

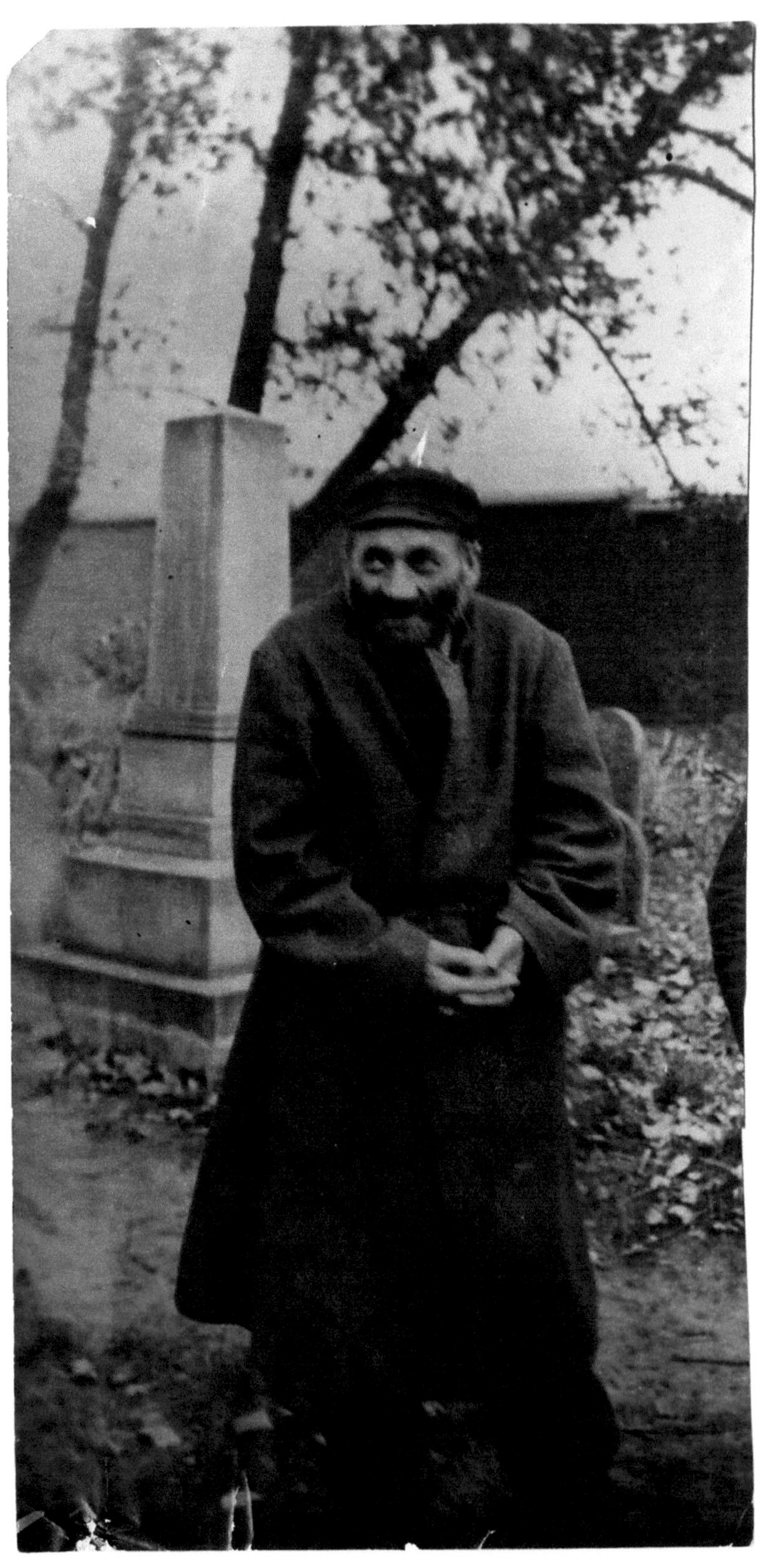

Keeper of the graveyard. (From the Photographic Archives, YIVO Institute for Jewish Research)

The Clever Servant

Someone came to Chelm and stayed at the inn. Before he went to sleep, he asked the servant to awaken him precisely at five in the morning, no later, so he wouldn't miss his wagon driver.

Three in the morning, the servant knocks on the door.

"Is it already five?" the guest asked angrily.

"No, it's only just three," answered the Chelmite, "but I woke you up on purpose to tell you that you only have two more hours to sleep."

How They Count in Chelm

A stranger arrived at the inn in Chelm. After breakfast, he asked how much he should pay.

"You had a roll with eggs, that's seven groshn," said the innkeeper's wife. "You drank a glass of tea with milk, that's seven groshn. Seven and seven make eleven groshn."

"No, seven plus seven isn't eleven; it's fourteen!" said the stranger.

"You think you're so smart," she said. "I'll show you in clear figures that seven plus seven make eleven."

"When I got married to my second husband, I already had four children, and my new husband also had four children from a previous marriage. After getting married, we had three more children. So I have seven children, and he has seven children, but when we count them all, we come to eleven!"

A Clear Sign

Once there was a great fire in Chelm. The bathhouse burned down, and there were a lot of casualties.

Afterward, the women came to identify their husbands, so that, God forbid, they wouldn't remain as *agunes* [chained, unable to remarry].

Each woman had to mention some sort of recognizable sign on her husband. One showed that her husband had a finger cut off. Another said that her husband had a wart on his hand. Each one came with a clear sign to identify her husband.

"Now you: What sign do you have to identify your husband?" the Rabbi asked a woman who was wandering among the corpses and couldn't find her husband.

"My husband was a stutterer!" the woman answered in tears.

"Go on now, foolish woman!" the Rabbi laughed. "You think there's only one stutterer in the world?"

The Chelmites Took a Bath

Nine Chelmites went to the river to bathe. When they had bathed well and came out of the river, they were afraid that maybe, God forbid, one of them had drowned. So one of them started counting to make sure they were all there, counting: not one, not two, not three, and so forth. But he forgot to count himself. It's terrible! Someone's missing. We only have eight.

Everyone looked about. They each realized they were themselves there; they had started out as nine, but the count came to eight.

Another started counting, and he also counted everyone but himself, and again the count stood at eight.

A third one tried to count, and a fourth, a fifth. Everyone counted the others but not himself, and it always came to eight.

The Chelmites sat naked on the sand at the river edge and cried. A stranger came by and asked them why they were crying. They told him the whole story, that they had gone to bathe, that they were nine, and now, having come out of the river, one is missing.

The stranger counted them and laughed:

OPPOSITE: Pub. July 18, 1926. Warsaw. Partners in troubles. A father and his son who deal together in old clothes, which they buy on the Warsaw courtyards and are mostly partners only in crying out "Trade! Trade" and to the sorrow which is spread over their faces. (People of a Thousand Towns, YIVO Institute for Jewish Research)

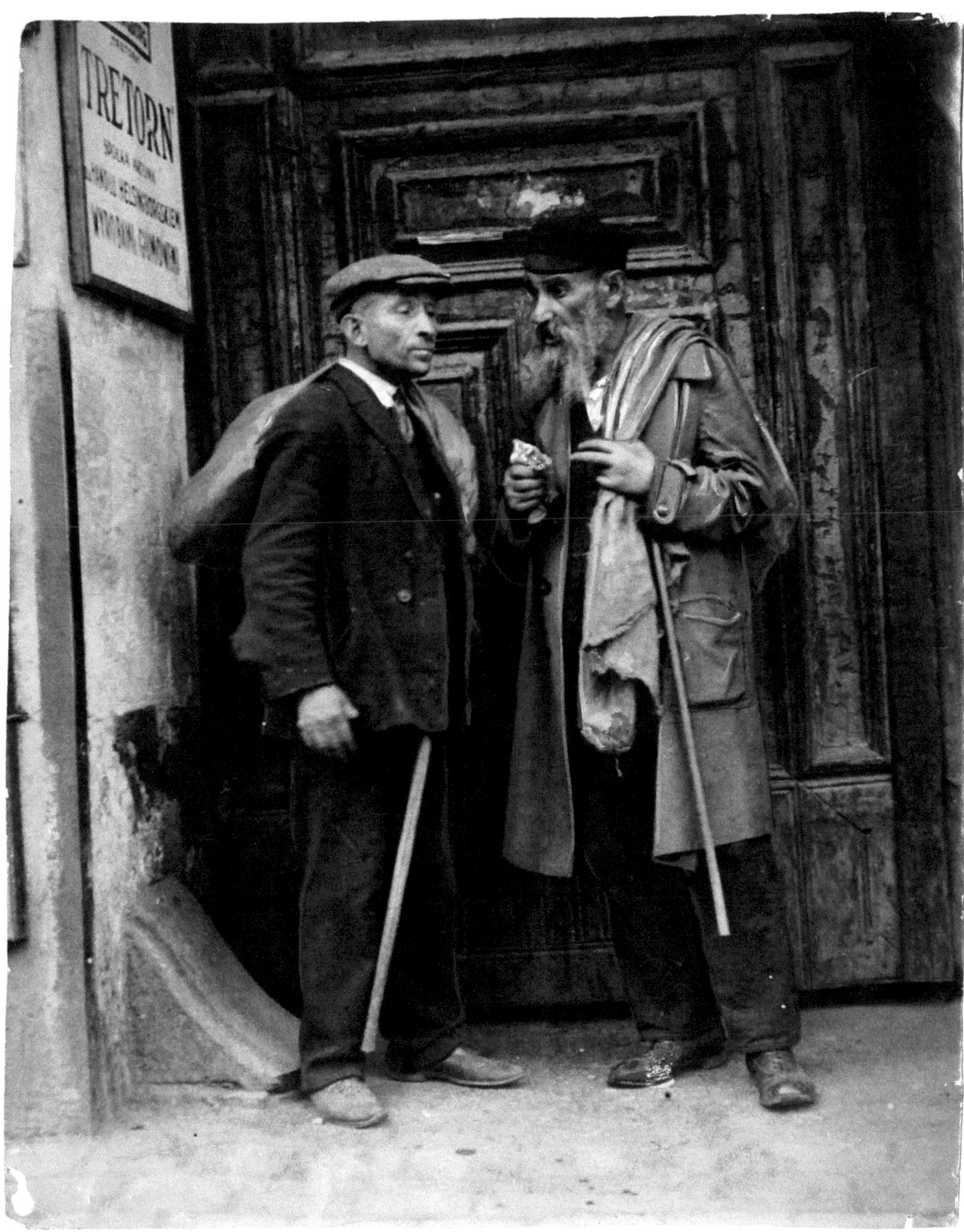
TRETORN

"Fools! No one is missing. You are all nine here!"

"Don't be such a wise guy!" they moved their hands in dismissal. "We have all counted, and it keeps coming to eight. This fellow counts and suddenly gets nine!"

"Do you know what?" the stranger asked. "If you want to convince yourselves for sure how many you are, take this advice: Each of you should stick his nose in the sand and then count the holes. You'll know for certain how many you are."

"Fine!" all the Chelmites shouted. And that's what they did. They poked their noses into the sand and then counted the holes. It came to nine.

That's when they finally were convinced that they were in fact nine and that nobody, God forbid, had drowned. With great pride they all pranced into town naked.

The Clever Guard

A clever fellow once arrived in Chelm. When he went out into the street early in the morning, he saw that the Chelmites were standing in their underwear and warming themselves in the sun. He started shouting:

"Chelm fools! Chelm fools!"

They grabbed him and threw him in jail.

So he was sitting in jail. Presently he felt like smoking. He went to the door and saw a guard standing there. He handed over six groshn so the guard would go and get some tobacco for him.

The guard took the six groshn and went to fetch some tobacco.

The stranger noticed that nobody was guarding the door, so he got up and went off home.

The next day he went out into the street and again shouted:

"Chelm fools! Chelm fools!"

So they grabbed him again and put him back in jail.

He sat there and got bored. He felt like smoking again, so he went to the door and saw the same guard as yesterday. He handed him another six groshn to fetch tobacco.

"Feh!" said the guard. "What were you up to yesterday? I'll go bring you tobacco, and you'll run away meanwhile? You're not going to play that trick on me. You want tobacco? Go get it yourself. I'm staying right here!"

The Chelm Jail

When they sentenced someone to jail in Chelm, they relied on his honesty. They brought him into a room, sat him on a chair, and said:

"You are now in jail, and you must not leave this spot until they tell you." And everyone obeyed and sat without a guard in an unlocked room until they told him he could leave.

Later, when the world became more sinful and people stopped obeying, they had to find other means, but they didn't want to require a guard.

In the walls of the Chelm jail there were narrow holes; only a hand could pass through. They would ask the prisoner to stretch his hand through the wall to the outside. On the outside they put a broom in his hand and said, "Hold this!" Since he couldn't pull his hand back holding the broom, and he wasn't supposed to let go of the broom (after all, they told him to hold it), he remained in jail.

Only much later, when the world became so sinful that honesty was no honesty at all and a promise was no longer a promise and the prisoners would drop the broom, pull back their hand and run away, that's when they finally established a guard in the Chelm jail.

The Chelmite in the Brest-Litovsk Hospital

They once took a Chelmite with a very sore foot to Brest-Litovsk and put him in the hospital there among other patients with foot problems.

When the doctor and the assistants came, and they started giving him massages and ointments, the patients started screaming in pain, so loudly that the screams reached the seventh heaven. But when they started massaging the Chelmite's foot, he lay there and even laughed.

That's how it went every day.

A young man who was lying nearby and who screamed in pain every time they massaged his foot, kept seeing that the Chelmite was lying in peace as they rubbed his foot, and not only did he not give a groan, but it was even giving him pleasure, so that he actually laughed. He leaned over to the Chelmite's bed and asked him:

"Tell me, please, how it happens that all the sick people scream as their sick feet are massaged, but you are actually laughing!"

"You're such a sage!" the Chelmite answered. "What sort of fool puts out his sick foot to massage and hurt? I hide my sick foot, and I put out my other foot to the assistant, the fool, and it's a real pleasure!"

The Chelm *Minyan*

In Chelm, ten men came together to pray as a group.

Before the prayers started, they started counting to make sure there was a minyan.

One started counting: "Not one, not two, not three, not four, not five, not six, not seven, not eight, not nine, but that's all."

He had forgotten to count himself.

"We don't have a minyan!" he called out. "Instead of ten, we only have nine."

"What do you mean, there's no minyan? Ten people came in!" they wondered.

A second one started counting, got up to nine, and forgot to count himself.

"Still nine, not ten!"

In short, each of the ten counted, and nobody included himself, and it always came to nine.

What to do? How can they count to reach ten so we can start the prayers?

They came upon an idea: Take a trough filled with clay, and everyone should stick a finger in to make a hole. They could then count how many holes there are in the trough. They would then know whether there was a minyan.

But one old fellow, whose fingers trembled, put in two fingers instead of one.

They counted anew, but now they found eleven holes.

That was really terrible. Earlier they had all counted and came up with nine.

And now they get eleven?

They pondered and pondered and concluded that each one should bring his wife. They could count the wives and know whether they had a minyan.

That's what they did.

They brought their wives and counted, and it came to ten.

They were finally convinced that there was a minyan, and they started praying.[34]

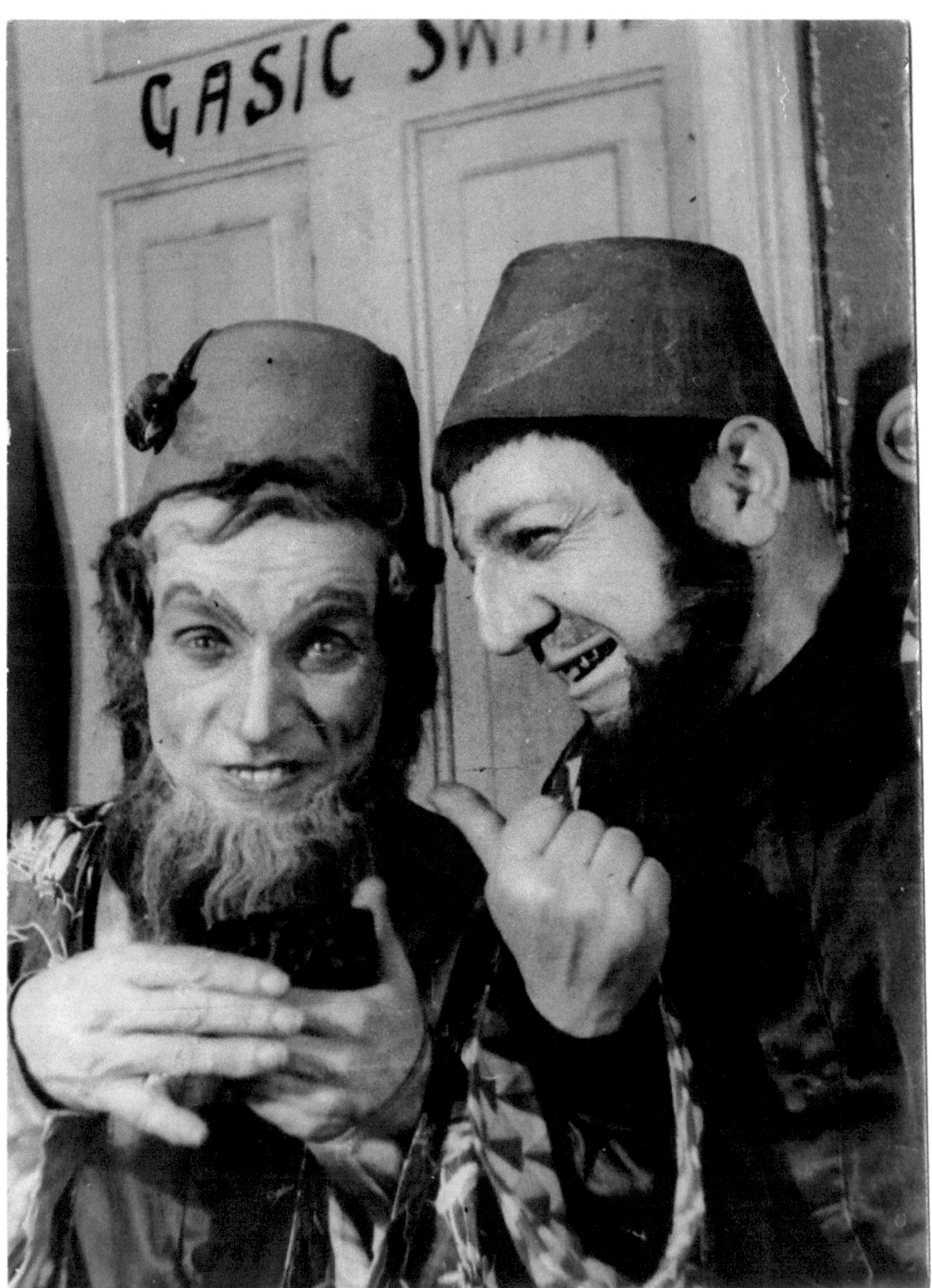
GASIC

They also tell this story about wives who were envious of their husbands and wanted to pray as a group.

Advice for Tight Boots

Once there was a fellow in Chelm who wore boots. Now they had never seen boots in Chelm before, so everyone ran up to inspect this marvel. The fellow quickly figured out that he was dealing with great sages, so he let it be known that he would sell this novelty for a high price.

But who could afford such an expensive thing? Most likely the town's rich man.

In short, they brought the rich man over, and he bought the boots for the enormous sum that the fellow demanded.

When the rich man took the boots, he discovered that they were too tight for him.

What to do?

The sages of the city sat down around the boots, pondered and pondered, and arrived at the wise result that there was nothing to be done except to cut open the fronts of the boots so they wouldn't be too tight.

What Comes First: Slaughter or Inspection?

A young fellow from Chelm once traveled to Vilna to study ritual slaughter.

After two years, when he returned to Chelm having finished his studies and wishing to start his business, he suddenly forgot the proper order: First to slaughter, then to inspect, or first to inspect and then to slaughter?

Meanwhile he saw a woman who was running about yelling:

OPPOSITE: Actors from the Warsaw Yiddish theater: Jacob Fisher (left) and S. Rattner (right). (From the Photographic Archive, YIVO Institute for Jewish Research)

"Help! They've murdered me! Help! They have slaughtered me!"

So he approached the woman.

"Dear woman, tell me, please, did they slaughter you first and then inspect you, or inspect you first and then slaughter you?

She answered:

"You crazy fellow! If they hadn't first inspected me, would they have slaughtered me?"

From then on he understood that you first inspect and then you slaughter.

The Shammes Waits for Spring

The shammes of Chelm went at dawn to awaken the congregation to recite Psalms.

Because the roads in Chelm were so muddy and overnight there had been a deep frost, his boots got frozen into the deep mud, and he couldn't pull them out.

People got up in the morning and saw that the shammes was stuck, frozen, to the mud.

What can we do?

They held a meeting, pondered and pondered, and concluded: If we drag the shammes out with force, it could, God forbid, pull off a foot. The only plan is to let him stay there until spring, when the ice melts; then we'll be able to pull him out. But to prevent his death from hunger, we should surround him with a barrier, and his wife should bring him food every day.

So the poor Chelm shammes stood all winter frozen into the mud and waited for spring.

A Charm for a Dead Person

A Chelmite wrote a missive with enormous letters.

"Why are you writing such enormous letters?" they asked him.

"I'm writing the letter to my uncle, and he is, may it not happen to you, stone deaf," he answered.

Unfortunately, She Can't See

A Chelmite woman came to Warsaw to see a doctor.

"Mr. Doctor," she started crying, "I'm sick."

"What is the problem, dear woman?" the doctor asked as he started his examination.

"It's terrible, Mr. Doctor. I can't see a thing."

"What do you mean, you can't see a thing?"

"It's like this, Mr. Doctor. Poor me, I can't see a thing. For example, Mr. Doctor, there on the wall is a little nail. You see it? Well, I can't."

It's Good That Father Won

A Chelm shoemaker recounted that when he was a small boy, his parents fought over him. His father wanted him to become a shoemaker, and his mother, a tailor. But thank God, his father won and made him a shoemaker. Because if his mother had, God forbid, won and made him a tailor, he and his wife and children would have died of hunger.

"How do you figure that?"

"What do you mean, how? I have a proof. Here I have been a shoemaker for thirty years, and not once has anyone come to me to sew some clothing. Everyone just comes to me for shoes."

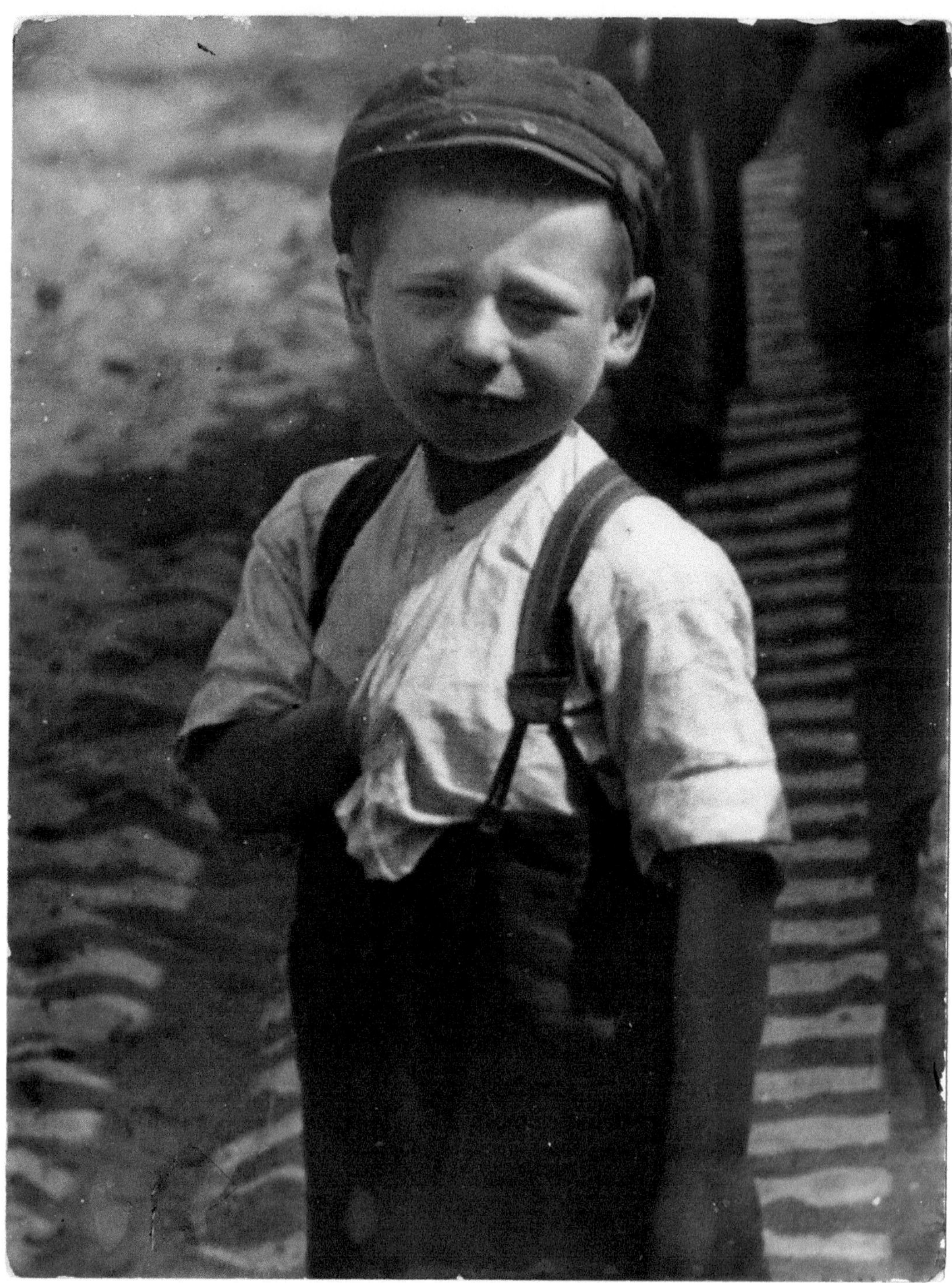

Day Has Broken in Zamość

In Chelm, suddenly all the clocks broke. The town folk didn't know how to establish the time by the sun, to know when to light Sabbath candles and the like.

They sent out a special emissary to carefully observe sunrise in order to use the calendar to figure out what time it was.

He traveled all night looking at the sky, and when he was close to Zamość, the sun rose.

He recited a praise to God for helping him succeed, and he headed back to Chelm.

He traveled back all day, and at nightfall, as he arrived at the outskirts, the finest householders and the mayor were awaiting him.

"What is the good news?" everyone started asking as they surrounded him.

"I have brought you important news," he shouted proudly. The day has begun in Zamość.

A Lack of One Sign Is Unimportant

A Chelm melamed went to a village to buy a cow.

Before he departed, his wife gave him several signs that a cow provides a lot of milk:

"You should notice that it has a long udder; its tail should be long, up to its ankles; and its horns should be wide and not too short."

"And what should I do if one of the signs is missing?"

"One sign missing is unimportant," his wife answered.

So the melamed went off and brought home an ox.

His wife went off to milk it: terrible!

OPPOSITE: pub. October 9, 1927. Falencia. Detail from [English] "Hail, Hail the gang's all here!" (People of a Thousand Towns, YIVO Institute for Jewish Research)

"Have yourself eighty demons!" his wife started cursing and complaining. "You brought me an ox!"

"How do you know that it's an ox?" he answered in his simplicity.

"You good-for-nothing! Where are your eyes!" his wife exclaimed. "It has no udder at all! I told you the signs!"

"You harpy!" he screamed in response. "You told me yourself that the lack of one sign didn't matter!"

A Headless Rabbi (Variant)

It once happened in Chelm that the Rabbi disappeared. Meanwhile at the town outskirts they found a headless corpse. They didn't know if it was the Rabbi and whether the Rabbi had actually had a head.

They went to ask the shammes. He answered: He knew for certain that the Rabbi had a beard, because he used to store all the hairs that fell out of his beard in his Talmud. But whether he had a head: that he didn't know.

They went to ask the bathhouse attendant. He said that the Rabbi had sidelocks, because every Eve of the Sabbath and holiday the Rabbi would wash them in hot water. But whether he had a head: that he didn't know.

They went to ask the Rabbi's wife. She answered that she knew for certain that the Rabbi had a nose, because every Eve of the Sabbath and holiday she would prepare snuff in a little box for him to sniff. But whether he had a head: that she didn't know.

Until this very day the matter has never been cleared up, whether the Rabbi had a head or was entirely without a head [without any sense].

The Difference Between a Rich Man and a Poor Man

A Chelmite recounted how he had become convinced that a rich man is a liar and a poor man is always trustworthy.

"Yesterday I was in Warsaw," he narrated. "I went all day around the big stores buying merchandise. At night I returned to the inn and what do you know? My cane is missing.

"Where is my cane?

"I got up early the next morning and went to all the wealthy businesses where I had been the day before, and everywhere I asked: Maybe they have seen my cane? They all denied it and said they hadn't. Finally, I arrived at the basement room of a poor fellow where I had eaten dinner, and I asked him about my cane. He said not a word and immediately gave me back the cane."

Only One in a Thousand

Two Chelmites were baring their hearts to each other. They were complaining that they couldn't find work, that they were sick, and that they had to bother with their wife and children all their life long.

"It's not for nothing that our sages have said, 'It is better for a person never to have been created [in Hebrew].' It would be better for a person never to have been born," one of them sighed.

"But who can merit such a prize?" groaned the other. "Maybe one person in a thousand."

The Greatest Fool in the Whole World

The world says that Chelm is a town of fools. It also says that a cantor is a fool, a turkey is a fool, and a dream is a fool. So just imagine: the dream of the Chelm cantor's turkey. Such a doubled and redoubled foolishness it must have.

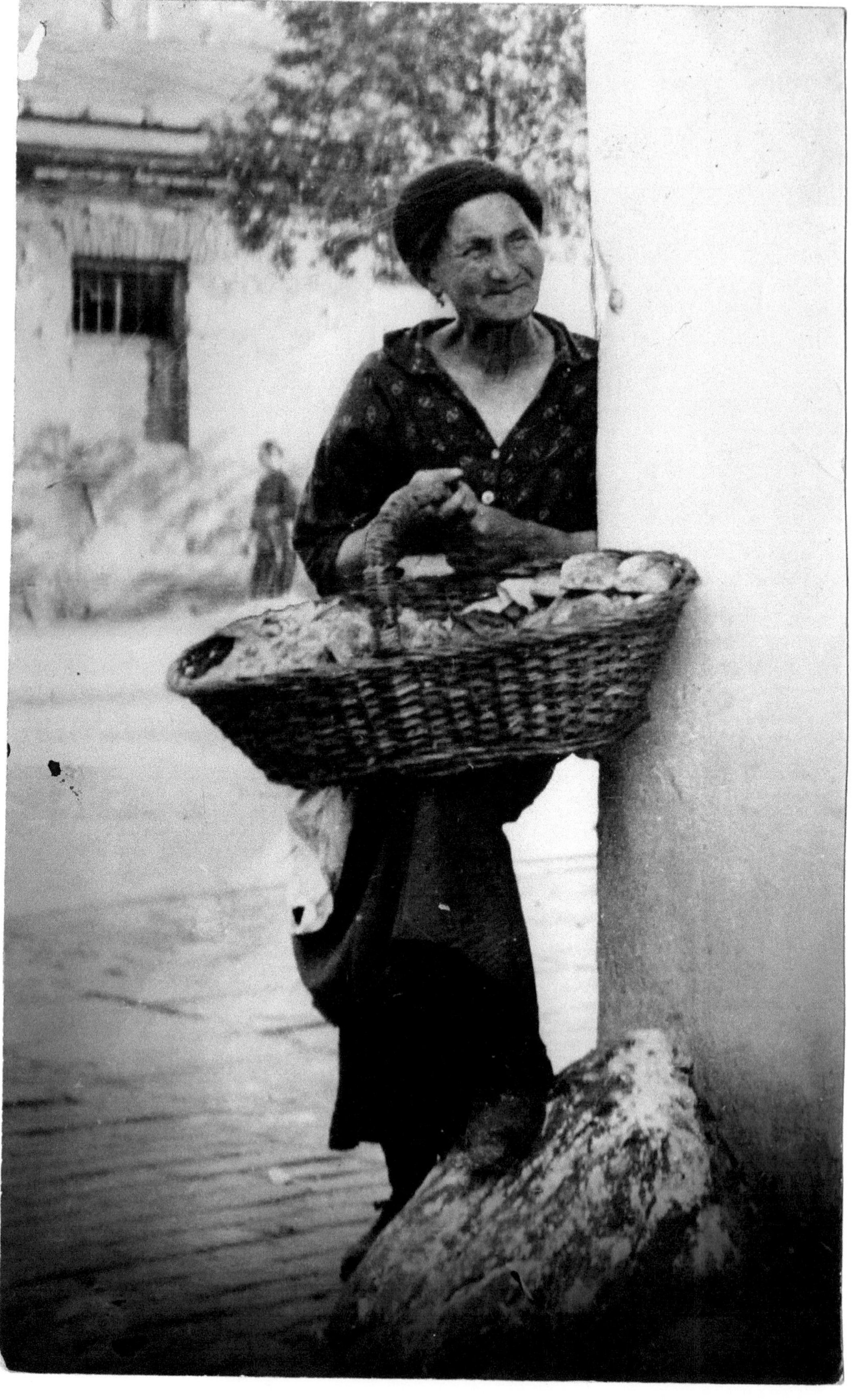

A True Heavenly Miracle

In Chelm one dark night a fire broke out. The whole town ran to the fire to put it out. Also the Rabbi came running. He stood to the side deep in thought.

"What is the Rabbi pondering?" they asked him.

"I'm marveling at this marvelous miracle from heaven, that a fire has broken out. If it weren't for the fire, nobody would have been able to see, in this darkness, how to put it out."

The Melamed in General's Clothing

A Chelm melamed once came to Warsaw. He stayed at a cheap inn on the Navelki street [the Jewish district] and went to sleep in a big communal room together with a few other guests.

Before he went to sleep, he asked the attendant to awaken him quite early so he wouldn't miss his train.

An old general slept in the next bed over.

When the attendant awakened him, it was only a few minutes before the train. He dressed himself in a hurry, and instead of his own clothes, he put on the old general's clothes, and he ran with his pack to the train.

On the way, he sees that the night watchman is greeting him.

"That's quite nice of him," he thinks.

He travels farther. The policeman salutes him with a hand to his visor.

"That's what a big town is like," thinks the Chelmite. "In Chelm, the smallest street urchin has no respect for him. But here is Warsaw: such honor!"

OPPOSITE: pub. September 25, 1927. Warsaw. [Yiddish] One man buys a "plats" [cemetery plot] and another, a "pletsl" [flat onion bread]. And those who buy "pletsl" in Warsaw's Jewish quarter know this "pletsl" peddler-woman, who is awaiting them. (People of a Thousand Towns, YIVO Institute for Jewish Research)

He arrives at the train, buys a third-class ticket, and heads to the wagons. He sees that they are saluting him on all sides. A soldier grabs his bag and carries it into the wagon. He enters the wagon. They open the door to the first-class section.

The melamed stands in the first-class compartment and wonders: "What am I doing being a melamed in Chelm, where everyone treats me like dirt, and here in Warsaw they bestow such honor! When I get home, I won't delay; I'll grab my wife, Keyle, and the kids, and I'll come to Warsaw to be a melamed here."

As he was thinking this, he glanced into the compartment mirror and screamed in fear:

"Just look what a terrible fool that attendant is! I asked him to wake *me* up, but, blockhead that he is, he went and woke up the general!"[35]

Two Rulings

In Chelm, they had to repair the women's gallery in the synagogue and rebuild the stairs. The workman started by demolishing the stairs from bottom to top. When he had removed the last stair, he was on the second floor with no way to get down.

That was terrible. How can we get the workman down without stairs?

They held a great meeting, pondered and pondered, and concluded that they should gather the pillows from all the houses and make a tall hill of them up to the women's gallery. That way the workman would be able to get down.

But in order to prevent a repetition of the problem, they made a ruling and wrote it in the town record that one must demolish stairs only from the top down.

One day it happened that they had to rebuild the stairs leading down to the mikve. Of course they knew about that ruling, that stairs should only be demolished from the top down. So, the

OPPOSITE: Pub. May 12–15, 1926. Warsaw. In the Jewish cemetery, a Polish military unit honors Jewish soldiers who died fighting on Pilsudski's side during the coup d'etat. (People of a Thousand Towns, YIVO Institute for Jewish Research)

workman took apart the mikve stairs from top to bottom. But then he couldn't get back up from the mikve.

That was terrible. They again held a great meeting, pondered and pondered until someone remembered that such a problem had occurred with rebuilding the stairs to the women's gallery, when they had built a hill of bedclothes in order to get the workman down.

So that's what they did again.

From all the houses they carried bedclothes and made a tall hill next to the mikve. Then the shammes called down to the workman that he could now come out of the mikve, because there was a big hill of bedclothes.

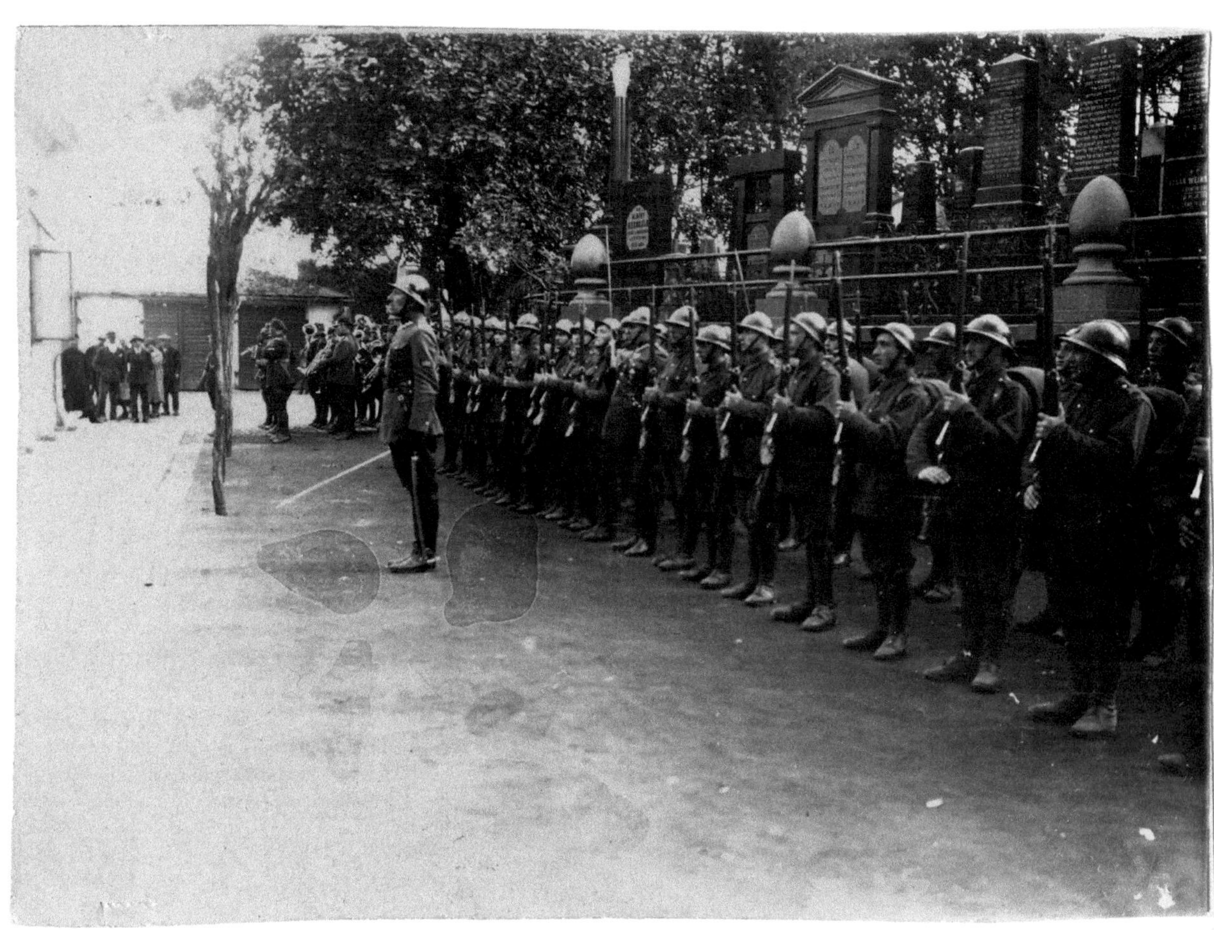

The workman, however, was still unable to climb out. He kept shouting up out of the mikve. Chelm had no idea what to do until a stranger passed by and burst out laughing.

"You fools! Toss the bedclothes down into the mikve; then he'll be able to climb out.

That's what they did. They covered the workman and the entire mikve.

In order that such a situation should not repeat, they made a second ruling, that stairs should be removed from bottom to top, not from top to bottom.

In a Leap Year You Recite It Twice

The women of Chelm always had a *zogerke* [prayer reciter] in their gallery in the synagogue for the High Holidays.[36] He would recite the prayers and supplications, and all the women would repeat them word for word. But because it isn't appropriate to put a man among all the women, they put the reciter in a corridor and set up a partition, so he would be separate but could still recite for them.

Yom Kippur at the Kol Nidre service, the women all stood near the corridor and repeated, sobbing, the stanzas of the Ya'aleh prayer. A cat ran by and jumped onto the partition.

"Scat! [*a kota*]," the reciter cried out to the cat in the middle of the prayer, and all the women repeated, "Scat!"

"Hannah, dear," one woman called to another, wiping her nose. "It seems to me that last year at the Ya'aleh we had 'scat' two times."

"Did you forget, dear Feyge, that last year was a leap year?" Hanna responded. "That's why we said it twice."

[The Ya'aleh prayer has two words that sound a bit like *a kota*: *naakateynu* and *enkateynu*, but in the Ashkenazic accent they are *naakoseynu* and *enkoseynu*.]

Moving the Synagogue

Chelm had to move the synagogue once, and they didn't know how to do it. They held a great meeting, pondered and pondered for three days and three nights, and discovered a method:

Chickpeas.

Since chickpeas are round, they poured chickpeas under one side of the synagogue, and all of Chelm started to push the synagogue onto the chickpeas, and then it continued on its own.

Renovating the Bathhouse

The Chelm bathhouse got old. They held a meeting and started considering: How can we have a new bathhouse and not have to put out much money?

They pondered and pondered and landed on an idea: renovating. All of Chelm had the custom of turning old cloaks inside out and thereby renovating them. Why couldn't they do the same to the old bathhouse?

So that's what they did.

They turned the bathhouse inside out so that the outer walls turned inward and the steam benches faced outside.

How the Chelm Cantor Became a Cow

The Chelm cantor saw in an old volume of Kabbalah that on Hoshana Raba,[37] after midnight, when the moon comes to the middle of the sky, everyone can determine their fate in the coming year. You just have to look at your own shadow. If it is full, that's a sign that you'll have a good year. If, God forbid, the shadow lacks a head, it's a sign that you'll die this year. Missing a hand: a sign that you'll be sick. It all depends on the shadow cast by the moon.

The cantor took this to heart and waited for the night of Hoshana Raba to find out his fortune in the coming year.

The night of Hoshana Raba arrived. The cantor went to the big synagogue to recite psalms with great devotion. When the psalms were finished, it was an hour past midnight, just when the moon would be in the middle of the sky. Everyone went home, but he stayed after. He wanted to be alone when he went out to examine his shadow, so nobody would interfere, and he could be sure that the shadow was his own.

When he went out and saw the Hoshana Raba moon in the sky, his heart started to pound, and he was unsure what to do. He was afraid to look at his shadow: Maybe it would lack a head! But if he didn't look, he wouldn't know what the coming year would be like. Finally, he couldn't contain himself, and with half-closed eyes he glanced at the shadow. It had a cow's head! (A cow was standing at the side chewing its cud, and it was its shadow that he saw.)

Like a corpse he just stood there, seeing that his shadow had a cow's head. His hands and feet were trembling. He dragged himself home with his last strength. He stumbled into his house and in a faint threw himself into bed.

"What's happened to you?" his wife began to ask, also alarmed.

"Woe is me! I'm a cow!" he screamed. "I saw my shadow cast by the moon. Tonight is Hoshana Raba, and I found in a volume of Kabbalah . . ."[38]

When the cantor's wife heard these words, she also began to believe, and she wrung her hands. "A curse has been my lot! Maybe it's true . . . ," and she started to examine him from all sides.

"Where is the mirror? Give me the mirror!" he screamed. "Let me look at myself!"

When he saw in the mirror that he was by no means a cow, he was not comforted. "Meanwhile," he explained, "I'm not yet a cow. But I will certainly become a cow: I saw the shadow myself!"

All night the cantor and his wife were weeping about their bitter misfortune. The next morning, he decided not to go to the synagogue.

"If I'm destined to become a cow, let me be a cow at home," he thought. If, God forbid, he should become a cow standing at the lectern in the synagogue, it would be terrible. The citizens would laugh at him, and the slaughterers would kill him for meat.

Early the next morning, the congregation assembled in the synagogue for the Hoshana prayers. But the cantor was missing. They had arrived at "haMelekh," introducing the morning service, and they didn't see him.

They sent the shammes to call him. But he wouldn't come; he was too afraid.

The shammes came back to the cantor with an urgent message: They are already at "haMelekh," and if he wouldn't come to lead the prayers, they would dismiss him from his position.

When he heard that they might dismiss him, it was doubly terrible. Meanwhile, whatever should happen, he could survive a while without income. He came upon a good idea and said to his wife:

"Listen, my wife! I'm going to go pray in the synagogue.
But you should accompany me. Here is a rope. Go up to the women's balcony and don't take your eyes off me. If you see me turning into a cow, come down into the back of the synagogue and lasso me and bring me home."

When the cantor entered the synagogue, all the annoyed citizens greeted him with curses because he was so late. He went to the lectern in fear and a little confused. It seemed to him that everyone was looking at him strangely, noticing something about him. He started to get dizzy, and his voice caught in his throat. Wanting to sing out "haMelekh," he just called out "hame," and that's all that came out. His voice was so strange that everyone laughed.

When he heard the congregation laughing, it seemed to him that he had started to creep like a cow. He became more confused and befogged. The pranksters, seeing that the cantor had called out "hame" like a cow, surrounded him and started chanting, "meh! meh! meh!" A commotion broke out. The congregation started slapping their lecterns and shouting, "Well, why isn't the cantor praying?" And the cantor stood like a statue,

OPPOSITE: 1920s–1930s. Rovno. A couple poses on the balcony of the butcher shop (in the photographer's words) "taking the May air." (People of a Thousand Towns, YIVO Institute for Jewish Research)

as pale as the wall, and he made all sorts of strange motions with his mouth. He turned to the women's gallery and shouted wildly:

"Help, Yente! Quick, the rope! Take me away from here!"

His wife quickly descended from the women's gallery, threw the rope on his neck, and pulled him home, wailing:

"Woe is me, destroyed is our luck. The cantor has become a cow!"

The cantor dragged himself behind his wife and he kept uttering, "hame, hame."

All of Chelm ran after.

The Chelm Cemetery: A Story in Verse

I

Chelm is a town of big fools.
If they say so, it must be true.
I tell a tale that happened
Five hundred years before.
Chelm was then a small settlement,
Without its own cantor or Rabbi.
The world had never heard of Chelm.
Chelm had to deal with Hrubishov.[39]
And there was a great problem:
Nobody was available to sermonize on *Shabbos Shuvah*
or *Shabbos HaGodl*.[40]
Whenever there was a wedding, Hrubishov came for the religious fees.
At a circumcision ceremony,
There was nobody to call as *sandek* [honoree to hold the child].
There was nobody to whom to sell the *khomets* [leavened food,
sold before Passover]
And when there was a ritual question:
They had to run off to Hrubishov.
The worst of all was the lack of a cemetery.
If someone should die,
He had to suffer the pains of the grave along with a
change of residence.
Traveling from Chelm to Hrubishov over hills and ditches,

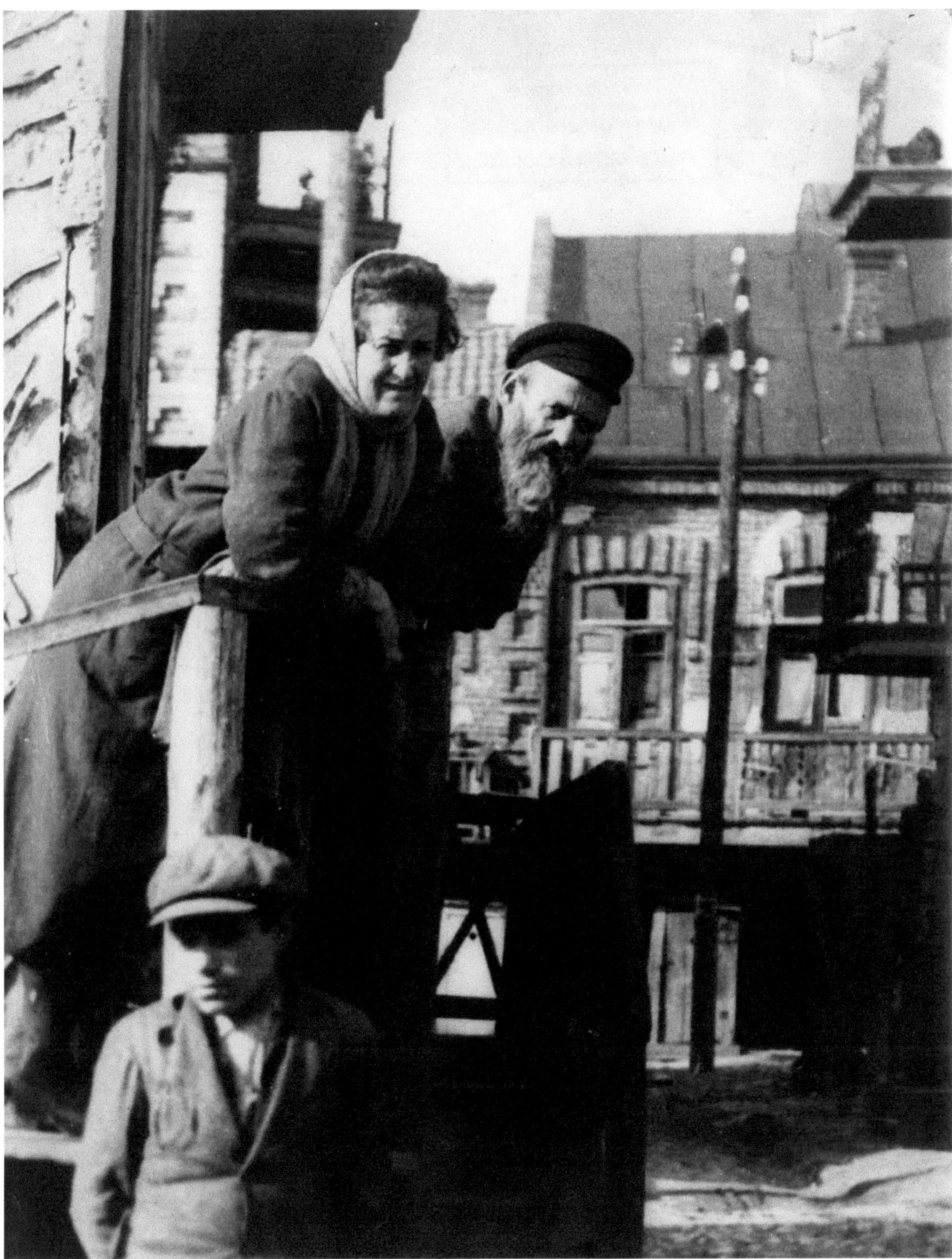

Shaking and breaking bones and limbs.
All the citizens gathered in a big meeting and started to ponder.
Whereas it is a terrible defect,
What good is it to travel after every death?
If they only had their own cemetery,
They would be able to avoid all of that.
Therefore, they sent a request to the governor,
To give them permission.
Whereas, they were in terrible need,
they want to have their own cemetery.
It cost a lot of money.
The important citizens stood up for them.
For months they dealt with the scriveners,
Even the police put out an effort for them,
Until they received the governor's seal of approval.

II

In Chelm there was joy and rejoicing.
They were singing and dancing in the streets.
It's no small matter: Our own cemetery!
We need all of Hrubishov like a hole in the head.
They were soon searching for a red heifer,
and the slaughterer, Mr. Judah,
Killed it for an enormous feast.
They were expecting a large attendance,
And as they were eating, they started thinking in earnest
about the cemetery.
What would be the best place for a cemetery?
What sort of fence
And what sort of lock?
One person said they should put the cemetery on the hilltop.
Another suggested: in his attic.
A third one pointed out that it would be a great defect:
If a dear departed should appear in someone's dream,
It would fall down and break its neck.
"It would be better," says he,
"In the market square,
Right in the middle."
Close and accessible to everyone.
Everyone would be able to keep watch
Over his own family.
Bringing a glass of coffee,
Or a glass of tea,

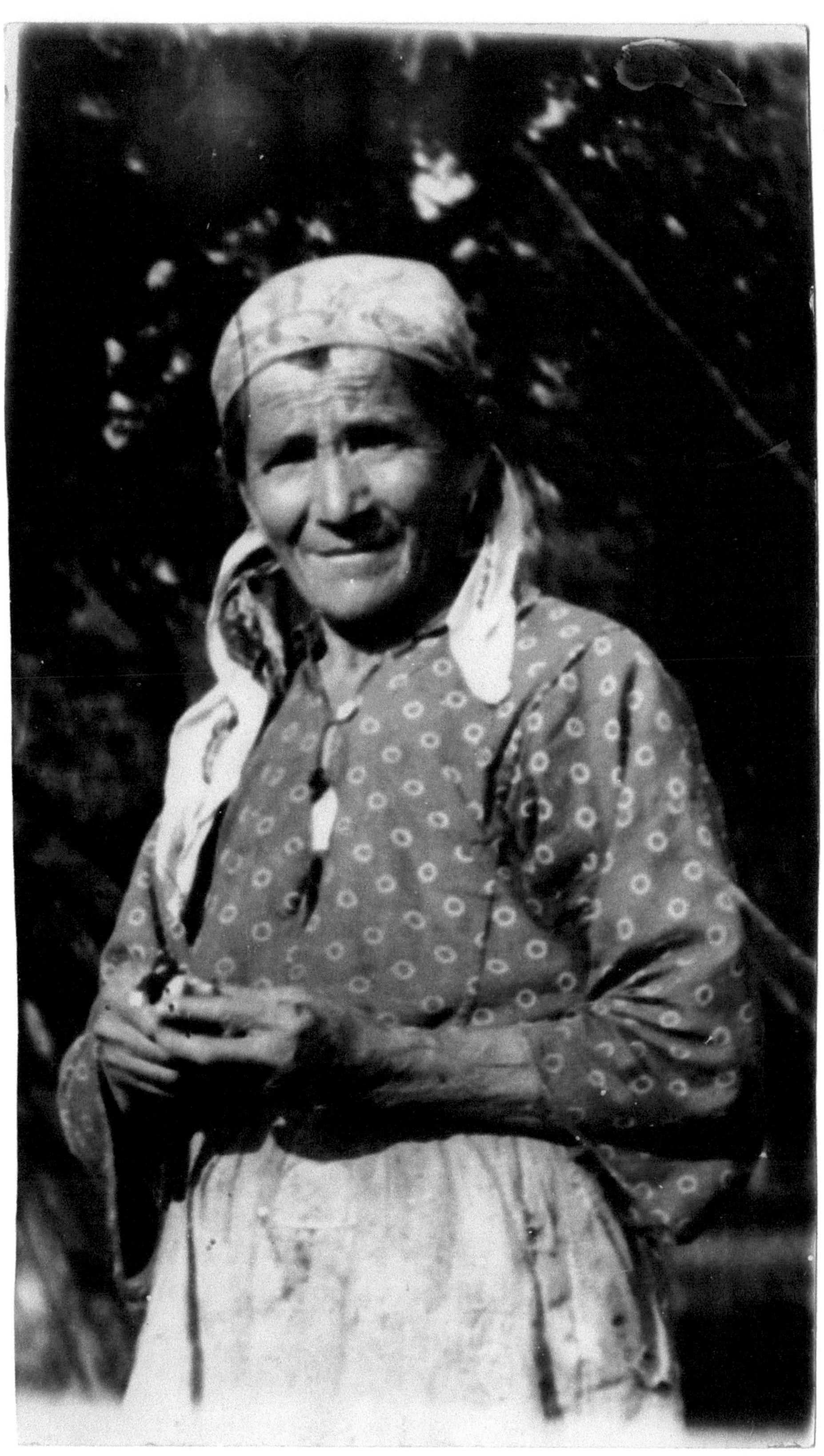

Woman with kerchief. (From the Photographic Archive, YIVO Institute for Jewish Research)

And setting out a bedstead
With a bit of fresh hay.
Someone arrived with a very new dream:
They should build two,
One for weekdays
And one for holidays.
So they pondered
Half the night,
Broke their brains.
It was too hard to consider.
Each had his own plan
And his advice.
Suddenly came forth a fellow with a new idea,
A pertinent question.
"How can we set up a cemetery?
How can an empty field get the name 'cemetery'
When nobody has yet been buried there?"
"That's right!" they all cried, "quite right!"
That idea made sense,
But please excuse me;
The question was quite tough.
How can they find a corpse at the very moment,
When just now nobody is dying in Chelm?
So that is a problem.
They sat and pondered and pondered anew,
All night through,
And concluded
That Chelm couldn't wait for a corpse.
They needed a cemetery right away.
But where can we find a corpse to bury?
We have to put out some effort.
If we can't find one here,
And no local resident can be gotten,
We'll have to buy one from elsewhere.

III

And so it was concluded.
They selected
Two of the important citizens,
Rented a wagon,
And collected money.
They got some from everyone.
Poor folk even donated money socked away in pillows.
It was without limit and measure.

And food for the road
All of Chelm accompanied them.
And with a song
Children from the cradle ran along.
And they wished the travelers
To have success
And not too far
At their first stop they should find a corpse.

IV

In short:
They arrived at a town
A city of regret
There they asked a tombstone engraver
If he didn't know a way
That they could buy a corpse.
Now that fellow was no fool.
He immediately understood that these were Chelm folk,
And however much he demanded, they wouldn't dicker.
So he told them:
You've hit the nail on the head.
Just today someone fell dead.
The community needs to repair the poorhouse,
So they surely will let him be removed.
But you'll need to pay accordingly
But what is the value of money when the need is great?
The Chelmites paid as much as he demanded.
But, poor fools, they never realized
That they were being treated like horses.
They were given a live person made up like a corpse,
As long as they could be tricked out of money.
Their happiness was so great
They didn't even examine the corpse.
They ran off to where pepper grows[41]
With the beautiful fish.

V

When they had traveled a few miles,
They needed to stop and rest.
They went into an inn to drink a glass of strong liquor.
The "corpse" on the wagon was also not feeling so well
He began to think:

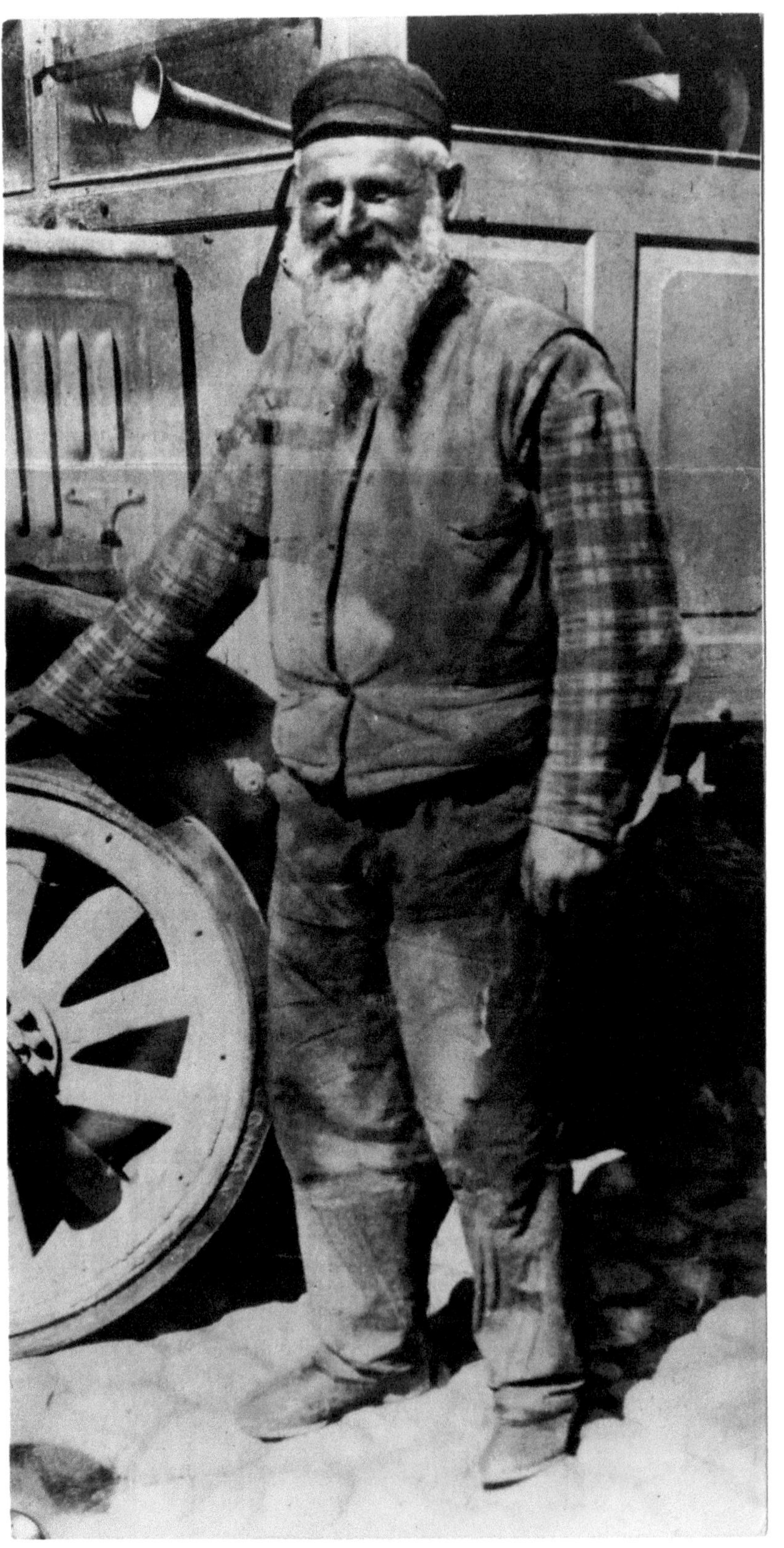

Pub. January 27, 1929. Nasielsk. Portrait study of Moyshe Hokhman with his new autobus. He rejoices at civilization. Before Moyshe Hokhman transported merchandise and passengers from Nasielsk to Warsaw and back with a team of horses. And today . . . with an automobile. (People of a Thousand Towns, YIVO Institute for Jewish Research)

"The devil will take you.
I'll sing you the dirge:
I'll turn back and make off with the horse and wagon.
You can just chase me!
And berate me in the prayer *Unetaneh Tokef*."[42]
The lad didn't pause for long,
And he turned about and made off with wagon and horse.
The Chelmites come out:
The wagon is not there in front.
Their world turned black:
It had cost them so much money.
How can they return to the community?
It's bad this way and bad that way.
They went back into the inn with a shout,
And the innkeeper treated them like a dead horse.
"You left a corpse alone?
You are supposed to guard it until it is deep in the ground.
You most likely left it alone,
And it made off to the Austrian Empire."

VI

The Chelmites returned home in sorrow and with heads hanging low.
In Chelm they were awaited
Just like the Messiah.
They barely crept there
And recounted what had happened to them.
Of course there was a wailing in Chelm
Up to the high heavens.
Terrible:
We need to buy another such hero,
But there is no more money.
And what's more, if he should run away too,
That's the awful problem.
They still had to establish the cemetery.
So they pondered and pondered,
Three days and a night.
They came upon a great plan:
From our own town folk
There has to be a corpse in time.
But since no Chelmite feels, out of spite, like dying just now,
Here's the plan:
We'll decree a fast.

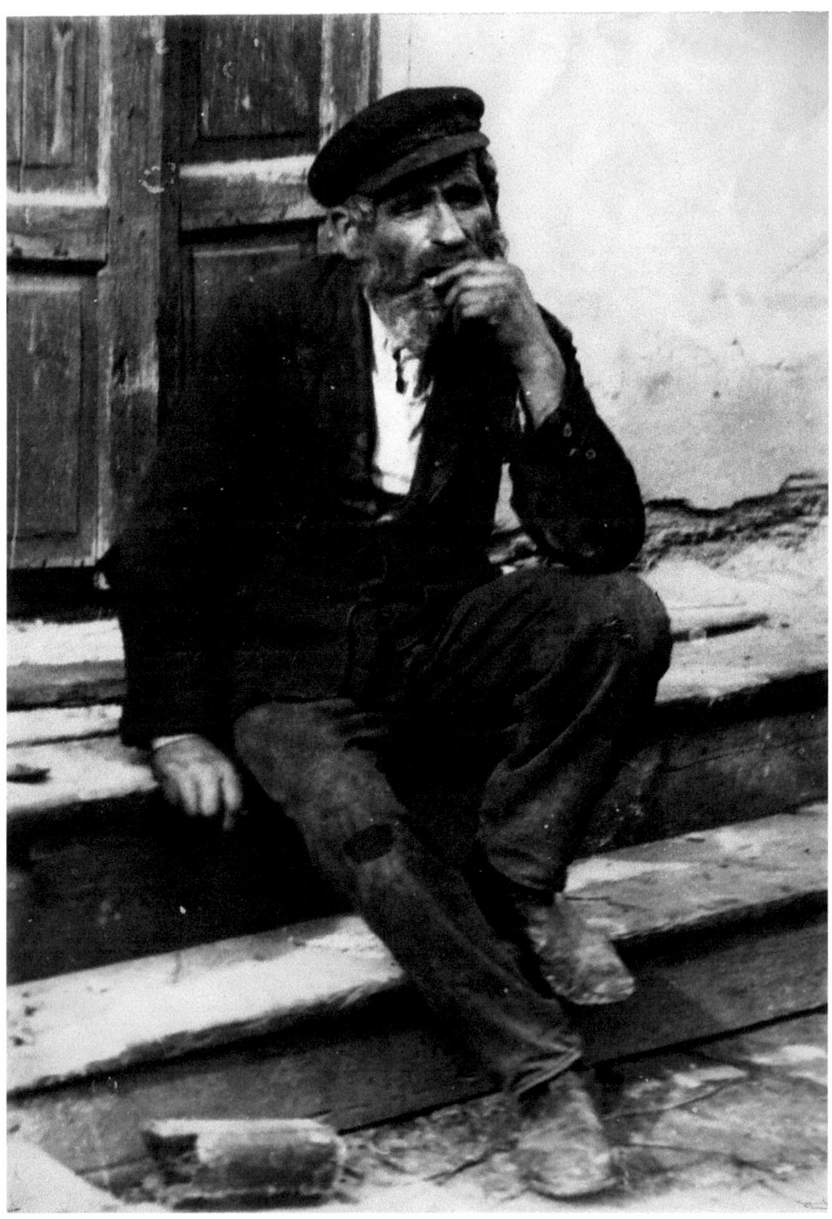

A man from Rovno[Poland] sits on the stair. (From the Photographic Archives, YIVO Institute for Jewish Research)

Men, women, and children should fast so long,
Until one of us is ready to be put in the coffin.
This plan met with general agreement.
First, we need to recite psalms eighteen times
And enunciate entire chapters.
And the whole town should allow itself to be flagellated.
So the community of fools started to fast so long
Until one became ill.
Well, in town it was joy and rejoicing.
The burial society was all ready.
The gabbai was ready with the *Maavor Yabbok*[43]
And handed out tobacco to all the society members.
Each member was ready to take a pulse
As soon as he would be roused from bed.
One of them suggested:
They should bring some candles.
Another took a penny from his pillow.
Anyway, they stood so long over the sick one
Until his soul departed.
One said,
"I'll tell you nicely:
Maybe he'll run off like that other one
Let me tell you a new thing:
We should bind him hand and foot.
Then we'll be certain
That he'll have to lie still until the Messiah arrives."
They took his picture
And bound him hand and foot with a bronze chain.
They performed the proper rites,
And then good night.

VII

Not eight days had passed—
A wailing and an outcry.
Just between afternoon and evening prayers, on the 17th of Tammuz[44]
The corpse showed up in the synagogue from the cemetery.
A fright, a commotion fell on young and old.
What's happening?
He was uncomfortable, he says, to lie alone.
He didn't want to go back and wait
Until they would prepare a second one.
Everyone ran home in a panic,
In tatters and cracks.

The corpse sat there three days and didn't depart.
He sees that nothing is being resolved.
So he took himself to thinking:
He grabbed the charity box and the *Kol Bo* book,[45]
He drank down the oil of the eternal light,
Overturned the reading desk,
Grabbed the shofar and the whole town's possessions.
And all the brooms from the bathhouse
And disappeared in a flash.

———

The community went and wrote this even in
their town record, but they kept it a secret,
That the corpse had run off from the cemetery
And disappeared as if in a big city.

———

Such a fear and trouble Chelm suffered as
it opened the first cemetery.

For the Sake of a Wall Calendar

The gabbai of the Chelm synagogue was once in Brest on business. While there, he bought a large wall calendar for the synagogue so that the congregation would know all year long about candle-lighting times, new moon details, and the like.

The assistant gabbai was also in Brest and also bought a wall calendar for the synagogue.

There arose a commotion in Chelm. Two wall calendars! What do we need two for?

They held a meeting, pondered for three days and three nights, and concluded that, given that they had an extra wall calendar, and it was a shame to waste the money: They would build a second synagogue.

And that's what they did.

The Clever Rabbi and the Wisdom Concerning the Keys

The Rabbi of Chelm was a great sage. He knew that whenever he conversed with people, he spouted foolishness. So he arrived at a plan: He arranged with his wife that whenever people would come and be immersed with him in conversation, she should enter and say, "The Rabbi should give me the keys to the money chest." Then he would realize that he was speaking foolishness, and he would stop.

One time some important citizens gathered. The Rabbi spoke with them and actually so cleverly that he was very satisfied with himself. Suddenly the door opened, and his wife came in and said, "The Rabbi should give me the keys to the money chest."

"Tell me, I beg you," said the Rabbi to the important citizens, "what sort of foolishness I have been uttering so that my wife should suddenly come in and ask me to hand over the keys to the money chest?"

Why They Refused to Give the Watchman a Raise

Chelm once heard that the Messiah was coming. They were afraid that he would pass Chelm by and not come in. They hired a watchman to stand day and night on the Chelm hill and watch for the Messiah. If he should pass by, the watchman should invite him to come into the town.

Meanwhile, the watchman noticed that ten *gildn* every week [about three rubles] was too little to support his wife and children. He came to ask the community for a raise.

The Rabbi refused to give him a raise.

"It's quite true," the Rabbi said, "that ten *gildn* a week is a small fee for the watchman. But, on the other hand, he has a job that will last forever."

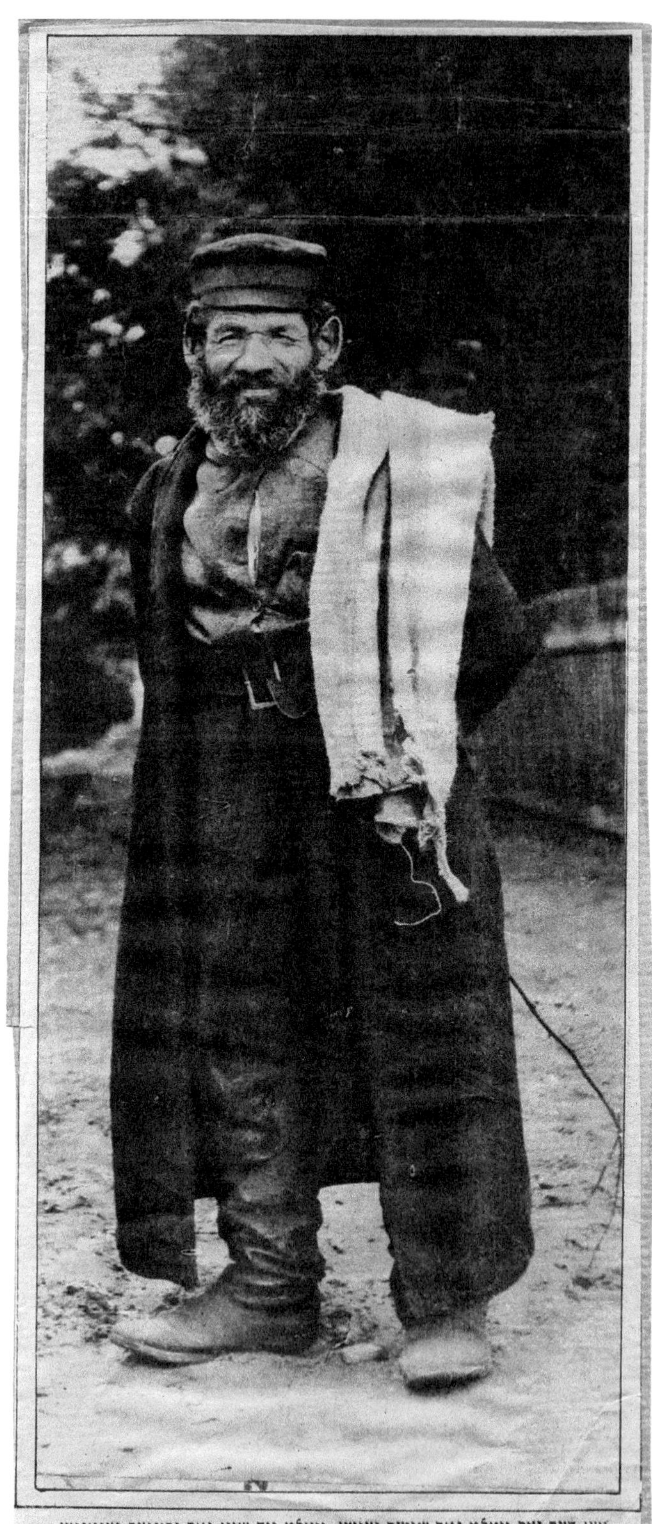

זועט דער זאק וואלט נאר שווער געווען, וואלט זיך שוין גאר גרינגער געגאנגען...— א אידישער טיפ. א שוסטער וועלכער געהט ארום זוכען ארבייט (אלטע שיך צו פארריכטען), אין אטוואצק, פוילען.

STICKING TO HIS LAST.—This is the itinerant cobbler of Otvotzk, Poland, looking for shoes to cobble. (*Kipnis*)

Pub. March 21, 1926. Otwock. [English] An itinerant cobbler. [Yiddish] If the sack were only heavier, his step would be lighter. (People of a Thousand Towns, YIVO Institute for Jewish Research)

The Sign in the Bath

A Chelmite was enjoying the steam in the bathhouse. Because he was naked, he was afraid that he might get confused with someone else. So he took a strand of red wool yarn and tied it around his leg. As he departed, we would look at his leg and see the red yarn and be assured that he was, in fact, himself.

When he went up to the highest bench to flagellate, the string got soaked and fell off. A second Chelmite took the string and tied it onto his own leg.

As he went out of the bathhouse to put on his clothes, he looked: What a misfortune! No red string! He had been exchanged.

He started to run about the bathhouse searching for himself.

He looked: There was someone standing with a red string on his leg. He ran up and said:

"It's lucky that you are wearing the red sign! Now I know that you are me. If it weren't for the sign, I would have gone home all mixed up.

The Wedding Canopy Rotated

In Chelm there was a wedding. They noticed that the groom and bride were facing west; they were supposed to be facing east.

They started to rotate the wedding canopy, but no matter how much they rotated it, the bride and groom were still facing west, not east.

"Fools that you are!" called out a stranger. "Don't rotate the canopy; rotate the bride and groom!"

So they did that. They realized that the stranger was right, and they never stopped commenting to each other how much wisdom one could find in the world.

Where the Chelm Fools Ended Up

I

Not far from Chelm, right outside town, a very clever Jewish farmer lived, called Berl. He wasn't doing well financially, but he had an idea:

Since he lived so close to Chelm, maybe with his clever mind he could dream up some way Chelm could help him.

He came to a decision, bought an old emaciated horse, traveled into town, stopped close to the synagogue, unharnessed the horse and set it with its head to the wagon and its rear pointing out, and placed a golden coin in its rear so that it was half visible. He sat nearby and waited to see what would happen.

A fellow came past having finished his prayers and saw: There is a horse, and something golden is shining from its rear. He grew curious to see what was going on and approached closer.

"What's so strange, Uncle?" Berl called out. "It's the sort of horse that takes in oats at one end and produces golden coins at the other end."

Seeing such a treasure, the fellow started bargaining with the farmer to sell him the horse.

A second person noticed them bargaining about some sort of horse, so he came up, too. When he was informed about the wonder-horse, he said that he alone would buy it. Up came a third, a fourth, a fifth person, until all of Chelm caught wind of this horse, that you feed oats at one end and it produces golden coins at the other end. A great tumult arose around the farmer and his horse, a riot where everyone wanted to get the horse, and however much one person offered, another offered more. It even came to blows, and they brought the Rabbi to the spot.

When the Rabbi arrived and saw what was happening and the reason for the fighting, without a pause, he pronounced the judgment that the horse should not be owned by any individual but rather belong to the town at large, which could then derive all the funding for communal needs. He then started to bargain with the farmer:

"What do you want, Berl, for the horse?"

OPPOSITE: 1930s, Krynki. Hasidim and others sitting on benches at one of the most popular spas in Poland. (People of a Thousand Towns, YIVO Institute for Jewish Research)

Berl hesitated.

"I'd rather not sell it at all," he says.

"You must sell it, Berl! Our congregation is poor. God himself sent you here!" the Rabbi tried to convince him.

"In that case, then I want five hundred rubles for the horse."

When the Rabbi heard "five hundred rubles," he paid Berl the money and took the horse.

Soon Chelm held a great meeting and started to ponder where to house the horse. One person suggested that they should place it in the Rabbi's house. Another suggested that they should lead it up to the women's gallery. In short, they pondered and pondered and decided to dig a deep pit in the synagogue courtyard, lower

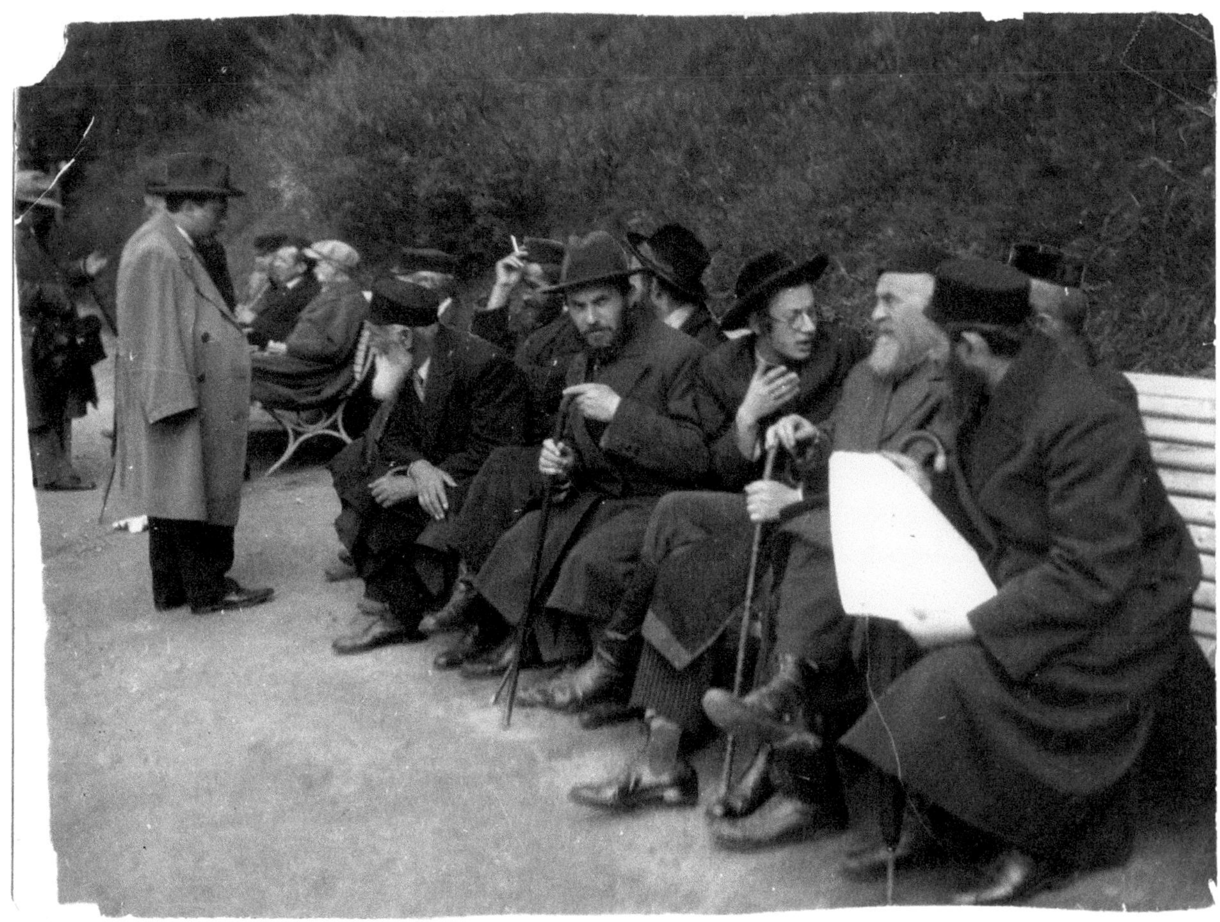

the horse into it, make a place in front to toss down oats and, on the other end, a deep receptacle for the coins.

That's what they did. They dug a deep pit in the synagogue courtyard, let the horse down into it, and waited for three days in order to collect lots of golden coins.

On the third day they held another meeting. Whom should we lower into the pit to collect the coins? They concluded that they could trust nobody except the Rabbi himself. They took him and lowered him into the pit.

The Rabbi searched and scraped but came up with nothing.

They didn't want to depend on the Rabbi, so they lowered the community leader himself. He busied himself there for a good while and also came out with nothing.

"Is that the story?" Chelm was in a commotion. "Is Berl the farmer a liar? Has he fooled all of Chelm? Well, let's pay him a visit!" So the Rabbi and two gabbais headed off to the farmer's house outside the town to pull him apart, root and branch.

II

The farmer knew quite well what was happening in Chelm and that any minute the Rabbi and the gabbais would show up. So he dreamed up a new joke.

He had two rabbits in his house. He gave one to his wife and told her that the Rabbi and gabbais would soon arrive and ask for him. She should take the rabbit, open the window, and say, "Run speedily, rabbit, into the forest and call Berl home!" In a short minute he would enter the other door with the second rabbit. The Rabbi and the gabbais would think that it's the same rabbit that his wife had sent through the window to summon him from the forest. They would see a new marvel, the rabbit, and they would forget all about the horse and golden coins.

When the Rabbi arrived with the gabbais and angrily asked, "Where is Berl?" his wife grabbed the rabbit, looked right in its face, and said, "Run, rabbit, quickly into the forest and call Berl home!" And she let it out through the window.

The Rabbi and gabbais looked on in astonishment as the wife spoke to the rabbit and sent it to call Berl. The rabbit quickly ran into the forest. They were even more astonished when they saw Berl coming in with the rabbit on his shoulders through the other door and announced:

"Here I am!" The Rabbi and gabbais were amazed at what they had witnessed with their own eyes.

They seemed to forget all about the horse and the gold coins. They had only one new idea in their heads: to buy the rabbit from Berl.

"Berl!" the Rabbi began. "We have come to ask you to sell the rabbit. Our community is poor and can't afford a shammes . We have come to buy the rabbit so it can become the town shammes.

Berl again doubted if he could agree, because he needed to send the rabbit on errands all the time. But after the Rabbi and the gabbais importuned him, he extracted a thousand rubles and handed over the rabbit.

The Rabbi and gabbais took the rabbit and proudly returned to Chelm.

"Great! Now we won't need a shammes," they rejoiced. "When the Rabbi needs to send out a summons to a meeting, it won't take hours. The rabbit will bring folks quickly, and it will be cheaper, too."

The community soon fired all the shammeses and made the rabbit the town shammes.

The next day they needed to hold a meeting. The Rabbi took the rabbit and told it, "Go, rabbit, and summon to a meeting: Saul the chief gabbai, David the assistant gabbai, Meyer-Simcha the meat-tax collector, Eli the slaughterer (son of Meyer Kuntsye). Also Joseph the mailman, Peysye the cantor, Shakhne the candle maker, Joel Boar, Hershl Kipke, Shmonye the tailor, and Zisye Holopuz. Do it immediately, do you understand?" And he let it out the window.

An hour passed. No rabbit. Two hours, three hours. It was already dusk. No rabbit. Already past the evening prayers. The meeting should be starting. No rabbit and no meeting.

"In that case, Berl the farmer must be a full-fledged liar," they realized. "Not only did he trick us with the horse that makes gold coins, he has tricked Chelm so dastardly with this town-shammes rabbit."

The Rabbi and the gabbais set off once again to the farmer, in a flaming rage. They would deal with him in a manner appropriate to such a liar.

III

Berl the farmer again understood what was happening in Chelm and expected that any minute the Rabbi and the gabbais would be coming to wreak judgment and to take away his money. He came upon a fresh inspiration and settled it with his wife that as soon as they would see the Rabbi and the gabbais coming, she should lie on the ground as if dead. He would weep and wail, and then he would take an egg out of the cupboard and knock it on her skull. She should then awaken and get up.

That's just what happened.

When the Rabbi and the gabbais arrived at his house full of rage to rip him to shreds, they quickly saw that a corpse was lying on the ground covered with a sheet. Berl was bent over it and was crying and wailing and shouting:

"Such a bright soul, my dear Hanna! What can I do without you in this foolish world?"

The anger disappeared in the hearts of the Rabbi and the gabbais. They stood around in terror, considering the sad spectacle, and they joined Berl in crying.

Suddenly Berl stood up and called out:

"No, you mustn't die! You haven't lived out your sixty years!" He went to the cupboard and took an egg out of a container. He went to the corpse and knocked the egg on its forehead. His wife awakened, stood up, and whole and hale went into the kitchen.

When the Rabbi saw this, he forgot all about the horse, the gold coins, the rabbit, and the town shammes, and he said:

"Berl, do you know why we have come here? We want you to sell us that egg that revives the dead. Our community is poor; the town can't support doctors or healers. Berl, sell us that egg!"

The farmer made all sorts of wild gestures. No, he couldn't sell it; the egg was an inheritance from his great-great-grandfather, who got it himself from his great-great-grandfather, and so on. It goes all the way back to the spies sent by Moses to inspect Canaan. "No, I simply cannot sell it!"

"But you must! If not for us, then for the sake of our poor Chelm community," the Rabbi and the gabbais begged for his mercy.

"But I'll need to get a full thousand rubles for it!" the farmer finally offered.

When they heard "a thousand rubles," the Rabbi and the gabbais hesitated not a second. They brought him the thousand rubles and took the egg to Chelm.

In Chelm there was happiness and rejoicing. "Finally! We'll have no fear of the Angel of Death! To hell with the healers and bloodletters. We have an egg that revives the dead!"

They immediately held a great meeting to consider whom to apply the egg to. It was concluded that the Rabbi himself was the best candidate, and they should place the egg in the silver case where he stored the *esreg*[46] for the Sukkos [holiday of booths].

That's what they did.

Suddenly, as it happens, who got sick? No more and no less than the Rabbi's wife. There was rejoicing and happiness. They didn't call for either a bloodletter or a healer. They called nobody. They had no need for anyone. They just had to wait for her to die. Then they would apply the egg and revive her.

And that's what happened.

In a lucky hour, she died. As soon as they placed her on the ground, the Rabbi himself took the egg and went and starting knocking it on his wife's forehead.

She didn't move. He started to knock harder. She didn't even think of moving a limb. He continued knocking harder and harder until the egg broke.

Seeing this, the town was in a fury. Such a liar, a swindler! As soon as they buried the Rabbi's wife in the cemetery, they decided: "A life for a life!" Not only the Rabbi but all of Chelm would go to Berl.

IV

When all of Chelm besieged Berl the farmer's house, he couldn't twist himself out of the community's hands. They quickly held a great meeting to ponder what to do with him.

Stoning, burning, decapitation, strangulation, slaughtering, impaling, breaking, hanging, shooting, broiling, flailing, ripping, biting: They thought up so many death penalties for Berl.[47] Finally they concluded that they shouldn't spill any blood but rather put him in a sack and toss him into the river so he would die on his own.

That's what they did. They placed the fellow in a sack and dragged it to the river.

When they arrived at the river, it was frozen, with no hole in which to pitch him.

What to do? We'll need an axe.

But this was, of course, Chelm. All of Chelm set off to bring an axe. Meanwhile, they left Berl under the bridge bound in the sack, all alone.

Lying under the bridge, he heard a nobleman traveling by. He came upon a clever idea and began to shout from the sack!

"[In Polish] I don't want to be the king! I don't want to!"

The nobleman heard that someone was calling out from under the bridge. He stopped his wagon and went down, untied the sack, and asked Berl what was going on. Why he was shouting, "I don't want to be the king!"

OPPOSITE: Pub. July 5, 1925. Ostrow. The house and yard of the Ostrovtser Rebbe, Meyer Yekhiel. The photographer wrote, [Yiddish] "In this house the Ostrovtser Rebbe has fasted now for forty years." (People of a Thousand Towns, YIVO Institute for Jewish Research)

Berl told him that all of Chelm had occupied themselves with him and wanted to make him king, but because he didn't want to, they had placed him bound here in a sack. Every two hours they would come and ask him if he was ready to become king.

"But if I were in your place, I would certainly want to be king," the nobleman said eagerly.

"You know what? So crawl into this sack, and I'll tie you, and they'll come and ask you if you want to be king. You should answer 'I do!' and you'll become king."

"Fine!" the nobleman agreed. He dragged Berl out and crawled into the sack.

Berl tied the sack and made off with the horse and wagon.

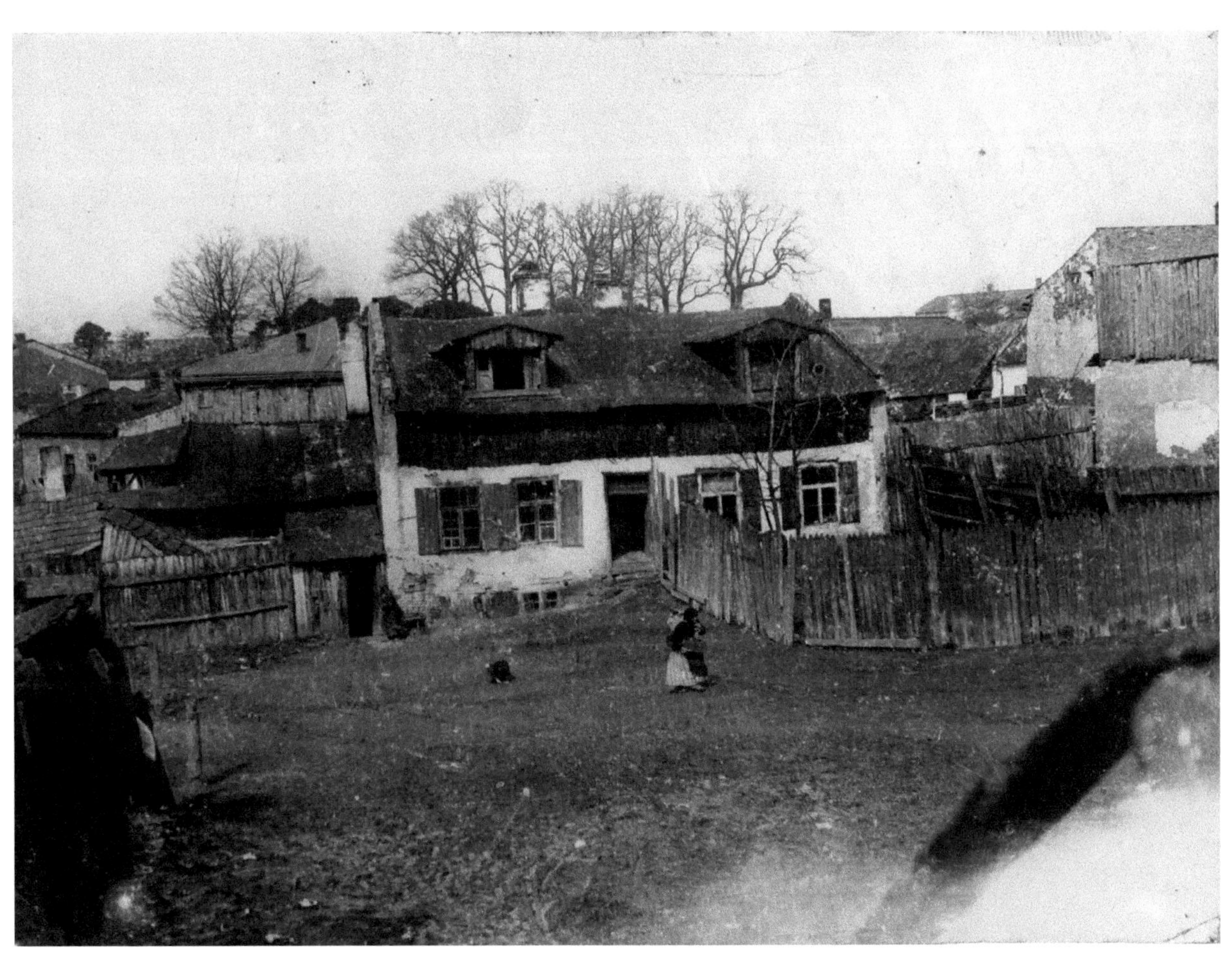

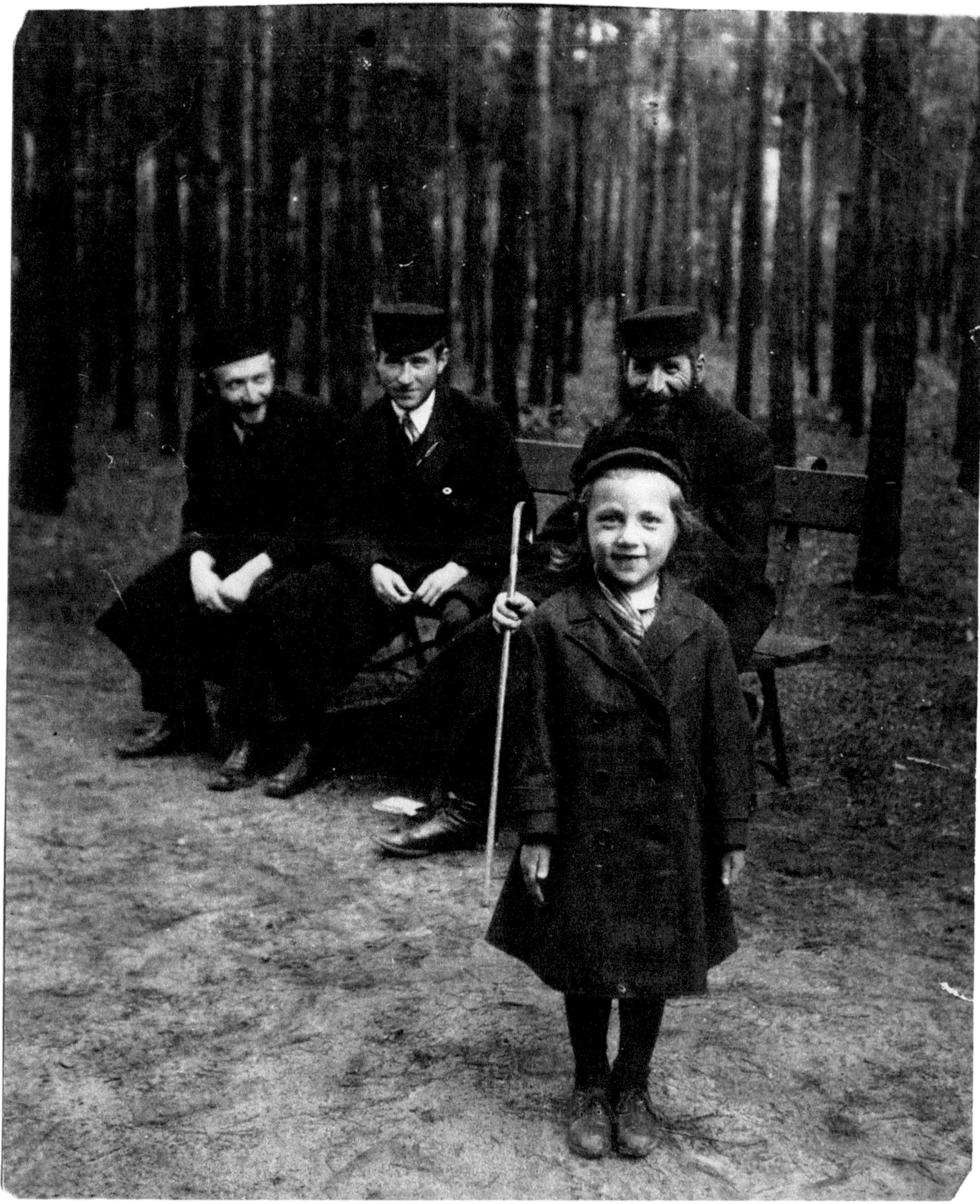

When the Chelmites returned with the axe, they quickly chopped a hole in the ice and tossed in the sack along with the nobleman.

V

Finally, Chelm quieted down. Exactly a month later, there appeared in the market a fine carriage with noble horses. The carriage drew up right in front of the Rabbi's house. Someone descended from the carriage and went right into the Rabbi's house.

They take a look: It's Berl!

"How did you manage to come here, Berl, from the other world?"

Folks came running up, men, women, and children. All of Chelm surrounded the Rabbi's house. Everyone wanted to catch sight of Berl the farmer, whom they had thrown into the river a month before, and hear what he could tell them of the other world.

So Berl stood in front of all of Chelm and started recounting what had happened to him. As soon as they had thrown him into the river, he had come upon a treasure of gold and silver, precious stones and diamonds. Because he was heading downward headfirst, he used his hands to gather the precious treasure, however much he could. He stuffed his pockets. Then he managed to climb out of the river on the far side.

Hearing this tale, they held a great meeting and concluded that in order to supply the needs of the Chelm community, all of Chelm should head to the other world for gold and silver and precious stones.

And in fact the very next day all of Chelm, from Rabbi to bathhouse attendant, went into the river under the ice to take themselves to the other world with gold, silver, and precious stones for the benefit of the Chelm community.

And that's how the ancient, well-beloved Chelm fools died and disappeared, a community about which the world continues to tell so many fine stories and precious folktales.[48]

OPPOSITE: Pub. August 22, 1926. Ciechocinek. [Yiddish] A little boy from Poland. With his broad earlocks and broad smile is the little son of the Aleksandrer Rebbe. The three men are his father's Hasidim and are honored to go walking with the Rebbe's child. (People of a Thousand Towns, YIVO Institute for Jewish Research)

JEWISH LIFE IN POLAND -- טיפען און בילדער פון אידישען לעבען אין פוילען

PHOTOGRAPHED BY M. Kipnis — פאטאגראפירט פון קיפניס

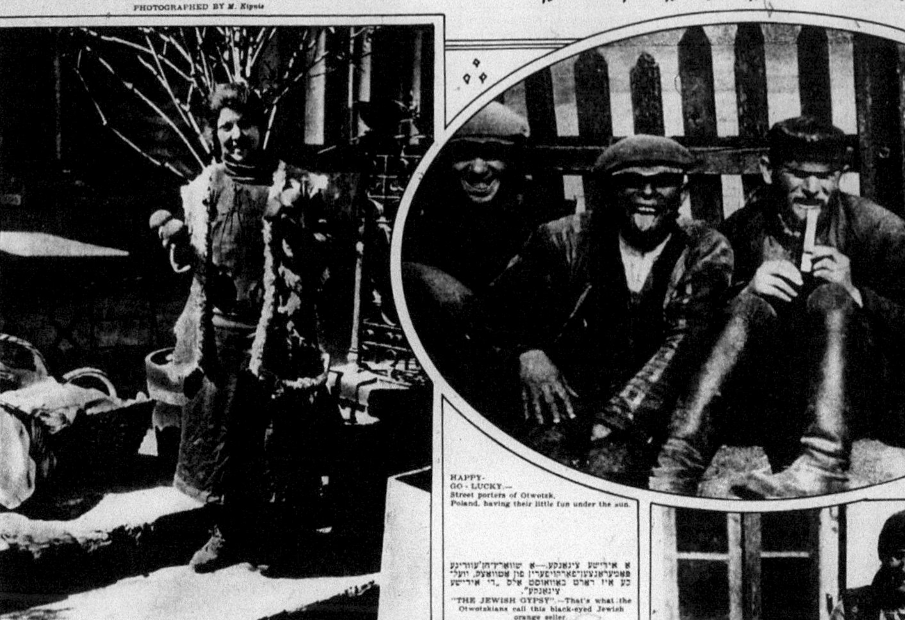

HAPPY-GO-LUCKY.—Street porters of Otwotzk, Poland, having their little fun under the sun.

א אידישע ציגאנקע.—א שווארצאויגיגע פאמעראנצען־פארקויפערין פון אטוואצק, וועלכע איז רופט באוואוסט אלס „די אידישע ציגאנקע".

"THE JEWISH GYPSY".—That's what the Otwotzkians call this black-eyed Jewish orange seller.

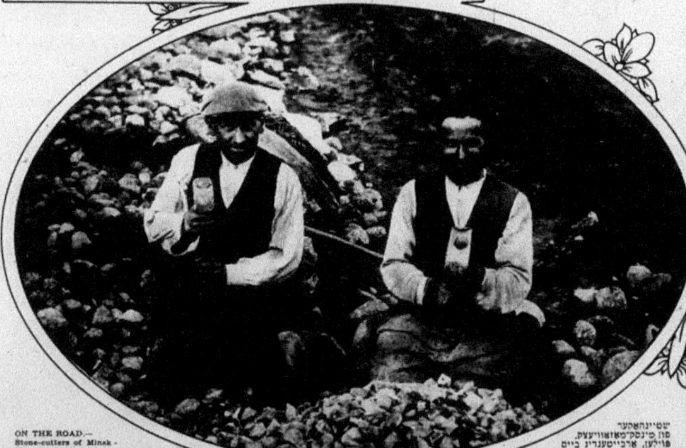

ON THE ROAD.—Stone-cutters of Minsk-Mazovietzki, Poland, working on a road.

שטיינהאקער פון מינסק־מאזאוויעצק, פוילען, ארבייטענדיג ביים קארטשעווער שאסיי, לעבען ווארשע.

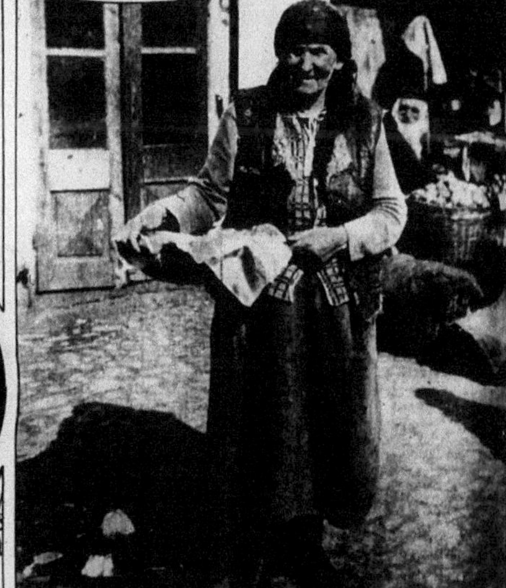

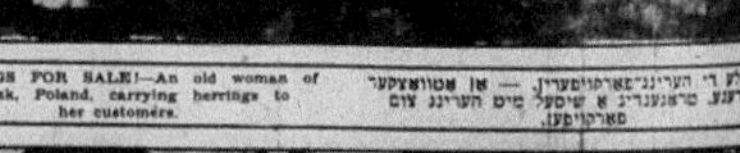

HERRINGS FOR SALE!—An old woman of Otwotzk, Poland, carrying herrings to her customers.

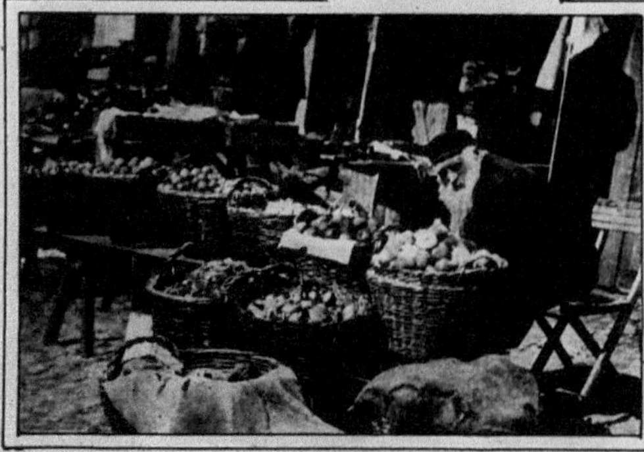

THE OLD FRUIT VENDOR.—An 83-year-old fruit-peddler in the market-place of Otwotzk.

יפותיאל דער פרוכט־הענדלער.—א 83־יעהריגער אטוואצקער פרוכט־הענדלער, וועלכער האט מעהר פרוכטען ווי קונים . . .

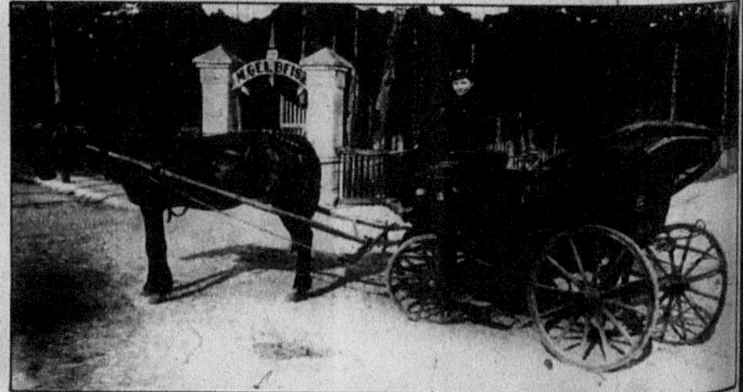

A LEADING YOUTH.—A 12-year-old youngster of Otwotzk, is the only cabman of that age in his town.

Epilogue

Between Yiddish and English

Sheila E. Jelen

The dialogue that arises between Kipnis's photographs and his Chelm stories is enhanced when we consider the dialogue between Yiddish and English that manifests in the photographs' bilingual captioning in the *Forverts* and in the Yiddish Chelm stories' journey to English and North America. In the *Forverts* arts section, Kipnis's photographs were captioned in both Yiddish and English, with the two captions not necessarily matching. The captions accompanying the photographs in this volume are mostly drawn from what has been published on the YIVO website in its "People of a Thousand Towns," which usually includes only the Yiddish captions, with occasional English ones.[1] In what follows, I provide several examples where both English and Yiddish captions exist for the same photographs on the "People of a Thousand Towns" site. Doing so leads us back to considerations of the "post-European" contextualization, or a fixation on place in Kipnis's photographs for an American audience during the interwar period.[2]

In comparing the narrative framing of these photographs in both English and Yiddish, a pattern emerges: In Yiddish, human subjects are named within the context of their locales, while in English, those human names disappear. To illustrate this, let us consider several images from Otwock, featured together on June 26, 1927.

In the center on the right, we see an image bearing the Yiddish caption, "Feygele the herring seller. A woman of Otwock carrying a [covered] bowl of herring for sale."[3] In English, we read, "Herrings for Sale! An old woman of Otwotzk [*sic*], Poland, carrying herrings to her customers."

Here, in Yiddish, the subject of the photograph is named, "Feygele," and identified by her role in the community as "the herring seller." In English, Feygele becomes an "old woman" without a name, and even the

OPPOSITE: Full-page spread from the *Forverts* Rotogravure Arts Section, June 26, 1927. (YIVO Institute for Jewish Research)

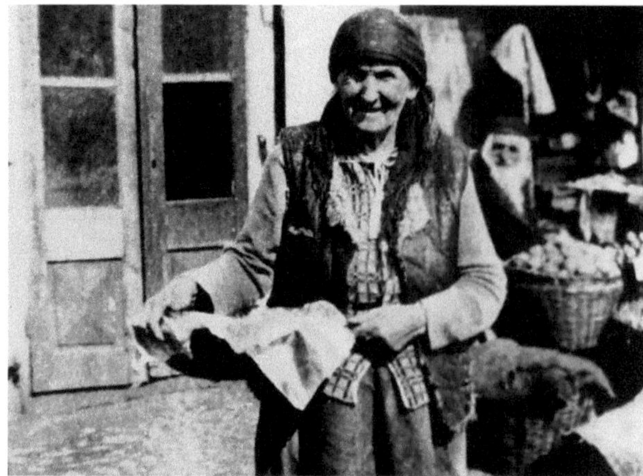

Pub. June 26, 1927. Otwock. [English] Herrings for Sale: An old woman of Otwotsk Poland carrying herrings to her customers. [Yiddish] Feygele the herring seller. A Jewish woman from Otwotsk. Carrying a bowl of herring to her customers. (YIVO Institute for Jewish Research)

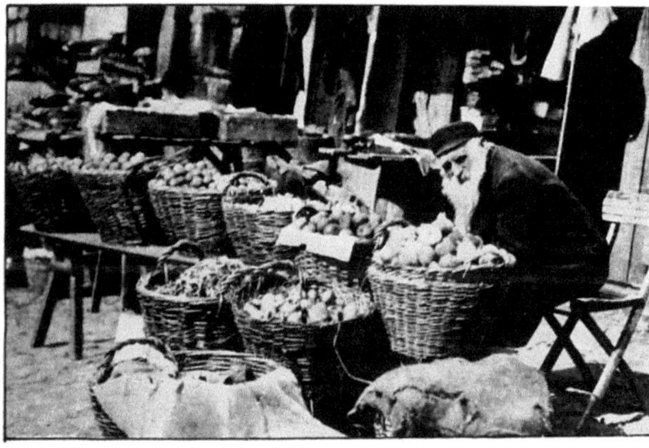

Pub. June 27, 1927. Otwock. [English] The Old Fruit Vendor—an 83-year-old fruit peddler in the marketplace of Otwotsk. [Yiddish] Yekusil the fruit peddler. An 83-year-old Otwotsk fruit peddler who has more fruit than customers. (YIVO Institute for Jewish Research)

city name, Otwotzk (*sic*), loses its specificity and is broadened to the more generic Poland. The Yiddish, therefore, is more intimate, affording a personal connection with the named woman, Feygele, while the English creates distance, taking away her name and featuring the city and its bustling street market within the context of the country, Poland, as the subject of the photograph.

Below Feygele and to her left is another photograph, captioned in Yiddish, as follows: "Yekusil the fruit peddler. An 83-year-old Otwock fruit peddler, who has more fruit than customers."[4] In English, we read, "The Old Fruit Vendor—an 83-year-old fruit vendor in the marketplace of Otwotsk [*sic*]." As in the previous caption, the Yiddish allows for personal identification, while the English insists on a more generic human identification, a typology, with the name of the place in the ultimate position, as the focus of the caption.

In a departure from this pattern, on the bottom right, we see an image with the Yiddish caption, "The young cabman. Yudl 'Droszkasz' [driver] . . . is only 12 years old and is already a big shot—with the whip." While here

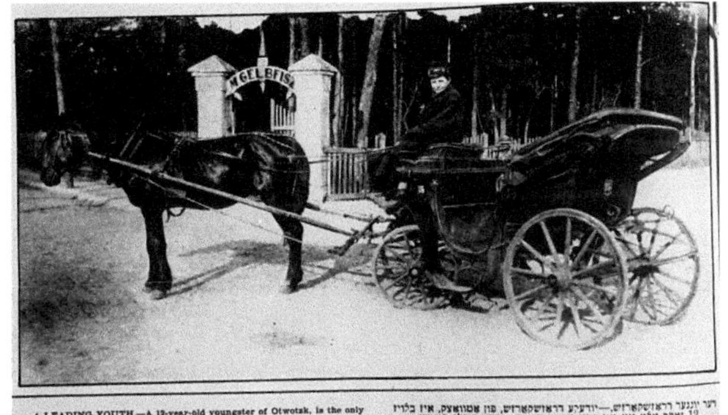

Pub. June 26, 1927. Otwock. [English] A Leading Youth—A 12-year-old youngster of Otwotsk is the only cabman of that age in his town. [Yiddish] The youngest cabman—Yudele the cabman from Otwotsk is only 12 years old and is quite the bruiser, with his whip. (YIVO Institute for Jewish Research)

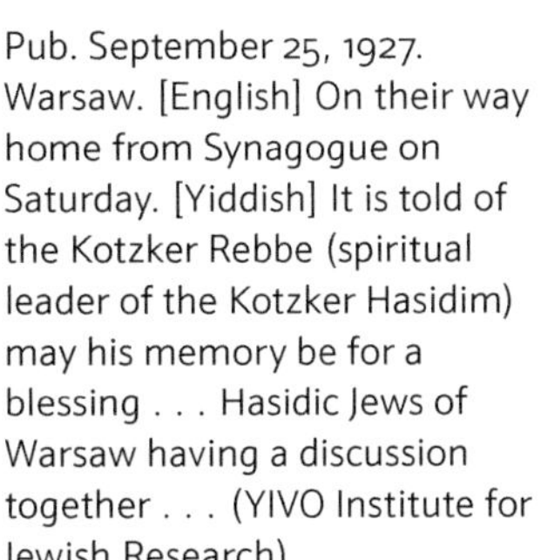

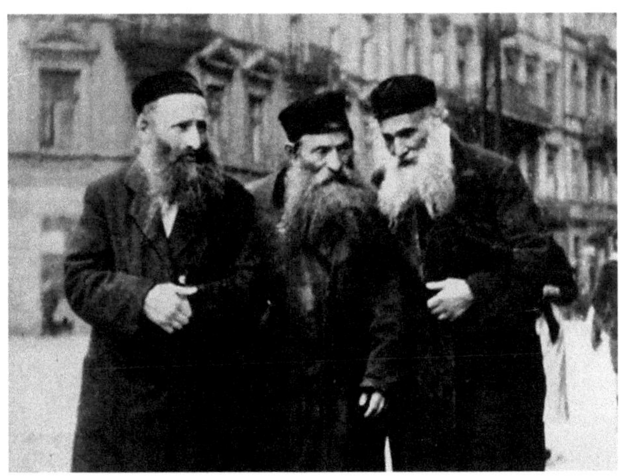

Pub. September 25, 1927. Warsaw. [English] On their way home from Synagogue on Saturday. [Yiddish] It is told of the Kotzker Rebbe (spiritual leader of the Kotzker Hasidim) may his memory be for a blessing . . . Hasidic Jews of Warsaw having a discussion together . . . (YIVO Institute for Jewish Research)

Otwock is implied by the placement of the photograph in a full-page spread of Otwock photographs, the Yiddish caption contains no explicit reference to the place. In the English, however, the driver is not named, while the city is: "A Leading Youth"—A 12 year old youngster of Otwozk [*sic*] is the only cabman of that age in his town."[5] In the English, the only named subject is the city, whereas in the Yiddish, the named subject, Yudl, does not become overshadowed by the name of the city.

A Warsaw image offers us a slightly different take on the question of a Yiddish-versus English-reading audience. On September 25, 1927, an image of three Orthodox men in conversation on a city street was published. The Yiddish caption is, "'It is told of the Kotzker "rebbe" [spiritual leader of the Kotzker Hasidim] may his memory be for a blessing . . .' Hasidic Jews of Warsaw having a discussion together." In English we read, "on their way home from the synagogue on Saturday."[6] Here, in the Yiddish, the men are not identified by name, nor do we know anything about their role in the Warsaw community. Yet the caption provides a frame for a Hasidic milieu through an allusion to the Kotzker rebbe via both its style, in its formulaic allusion to the Kotzker rebbe, and its mention of this personality.[7] In

English, however, any specificity of content is missing. Because English-reading Jews are not expected to have any familiarity with the Kotzker rebbe or what he represents, he is entirely omitted from the English caption.

The simultaneous presentation of these photographs to both Yiddish- and English-reading audiences required captions in both languages. But we have seen how distinctions between the Yiddish ones and the English ones reflect a substantial difference, with the Yiddish captions intent on personal human identifications, while the English ones focus on place names and Old World character types. How does the transformation of Kipnis's Chelm stories in the United States compare to this?

Kipnis's adaptation and publication of Chelm stories in the Yiddish press in the 1920s made its way to the United States during those same years. According to Ruth von Bernuth, Ben Mordkhe's 1929 Yiddish publication *Khelmer naromin: Geklibene mayselekh* (Chelm fools: Selected stories) in New York was based on Kipnis's column in *Haynt* and even preceded the publication of Kipnis's own 1930 *Chelm Tales* by one year.[8] Ben Mordkhe's text, in turn, became the basis for a variety of American adaptations, including Solomon Simon's *Wise Men of Chelm* (1945) and even Isaac Bashevis Singer's *The Fools of Chelm* (1973).[9] Many anthologies of Jewish folklore published in the United States during the post-Holocaust years, such as Nathan Ausubel's *A Treasury of Jewish Folklore* (1948) and Jacob Richman's *Jewish Wit and Wisdom* (1952), consistently included selected Chelm stories, most likely gleaned from Kipnis's adaptations.[10] While other folklorists in Europe, such as Noyekh Prelutski (1882–1941) and Shloyme Bastomski (1891–1941), collected and anthologized Chelm tales in Europe, only Kipnis's appeared in the popular European press, lending them far more influence and longevity than the others and perhaps explaining why Kipnis's collection traveled to the United States and theirs did not.[11]

It is instructive, then, to compare American versions of selected Chelm stories to their precursors in Kipnis's column. Solomon Simon's *The Wise Men of Chelm*, for example, weaves the stories together into a single sustained narrative, with transitions connecting one story to the next.[12] Thus, a pastiche of individual stories in Kipnis's corpus becomes one unified story in Simon's. Simon also gives his characters names and weaves one main character through all the stories: Gimpel, who is the ultimate Chelm genius, having the final word in all situations, great and small. I. B. Singer's "Gimpel the Fool," an expanded, elaborated, and personalized Chelm story replete with names and a sustained plot, was published in English in 1953 in the *Partisan Review*, translated from the Yiddish by Saul Bellow.[13] Simon's 1945 English adaptation was first published in Yiddish in 1942 and may very well have inspired Singer's 1945 Yiddish original of "Gimpel." In any case, the movement, in English, from the anonymous types and brief anecdotes in the Yiddish Chelm texts to sustained, elaborated, and unified narratives with named characters and character development reflects an interesting trend in the United States. What had previously been a piece of folklore became a work of fiction, and what had previously sufficed for European audiences—comedy at a cultural distance—was no longer enough for Americans seeking to use Chelm stories as a window into a lost world. Why were Chelm stories so naturally embraced as a representation of eastern Europe? Because, in the decade after the Holocaust, Americans had already been schooled in a "post-European" poetics of place by their earlier engagement with photographs from eastern Europe in the pages of the *Forverts* during the interwar period. As discussed earlier, the English captions accompanying these photographs focused not on individuals but on places in their presentation to an American English-reading audience. A "post-European" poetics of place created a bond between American Jewish audiences and east European Jewry on the basis of geographic identifications but not personal, individual ones.

Thus, in the movement of Kipnis's photographs from Europe to the United States, or from Yiddish to English, we see a journey away from names of individuals toward a fixation on place names. In the Chelm stories, this same movement from Europe to the United States might appear to be moving in the opposite direction, toward specificity, with character "types" transformed into actual characters and an expansion of vignettes into stories; however, the power of place continues to dominate in the presentation of these stories. In the American adaptations, it becomes important for Chelm to be construed as a fleshed-out "place" where drama unfolds and characters develop, but that is not to say that the English versions present Chelm as real. Rather, they seek to present Chelm as relevant in its identity as a place that might represent, metonymically, eastern European Jewish culture in a sustained and engaging way. In other words, what we see is the expansion of a folklorically valuable curiosity into a narratively ramified literary work that might be understood as folklore by those who care to understand it that way; but it can also be received as representative of a real culture, thus connecting a post-European pre-Holocaust American Jewry to their coreligionists who have remained in eastern Europe, or a postwar and post-Holocaust generation to a world destroyed in the Holocaust.

Acknowledgments

This book is the result of years of cooperation and collaboration. Thank you, first and foremost, to Raphael Finkel, who offered to study these stories with me in the context of a Yiddish reading group at the University of Kentucky and subsequently agreed to translate them. Thank you, as well, to the University of Kentucky Office of the Vice President for Research (VPR), which funded the reproduction rights for the photographs that appear in this book. I am grateful to Vital Zajka, the photo archivist at the YIVO Institute for Jewish Research, who has graciously assisted me in acquiring the rights to the photographs that appear in this book. The photographs are drawn from the online archive at YIVO ("People of a Thousand Towns") as well as from the undigitized Kipnis collection and are identified as such in the captions that accompany them. Thank you to the YIVO librarian who approached me sixteen years ago when I was in the archive researching, for an earlier book, photographs published during the 1920s and 1930s and asked me if I might be interested in editing a volume of Kipnis's photographs. I did not know him at the time, but as an early-career scholar, I was gratified to be invited to engage in what he presented as an important act of cultural salvage. I suspect, in hindsight, that the librarian in question was Marek Web (1938–2021) who coedited, with Sulamita Kacyzne-Reale, a volume of Alter Kacyzne's (1885–1941) photographs in *Poyln: Life in the Old Country* (1999). I am grateful to the National Yiddish Book Center for their outstanding work as a repository of Yiddish literature. It is thanks to their digitization of Kipnis's collection of Chelm stories, published in 1930, that I was able to complete this project. Finally, as always, I am grateful to my brilliant and loving life partner, Seth Himelhoch, for supporting me in everything that I do and to my children, Malka, Nava, Akiva, and Meirav, for helping me to remember that there is more to life than work.

This book is dedicated to the memory of Menachem Kipnis, who died in the Warsaw Ghetto in 1942, to his wife, Zimre Zeligfeld, who died at Treblinka, also in 1942, and to the men and women of Chelm, a real city in eastern Poland (where my own paternal great grandfather, Aaron Honorow, was born) about twenty-five miles from the Ukrainian border and the site of a Jewish ghetto during the Holocaust. May their memories be a blessing.

Notes

Introduction

1. For a brief discussion of Zeligfeld, see Julie Riegel, "'Jewish Musicians Are the Crowning Achievements of Foreign Nations': Jewish Identity and Yiddish Nationalism in the Writings of Menachem Kipnis," in *Jews and Music-Making in the Polish Lands*, Polin: Studies in Polish Jewry 32 (London: Littman Library of Jewish Civilization, 2020), 311–313.
2. Itzik Gottesman, *Defining the Yiddish Nation: The Jewish Folklorists of Poland* (Detroit: Wayne State University Press, 2003), 59.
3. Gottesman, *Defining the Yiddish Nation*, 56.
4. Gottesman, *Defining the Yiddish Nation*, 56.
5. Ruth von Bernuth identifies three sources for Kipnis's stories: existing literary and ethnographic collections, stories sent in by readers, and popular tales not previously attached to Chelm. Ruth von Bernuth, *How the Wise Men Got to Chelm: The Life and Times of a Yiddish Folk Tradition* (New York: New York University Press, 2016), 188–202.
6. Von Bernuth, *Wise Men*, 197.
7. Menachem Kipnis, *60 Yidishe folkslider mit notn: Fun M. Kipnis un Z. Seligfelds repertuar* (Warsaw: A. Gitlin, n.d. [1918]); Menachem Kipnis, *80 Yidishe folkslider: Fun M. Kipnis un Z. Zeligfelds repertuar* (Warsaw: A. Gitlin, n.d. [1925]); Menachem Kipnis, *Khelmer mayses* (Warsaw: Sz. Cukier, 1930). Cited in Gottesman, *Defining the Yiddish Nation*, 57.
8. Von Bernuth, *Wise Men*, 198.
9. On S. Ansky's expedition, see Benyamin Lukin, "An-ski Ethnographic Expedition and Museum," trans. I. Michael Aronson, in *The YIVO Encyclopedia of Jews in Eastern Europe*, accessed September 4, 2025 https://encyclopedia.yivo.org/article/2074. On the popularity of folklore collecting in part as a result of Ansky's expedition, see Jeffrey Shandler, *Shtetl: A Vernacular Intellectual History* (New Brunswick, NJ: Rutgers University Press, 2014), 59–64. There he discusses how the *landkantenesch* movement, which encouraged individuals to acquaint themselves with the provincial towns they or their forbears had left behind, motivated YIVO to introduce contests in 1926 and 1929 to see how many artifacts, photographs, and stories of their European origins American Jews could produce for archiving at YIVO.

10. S. Anski, "Jewish Ethnopoetics," in *Pioneers of Jewish Ethnography and Folkloristics in Eastern Europe*, ed. Haya Bar-Ithak, trans. Lenn Schramm (Ljubljana: Scientific Research Center of the Slovenian Academy of Sciences and Arts, 2010), 34–75.
11. Gottesman, *Defining the Yiddish Nation*, 59.
12. Gottesman, *Defining the Yiddish Nation*, 309.
13. For a contemporary treatment of Kipnis's role in the field of Jewish ethnomusicology, see Evgenia Khazdan, "The Folk Song of the Ashkenazim: The Problem of Genre Definition," *Shofar: An Interdisciplinary Journal of Jewish Studies* 40, no. 2 (2022): 58–88.
14. Sheila E. Jelen, *Salvage Poetics: Post-Holocaust American Jewish Folk Ethnographies* (Detroit: Wayne State University Press, 2020).
15. Alter Kacyzne, *Poyln: Jewish Life in the Old Country* (New York: Metropolitan Books, 1999). On Marek Web, see YIVO Institute for Jewish Research, "YIVO Mourns the passing of Marek Web," May 17, 2021, accessed September 16, 2025, https://www.yivo.org/Marek-Web.
16. Lucjan Dobroszycki and Barbara Kirshenblatt-Gimblett, *Image Before My Eyes: A Photographic History of Jewish Life in Poland, 1864–1939* (New York: Schocken Books, 1977), 25.
17. Dobroszycki and Kirshenblatt-Gimblett, *Image*, 26.
18. Marianne Hirsch, "The Generation of Postmemory," *Poetics Today* 29, no. 1 (2008): 106.
19. Alison Landsberg, *Prosthetic Memory: The Transformation of American Remembrance in the Age of Mass Culture* (New York: Columbia University Press, 2004). Also see allusions to variations on "absent memory" in the works of Nadine Fresco, Berel Lang, Ulrich Baer, and Victoria Aarons. Nadine Fresco, "Remembering the Unknown," *International Review of Psychoanalysis* 11 (1984): 417–427; Berel Lang, *Post-Holocaust: Interpretation, Misinterpretation, and the Claims of History* (Bloomington: Indiana University Press, 1998); Ulrich Baer, "To Give Memory a Place: Holocaust Photography and the Landscape Tradition," *Representations* 69 (2000): 38–62; Victoria Aarons and Alan Berger, *Third-Generation Holocaust Representation* (Evanston, IL: Northwestern University Press, 2017).
20. Hirsch, "Generation of Postmemory," 106.
21. Krakow, amateur film footage of Krakow, Poland, YIVO Film Collection, RG 105, YIVO VM 1 81/87 (1945). Also see Natan Gross, *Toldot ha-Kolnoa ha-Yehudi be-Polin: 1910–1950* (Jerusalem: Magnes, 1990).
22. Chaim Finkelstein, "Eyle toldos *Haynt*" (These are the chronicles of *Haynt*), accessed September 4, 2025, https://web.archive.org/web/20150208104655/http://haynt.org/chronicles.htm; Also see Chaim Finkelstein, *Haynt: A Tsaytung baym Yidn 1908–1939* (Tel Aviv: Farlag Y.L. Peretz, 1978) [Yiddish]
23. Dan Miron, *The Image of the Shtetl and Other Studies of Modern Jewish Literary Imagination* (Syracuse, NY: Syracuse University Press, 2000).
24. Robert Alter, *The Invention of Hebrew Prose: Modern Fiction and the Language of Realism* (Seattle: University of Washington Press, 1988).
25. See Shandler, *Shtetl*; Antony Polonsky, ed. , *The Shtetl: Myth and Reality*, Polin: Studies in Polish Jewry 17 (Oxford: Littman Library of Jewish Civilization, 2004); Steven T. Katz, ed., *The Shtetl: New Evaluations*, Elie Wiesel Center for Judaic Studies (New York: New York University Press, 2007); Yohanan Petrovsky-Shtern, *The Golden Age Shtetl: A New History of Jewish Life in East Europe* (Princeton: Princeton University Press, 2014).
26. Von Bernuth, *Wise Men*, 2.
27. Von Bernuth, *Wise Men*, 2.
28. Kipnis, *Khelmer mayses*, n.p. (Finkel translation).
29. The literature on nationalism and literature is immense, but for a brief, foundational discussion of literature's role in the construction of

nationalism, see Benedict Anderson, *Imagined Communities: Reflections on the Origins and Spread of Nationalism* (London: Verso, 1983).

30. Jelen, *Salvage Poetics*; Sheila E. Jelen, *Israeli Salvage Poetics* (Detroit: Wayne State University Press, 2023).
31. James Agee and Walker Evans, *Let Us Now Praise Famous Men* (Boston: Houghton Mifflin, 1941), xv.

Chelm Stories

1. A "Shabbos goy" is a non-Jew who is hired before the Sabbath or holiday to do forbidden work on Sabbath or holidays for the Jews, such as lighting a fire or carrying something out of the Sabbath perimeter.
2. Throughout these stories, there is a mapping of Jewish, eastern European geographical space. The storyteller, in other words, insists on reminding us that despite the foolishness of Chelm's inhabitants, Chelm is a real place in real space. Indeed, Kipnis incorporated actual geographical landmarks from the city, such as a hill with a well-known Basilica of the birth of the Virgin Mary, which features prominently in the Chelm fools' antics. In the *Haynt* column, Kipnis further reinforces the sense of reality when he presents his readers with the pretense of himself as a correspondent reporting from Chelm with subtitles such as "Ayndrikn fun Khelm gufe" (impressions from Chelm itself) and "Khelmer mayses oyfgenumen in Khelm gufe" (Chelm stories actually recorded in Chelm). Von Bernuth says, "This underscores one of the original features of the columns that contributed greatly to their popularity. In them, Kipnis presented himself as the paper's special correspondent in Chelm, on assignment to research the history of the town and the antecedents of its perfectly normal-seeming present-day Jewish community." Ruth von Bernuth, *How the Wise Men Got to Chelm: The Life and Times of a Yiddish Folk Tradition* (New York: New York University Press, 2016), 198.
3. The ending of this story has absolutely nothing to do with the beginning of the story, highlighting an important aspect of Chelm narratives: Oftentimes there is no resolution to the main problem. In this case, the main problem is the fact that the nanny goat is really a billy goat and the melamed keeps stopping at the same inn, where the same trick gets played on him repeatedly. The form of this story undermines the notion of narrative as we understand it; it meanders and fizzles out, not honoring its own intentions and changing its mind about what it is about. Perhaps the story sputtering out this way after a digression is meant to echo Talmudic literature, which is rife with digressions. Are the Chelm stories making fun of the Talmud in cases like this?
4. A holiday in early summer which commemorates the harvest and the giving of the Law.
5. Tisha B'Av commemorates the destruction of the first and second temples (586 BCE and 70 CE). Although it is rabbinically ordained, not biblically, it is still considered a major Jewish fast day, akin to Yom Kippur.
6. This tale of a mistaken date for Yom Kippur invokes the famous story from the Talmud of a conflict between Rabban Gamliel, the head of the Sanhedrin, or the high court, and the sage Rabbi Joshua. They have a difference of opinion about the date of Yom Kippur, and Rabban Gamliel, to reinforce the necessity for a universal consensus on the dates of the Jewish holidays, forces Rabbi Joshua to carry his cane and his wallet to the court on the day that he has designated as Yom Kippur as a sign of obedience to

Rabban Gamliel's authority. Rabban Gamliel, indeed, becomes demoted as a result of the shame he has inflicted on Rabbi Joshua. See Babylonian Talmud, Rosh HaShanah 25a. To what extent does this Chelm story evoke this very serious tale of the struggle for authority and the rise and fall of rabbinic figures? The yoking together of the literature of the folk (Chelm) and the literature of the scholarly class (Talmud) can be discerned, throughout this collection, from the intertextual allusions to the rabbinic literature.

7. A phrase that has "become an expression triumphantly uttered by dupers in defiance of their victims." See Alexander Harkavy, *English and Yiddish Dictionary* (New York: Hebrew Publishing Company), 70.
8. The allusion to variants throughout the volume reminds us that these stories were collected as a folkloric corpus. Sometimes variants appear without a special note to that effect, while at other times, such as here, Kipnis makes himself known as an editor and folklorist by pointing out the variants. In *Haynt*, the variants were identified within the context of those who contributed these stories to Kipnis. In the book, these sources are left out. Von Bernuth, *Wise Men*, 202.
9. Hershele Ostropoler and Efrayim Greydiger are two well-known fools in Yiddish literature. Kipnis incorporated Greydiger into his Chelm stories, creating the opportunity for an outsider fool to make the Chelmites look even more foolish. According to Ruth von Bernuth, Kipnis took many liberties with the stories, introducing elements into them that were not originally there, like Greydiger. Von Bernuth, *Wise Men*, 198.
10. This is another example of a story that meanders to the wrong conclusion, allowing the form of the stories to match their absurd content.
11. "Joy and gladness" is a quote from the Book of Esther. See Esther 8:16.
12. The "pondering" that goes on in these stories, the committees of men who discuss and think for days and nights, emphasizes the intellectual pretenses of this town of fools. More important, however, might be the allusion, again, to the sacred literature that these stories appear to be parodying. Think, for example, of the famous story from the Passover Haggadah of the five rabbis conferring about the exile from Egypt until dawn.
13. Periodically the narration shifts to the present tense, so we are thinking along with the Chelmites, sharing, perhaps, in their foolishness.
14. In a story of the BeShT (the Ba'al Shem Tov, or Eliezer Ben Israel [1698–1760]), the founder of the Hasidic movement is said to have made every one of his followers crowded into a room feel as if he had spoken exclusively and directly to them. See Martin Buber, "The Address," in *Tales of the Hasidim* (New York: Schocken Books, 1947), 55. The reverence and beauty of this concept is twisted here, in this Chelm tale, perhaps in the tradition of the parodic literature of the Jewish Enlightenment (the Haskalah), which often addressed itself to the Hasidic community, ridiculing its hagiographical tales and folk beliefs.
15. It is highly unusual for anyone in these stories to have a name (with the exception of place names). Here, not only is a character named, but a female character is named. Are the females in these stories more or less foolish than the men? It is hard to say.
16. An expression of horror.
17. The stories within the story here are typical of the literature of Jewish modernity written at the turn of the twentieth century in Yiddish as well as in Hebrew. The notion of a "found text" or a "spoken text" within the broader narrative or constitutive of the broader narrative was part of the project of vernacularizing Jewish literature or turning Jewish literature into a representation of "the Jewish street," as opposed to the house of

study or the house of prayer. Thematizing and highlighting the individual voice, or the text authored in the present moment, creates a more intimate encounter with the reader and emphasizes the presentness of the text.

18. Some of these stories resemble what we understand to be a "Jewish joke," with the protagonists representing "types" and playing off one another. This makes sense because, according to Ruth von Bernuth, one of Kipnis's main sources for the Chelm stories was Alter Druyanov's (1870–1938) Hebrew anthology of Jewish jokes, which was published the same year that Kipnis's column in *Haynt* was launched (1922). The first edition included twenty-five Chelm stories, and later editions included even more. Von Bernuth, *Wise Men*, 202. Also see Alter Druyanov, *Sefer ha-bedihah veha-hidud* (Frankfurt: Omanut, 1922).
19. One of the common mistakes Chelmites make is failing to understand linguistic cues and concretizing metaphoric idioms. This becomes the main theme of perhaps the most famous Chelm story available to English readers, Isaac Bashevis Singer's "Gimpel the Fool" (Yiddish, 1945; English, 1953). There, Gimpel takes Yiddish idioms literally and is thus understood as especially gullible or "foolish."
20. See note 7.
21. The Litvaks (Jews from Lithuania) and the Galicianers (Jews from Galicia) were at odds with one another. The seat of Hasidism was Galicia, and the seat of Mitnagdim (or those who opposed the Hasidim) was Lithuania. Galicianer Yiddish was different from Litvak Yiddish, with Litvak Yiddish being more German inflected and the Galicianer Yiddish more Slavically inflected. This moment in the story pays obeisance to this divide, emphasizing the intellectualism with which the Litvaks are traditionally associated and the lack of intellectualism (because Hasidism was a populist movement at its inception) with which Galicianers are associated. Thus, the fools of Chelm are likened to the foolish (presumably Hasidic) Galicianers.
22. Harkavy, *Dictionary*, 308.
23. This is reminiscent of a famous scene from Sholem Aleichem's Tevye the Milkman, where Tevye takes a break from driving to say the afternoon prayers and in the course of the silent Amidah where the correct posture is to stand with your feet together at attention for the duration of the rather long prayer, his horse runs off and Tevye screams the prayer at a run. See, Sholem Aleichem, "Tevye Strikes it Rich" from *Tevye the Dairyman and the Railroad Stories*, Trans. Hillel Halkin, (New York: Shocken Books, 1987), 6.
24. The first variant of this story falls under the rubric of religious observance. This one falls within the rubric of business. Almost all the stories fit into one or the other of the two models.
25. With the narrator drawing attention to himself here for the first time in the collection, perhaps this is a relic of the framing in the *Haynt* column, wherein Kipnis is a correspondent sending reports back from Chelm (see note 1).
26. The different lengths of time for pondering presented in these stories (three days or seven days) create motifs that help to unify the stories. This was a Kipnis innovation, according to Ruth von Bernuth. Von Bernuth, *Wise Men*, 201.
27. Who is this "us?" This is the first time that the first-person collective pronoun is invoked. Are the Chelmites authoring these stories about themselves? Is the author a Chelmite? Either answer would have interesting implications.
28. This is reminiscent of Y.L. Peretz's famous story "If not Higher," in which the Rabbi of Nemirov dresses like a peasant during the high holy days, and says his penitentiary prayers while he does chores for a bedridden woman who has no idea who he really

is. In dialogue with traditional Jewish literature, these stories also engage with high Yiddish literature, as Peretz was one of the "Classikers" or the founding fathers of modern Yiddish literature.

29. Vilna is called "The Jerusalem of Lithuania," a city renowned in Eastern European Jewish society, for its rabbinic figures, its libraries, its houses of study. It presents a sharp contrast to Chelm, the "city of fools."
30. A greeting and its response: "Peace be upon you," and "Upon you be peace."
31. This is traditionally done during the Aleinu prayer on the High Holidays.
32. A spring holiday preceding Passover by a month.
33. A scroll of parchment, usually containing the Book of Esther. This book is read communally on the holiday of Purim.
34. This is a particularly interesting innovation because in traditional Jewish culture, women do not count in a minyan. Ascertaining that there is a minyan by counting wives, while framed as absurd, is rather revolutionary.
35. This is a retelling of Sholem Aleichem's well-known 1913 story "Iber a hitl" ("On Account of a Hat"). Again, Kipnis took liberties with the genre. In later publications, many Sholem Aleichem stories like this are remade into Chelm stories. Von Bernuth, *Wise Men*, 202.
36. Because Jewish women were not usually literate in Hebrew, they could not read the Hebrew prayers. Therefore, the recited the prayers by repeating after a "zogerke" or a prayer reciter who either could read the Hebrew or knew all the prayers by heart.
37. A holiday on the fifth day of the week of Sukkot.
38. Kabbalah is Jewish mysticism.
39. A village in the Chelm region.
40. Special sabbaths preceding major holidays. Shabbos Shuvah is between Rosh Hashanah and Yom Kippur. Shabbos HaGodl is before Passover.
41. "Where the pepper grows" is an idiom meaning "to the ends of the earth."
42. A solemn prayer from the High Holiday liturgy, about who shall live and who shall die.
43. A collection of prayers for the dead.
44. A fast day during the summer.
45. A book that contains all the rituals for the Jewish year.
46. The citron, a part of the four species blessed during Sukkoth, the Holiday of Booths.
47. Again, from the High Holiday liturgy—different ways of dying. Throughout these stories, there is a yoking of opposites together—the most sacred with the most ridiculous, ritual objects with the mundane tools of everyday life. The fact that the High Holiday liturgy is so often invoked within the most ridiculous situations articulates the very premise of a modern Jewish literature—finding a way to infuse sacred languages with the mundane vernacular, the "Jewish street."
48. A complete cycle, from the birth of the community in the first story to the death of the community in its last.

Epilogue

1. With the exception of those photographs in the archive that have not yet been digitized, a few of which are featured here.
2. For a discussion and definition of "post-European," see the introduction to this volume.
3. *Forverts*, arts section, June 26, 1927, Collection: PO, Record ID: 6509, Catalog No.: Forward, Frame: 43155, YIVO Archives, http://yivo1000towns.cjh.org/frame_viewer.asp?PictureSetID=6509&PictureSetIndex=1&ImageID=43155.
4. *Forverts*, arts section, June 26, 1927, Collection: PO, Record ID 6510, Catalog No.: Forward, Frame: 43156, YIVO Archives, http://yivo1000towns

.cjh.org/frame_viewer.asp?PictureSetID=6510&PictureSetIndex=2&ImageID=43156.

5. *Forverts,* arts section, June 26, 1927, Collection: Po, Record ID: 6511, Catalog No: Forward, Frame: 43157, YIVO Archives, http://yivo1000towns.cjh.org/frame_viewer.asp?PictureSetID=6511&PictureSetIndex=1&ImageID=43157.
6. *Forverts,* arts section, September 25, 1927, Collection: PO, Record ID: 6559, Catalog No: F4258.01, Frame: 43237, YIVO Archives, http://yivo1000towns.cjh.org/frame_viewer.asp?PictureSetID=6559&PictureSetIndex=1&ImageID=43237.
7. The Kotzker rebbe (Menachem Mendel of Kotzk [1787–1859]) was known for his severity and his ascetism despite the fact that Hasidim were generally identified with ecstasy and laxity. On the Kotzker rebbe, see Abraham Joshua Heschel, *A Passion for Truth* (New York: Macmillan, 1973); also see Morris Faierstein, "Menahem Mendel of Kotzk," *The YIVO Encyclopedia of Jews in Eastern Europe,* accessed September 4, 2025> https://encyclopedia.yivo.org/article/1226.
8. Ben Mordkhe, *Khelmer naronim: Geklibene mayselekh* (New York: Hebrew Publishing Company, 1929).
9. Ruth von Bernuth, *How the Wise Men Got to Chelm: The Life and Times of a Yiddish Folk Tradition* (New York: New York University Press, 2016), 10. See Solomon Simon, *The Wise Men of Chelm* (New York: Behrman House, 1952); Isaac Bashevis Singer, *The Fools of Chelm and Their History* (New York: Farrar, Straus and Giroux, 1973).
10. Nathan Ausubel, *A Treasury of Jewish Folklore* (New York: Crown, 1948); Jacob Richman, *Jewish Wit and Wisdom* (New York: Pardes, 1952).
11. Itzik Gottesman, *Defining the Yiddish Nation: The Jewish Folklorists of Poland* (Detroit: Wayne State university Press, 2000), 64.
12. Solomon Simon, *The Wise Men of Helm and Their Merry Tales* (New York: Behrman House, 1945).
13. Isaac Bashevis Singer, "Gimpel the Fool," trans. Saul Bellow, *The Partisan Review,* May–June 1953, 300–313.

Glossary

ALIYE—The honor of being called to the Torah during synagogue services.

ENKAS MESALDECHO—A prayer from the final service of Yom Kippur.

GABBAI—A synagogue service coordinator.

GEVALD—An expression of horror: "Oh no!"

GOYMEL—A prayer recited over the Torah when one has gotten safely through a dangerous situation.

HAMELEKH—Lit. "the king," but a transitional prayer in the Rosh Hashanah morning service.

HOSHANA RABBA—The last intermediate day of the Feast of Tabernacles.

KABBALAH—Jewish mysticism.

KHEVRE KADISHE—A Jewish organization of volunteers dedicated to tending to the dead and overseeing the process of burial and mourning.

MAAVOR YABOK—A seventeenth-century Jewish mystical text that features prayers pertaining to the Jewish rituals of death and mourning.

MIKVE—A ritual bath.

MINYAN—A quorum of ten adults, required for communal prayer.

MORNING WATCH SOCIETY—The morning watch, in Jewish tradition, is the final period of the night, just before the dawn. Traditional Jews often used that time of day for self-reflection, personal prayers, and preparation for communal prayer that takes place at the break of day.

MUSEF—A prayer added to the morning service of every Sabbath and holiday.

NEILE—The final service at Yom Kippur.

PEYSACH—Passover.

PURIM—A carnivalesque holiday in the early spring commemorating a reversal of fortunes for the Jewish population in Persia, as described in the Book of Esther.

ROSH HASHANAH—The New Year.

SHABBOS—The Sabbath.

SHABBOS GOY—A non-Jew who performs tasks on the Sabbath that Jews cannot perform for themselves, such as lighting or extinguishing a flame. They are asked (and sometimes paid) before the Sabbath to do so.

SHAMMES—A synagogue sexton.

SHAVUOS—The Feast of Weeks.

SHOFAR—A ram's horn, blown throughout the penitential month of Elul and on Rosh Hashanah.

SHOLEM ALEICHEM—A greeting: "Hello! How are you?"

SLIKHES—Penitential prayers recited during the month of Elul, in the lead-up to the high holidays.

TALLIS—A prayer shawl.

TIKKUN—Spiritual repair.

TISHA B'AV—The ninth of the month of Av, a major fast day commemorating the destruction of the two temples (586 BCE and 70 CE).

VIDUY—Confessional prayers during the high holidays and on the deathbed.

YOM KIPPUR—The Day of Atonement.

ZOGERKE—A woman tasked with leading the other women in prayer orally.

About the Contributors

MENACHEM KIPNIS (1878–1942) was born in Ushomyr of what is now Ukraine, into a family of cantors. Distinguishing himself as a talented musical performer at a young age, by eighteen he became a cantorial soloist, and by twenty he had become first tenor in the chorus of the Warsaw National Opera, a position he occupied for sixteen years. He performed Yiddish songs, along with his wife, Zimre Zeligfeld, throughout Poland, and he documented those songs in several books, published in 1918 and 1925. Kipnis first became interested in photography in 1902 when he used photographs to illustrate his song transcriptions and musical notations. Throughout the 1920s, he was commissioned to send photographs of Jewish life in eastern Europe to the Yiddish newspaper with the widest circulation in the United States, the Yiddish daily *Forverts* (Forward). At the same time, he published Chelm stories, stories of a town of fools, in a column in the Warsaw Yiddish daily *Haynt* (Today). The Chelm stories were published as a book in 1930 under the title of *Khelmer mayses* (Chelm tales). Kipnis's work as an ethnomusicologist, singer, photographer, and folklorist unfolded at the height of Jewish folkloristic activity in Europe between the world wars. Kipnis died of a stroke in the Warsaw Ghetto in 1942.

SHEILA E. JELEN is a professor of religion, literature, and visual culture and the history of Judaism in the Divinity School at the University of Chicago. Her recent publications include *Olga Lengyel, Auschwitz Survivor: Interdisciplinary Approaches, Testimonial Montage: A Family of Israeli Holocaust Testimonies from the Cracow Ghetto Resistance, Israeli Salvage Poetics,* and *Salvage Poetics: Post Holocaust American Jewish Folk Ethnographies.* Her edited volumes include *Building a City: Writings on Agnon's Buczacz in Memory of Alan Mintz* and *Reconstructing the Old Country: American Jewry in the Post-Holocaust Decades*. She is an associate editor for *Prooftexts: A Journal of Jewish Literary History*. She was a fellow at Yad Vashem in Jerusalem during the summer of 2025 and will be a fellow at the United States Holocaust Memorial Museum during the summer of 2026 as she researches a new book, *Recognize Someone? Crowdsourcing Holocaust Memory*.

RAPHAEL FINKEL is a professor emeritus of computer science at the University of Kentucky. He compiled the first version of the Jargon File. Finkel is also an activist for the survival of the Yiddish language.